SAILING BEYOND THE SEA

SAILING BEYOND THE SEA

By

Jim d'Urfe Proctor DVM

PUBLISHING COMPANY
P.O Box 42028 Santa Barbara, CA 93140-2028
(800) 647-9882 • (805) 957-4893 • Fax: (805) 957-1631

©1996 Queenship Publishing

Published by:
  Queenship Publishing
  P.O. Box 42028
  Santa Barbara, CA 93140-2028
  (800) 647-9882 • (805) 957-4893 • Fax: (805) 957-1631

Printed in the United States of America

ISBN: 1-882972-86-4

Where from your love can I flee?
If I go up to the heavens you are there;
If I take wing to the sunrise or sail beyond the sea,
Still you are present even there. (Psalm 139)

FOREWORD

This book was written for a purpose. The author's parents have progeny numbering over a hundred. Some of these as well as the children of many friends and families everywhere have strayed from the teachings of their Creator and His Church. Many admire the exciting life that Jim and Carole have led. The hope is that they will be impressed with the story of the long slow change of direction in their lives andthe lives of friends. They have been invited to share their stories to others and were instrumental in organizing conferences and other events that have helped others turn toward a more satisfying and fruitful life. The hope is that this story may increase that effect.

Chapter 1—No Matter Where You Go There You Are
The book starts with early adventures of a veterinarian and his wife who is an extraordinary woman but who is also blind. A possible theme for the book is suggested here. "I have been a jerk most of my life; perhaps I'm still a jerk but at least now I'm trying to change.

Chapter 2—From Terrace to Tintagel, or North to Alaska Almost
Moving to the wilderness of northern British Columbia with a blind wife and four small children they began a search of adventure and riches. One of the largest veterinary practice areas in North America results in unusual experiences. A final count of six children is achieved.

Chapter 3—Attention Getting Device
A playboy is confronted with early spiritual intervention, including an unusual narrow escape from an avalanche which destroyed the lives of eight other people.

Chapter 4—Running Away
A blind lady becomes first mate on a fifty one foot sailing vessel. When Christian values are put on hold, raising six children becomes difficult. Many young people were starting to experiment with drugs and sex with serious consequences. One answer, buy a fifty foot sailboat and run away from the world to the South Pacific.

Chapter 5—Mexican Jail
On the way south playboy parents end up in a Mexican jail. Some people are slow learners, but the adventure was unique.

Chapter 6—On to the South Pacific.
With fear and trepidation the inexperienced family-crew of eight set out across the largest body of water in the world. Age of the crew members ranged from ten to seventeen. At some points the waves became half the height of the sixty foot mast on the fifty one foot boat. Boy, if you ever forget how to pray and find yourself in this kind of situation, and suddenly it dawns on you that the nearest land is straight down, it is amazing how quickly you learn how to pray all over again with genuine sincerity!

Chapter 7—Equator
A life of hazards and excitement on the open ocean for a three week crossing to the South Pacific. The family was drawn closer together through hardship and adventure.

Chapter 8—Paradise is Many Islands
This chapter describes many adventures with natives and the beauty of the exotic South Pacific as seen from the eyes of sailors, but unseen by the average tourist.

Chapter 9—Tahiti
Describes life and adventures and misadventures of five kids in the capital city of the South Pacific.

Chapter 10—Return Toward Solid Ground
Life aboard a sailboat could go on forever but something was calling the parents back to land and a change in attitude. On the way home the family brushed close to a murder scene on the island of Palmyra.

Chapter 11—Intrigue Continues in the North Pacific
Sailing north to Hawaii, another close encounter with the evil side of life.

Chapter 12—Attempt at Being a Land Lubber
Final Crossing to Hawaii, then return to Washington, gold mining in the Yukon and the increase in the Creator's relentless pursuit, shades from "The Hound of Heaven."

Chapter 13—Vancouver Island
Final destiny to Vancouver Island and an explosion of events was rapidly causing changes in a stubborn heart.

Chapter 14—Campbell River
More moves and continued miracles including the miraculous healing of a sick cat by way of a humble priest. Answers the question, "Why on earth would God heal a domestic cat?"

Chapter 15—You are Losing it Doc
After amassing a six million dollar fortune, can the loss of everything turn out for good?

Chapter 16—A Slight Attitude Adjustment
The change in other's lives results in a contagious conversion. The final effects of going down the financial tube is told.

Chapter 17—Pilgrimage to Europe
An invitation to the Vatican, an encounter with Mother Teresa and challenged by a Cardinal in Rome all have a dramatic effect.

Chapter 18—Medjugorje
Encouraged by priests at the Vatican to visit Medjugorje in spite of the Catholic media discouragement.

Chapter 19—Munich to Lourdes
A description of the miracle of Lourdes with an explanation of the efforts against it by the adversary.

Chapter 20—Short but Not So Sweet Visit to Paris
None of the adventures in Paris were positive. Maybe the tour guide we employed, the Paraclete, didn't feel we needed any more secular events.

Chapter 21—Marguerite
An inspiring meeting with Marguerite and The Message of Merciful Love, a chosen mystic in Belgium.

Chapter 22—Native Pilgrimage and Cursillo
A surge of spiritual reawakening in the natives of Montana, Washington and Canada. The story of alcohol and drugs and their efforts to escape.

Chapter 23—Medjugorje Two More Times
After minimal financial recovery a return to Medjugorje. Most enjoy peace and joyful encounters in Medjugorje, why the devil for us?

Chapter 24—Cenacles and Marian Conferences
The spread of Marian devotion on Vancouver Island. The seed is planted here for all of Canada in spite of the controversy. This was an effort to accept the cardinal's challenge.

Chapter 25—Whatever is not Dead is Alive
Adventures in the battle for the respect of life.

Chapter 26—Sailing On
Final adventures and thoughts on changes in attitude.

DEDICATION

To the Gospa, my wife Carole and the entire crew of the Maritashan. All of who have given so much love and meaning to life.

ACKNOWLEDGMENTS

A heartfelt thank you to all who helped make this story readable, especially Ted Flynn, the lieterary physician who once said, "It's a great story but in need of a lot of surgury." Also, Elizabeth Senson, Maureen Larson, Emilie Melanson, Frank Straub and others who helped perform the surgury.

CHAPTER 1

No Matter Where You Go, There You Are

We were in the middle of the Pacific Ocean. The wind was blowing 30 knots from the northeast, building waves that reached nearly half as high as the sixty foot mast on our fifty one foot sailing vessel. The first mate, my wife Carole, is blind. I, the captain, was not all that brave in spite of feigned confidence. Five of our six beautiful, young children, age 10 to 17, took their turn steering, while trusting their lives to this fifty-one foot sailing ketch and its captain.

Plunging toward the South Pacific from our home in British Columbia, the last sight of land had disappeared nine days before. That was Clarion Island, an exotic little lump of volcanic rock lying some 400 miles southwest of Cabo San Lucas, Mexico. Cabo was now 1400 miles behind to the north. The ship alternately climbed high on giant waves, balanced on the crest, and then careened down its steep slope only to repeat the same maneuver over and over like an eternal roller coaster. Would this precious little family ever see land again?

Boy, if you ever forget how to pray and find yourself in this kind of predicament, then suddenly it dawns on you that the nearest land is straight down...it is amazing how quickly you learn how to pray with true sincerity all over again!

Many dreamers fantasize of someday sailing off to the South Pacific in a boat. In spite of the apprehensions, we felt extremely privileged having the opportunity to attempt this adventure.

Before leaving home in Terrace, British Columbia, I asked the high school Vice-Principal, Walt Macintyre, "Walt, do you think we are making a big mistake dragging all these six young kids out of school, away from their friends, putting them on a boat, and risking their very lives sailing across the big pond?"

After an abbreviated pause, he responded, "You are only making one big mistake. You are not taking the Vice-Principal with you!"

Unique circumstances, signs and wonders have always been a part of our lives. I will attempt to describe how events in our lives and others, led up to this sailing adventure and beyond to produce a notable change in attitude. I have spent a good share of my life being a jerk. I am still a jerk, but at least now I am trying to do something about it. Hopefully, if some of you who read this feel you might need a change of focus, you will find some consolation here.

My mother was a school teacher. Around 1914, she rode on horseback into the little town of Proctor, Montana, to accept her first teaching assignment. There she met Dad. Proctor, Montana was my Grandfather's homestead, and was named after him. Even now it can be located on maps of Montana. Granddad heard the railroad was coming through the area, so he bought up all the surrounding land and escalated the price. The railroad retaliated and rerouted the railroad. The town then mushroomed to its present population (11 people at the last census.) Several years later my parents moved to Kalispell, Montana, where I was born in 1933. The country was experiencing the Great Depression at the time and Dad worked at anything he could find to earn a living. He sold subscriptions to the *Montana Farmer* Magazine and samples for The Macabees, a woolen clothing marketing company. Sometimes, in trade for his sales, he accepted things like chickens and eggs. When the poor people were eating beans, we got to eat chicken and beans. I made pets out of these little feathery friends. (Could this have been early evidence of my future vocation?) My sister, Lois, remembers that I cried one night at supper. "Are we eating Blacky?"

When I was in the third grade, we moved to Philipsburg, Montana, to be near my ailing grandfather, Judge Durfee, who died shortly thereafter.

No Matter Where You Go, There You Are

On our way home from school one day, Jerry Ryan and I stuffed a post office box with discarded cigarette packages, dripping with mud. The postmaster caught Jerry. I was certain he would be put to a horrible death, or at least imprisoned. I managed to escape with my life by dashing away and ducking down the alley. I discovered later, Jerry only got a good boot in the rear. The very next day, Mom announced we were moving to Spokane, Washington. She never understood why I was so tickled about that move.

Mom and Dad were separated for a good share of their married life. I don't think they realized how traumatic their separation was for us kids. To me, the pain was equal to what I imagine loosing an only child would be. They lived apart for many years, but at least they never divorced. The respect for their vows made a definite impression on their six offspring. Toward the end of Dad's life, he and Mom became caring and cautiously friendly.

Dad moved to Alaska by himself in 1941 and worked there during World War Two. I will never forget the day he returned home unexpectedly after six years. He quietly entered my bedroom early one morning and woke me by sitting on my bed. When I peaked out from under the covers, I couldn't believe my eyes! All I could do was hug him, cry, and stutter senselessly for half an hour. For days, I never let him out of my sight. My love for my mother was equal to the love for Dad, but it never became a challenge because she was always there.

Two years later, Dad purchased a 600-acre wilderness stump ranch north of Spokane for $3000. Us kids thought he had just procured a piece of heaven. A beautiful gem of a lake (one of the Chain Lakes) lay at one corner of the ranch, and the Little Spokane River meandered for a mile through the property. Trees, wild animals, and fresh water springs were everywhere.

Dad was a dedicated atheist and Mom a dedicated Catholic, a strange combination. But Dad was a good atheist; he believed and preached it. Then, one day in 1950, he had a tremendous experience which jolted him into a complete shift in philosophy. It was like a life after life experience. He was totally astounded and told me what he saw was more real than standing there describing the vision to me. He saw colors that didn't exist on earth and became frustrated because the scene was so extraordinary, he couldn't find words that could describe what he saw.

Then to my surprise, he said, "There is no way that God does not exist!"

I was seventeen at the time and didn't think all this was too cool, but fortunately I withheld comment. If anyone reading this has ever been seventeen, they might understand. More on this later.

After graduating from high school in the town of Lind, I attended Washington State University and somehow, in 1957, received a DVM degree...Doctor of Veterinary Medicine.

The greatest gift of my lifetime was meeting my wife, Carole. We met on a blind date while attending university. Carole is blind and has been blind since the age of seventeen.

She likes to tell people, "We met on a blind date and have been on a blind date ever since."

Her blindness was thought to be a result of rheumatic fever. At one time, she was confined to a wheel chair from arthritis, and told she would probably never walk again. One day, this determined little girl came home from school pushing her wheelchair in front. She hasn't stopped pushing since.

A research group made a study of the fifteen most serious conditions that afflict humanity. Cancer and several fatal diseases were listed, as well as non fatal conditions such as deafness and blindness. Respondents were asked to list, in order, the conditions they dreaded most. It was interesting to note that most people placed blindness at the top of their list.

I was particularly impressed by Carole's spirit on one of our early "blind dates." We were discussing suicide, and Carole summed up her attitude toward her handicap, "I can't understand people committing suicide when living is so much fun!"

We were married a year later and graduation followed the year after. Dad always liked Carole, but Mom was not impressed. She feared that I was marrying what would become a terrible burden. Carole was depressed over Mom's aloof behavior.

One day, she asked my aunt Eula, "Why doesn't Mom like me?"

Aunt Eula, a very loving and gentle lady, asked in return, "Carole, dear, don't you realize you just stole her baby boy?"

No Matter Where You Go, There You Are

Carole warned me before we were married that she would like to have six kids. We started right away fulfilling her request. These six were our next greatest gifts. Mom quickly discovered what a sweetheart Carole was and what a great job she was doing raising six kids. It soon became obvious that Mom was often more impressed with her daughter-in-law than she was with her son.

With mixed emotions, it became awe-inspiring to watch those six little guys grow, develop, and change over the years. Often, these six little gifts would reward me with their cheeky humor.

For instance, as the date of my graduation faded into the past, they made remarks like, "Gee, Dad, you must have found the study of Dinosaur Medicine intriguing," or, "Good thing you found a blind girl, Dad. Otherwise, you might never have gotten married."

Right after graduation, a job in a veterinary hospital opened in Newport, Washington. This was great; it was only fifteen miles from Dad's ranch. The following year, I purchased the business from the retiring doctor and practiced there for three more years.

Carole assisted with surgery, helped out in the office, and continued raising our family. She often recalls the most embarrassing moment of her life, which took place during our third year in Newport. She used to write down phone messages and leave them near the telephone. After returning from farm calls, and before removing my black navy peacoat, I would sit down to return phone calls. One day, she heard me enter the house and start the routine. Carole's hands were chilled from serving ice cream to the kids. She tip-toed up behind me and quickly slipped her cold hands down the back of my neck, under my heavy coat collar and giddily chortled, "Cold, huh?" Only one problem. Instead of me at the phone, it was the telephone repairman wearing a coat identical to mine.

His only comment was, "Hey, what's going on here?

In fits of tears, she related the story to Lilian, my veterinary assistant, and myself. "It was the closest I ever came to fainting!" she sobbed.

In spite of this heart rending story, Lilian and I were both seized with uncontrollable laughter. Lilian laughed so hard, she fell off her chair to the floor. And then, even Carole started to laugh. Carole handled her challenge better than anyone I know, but there were some trying moments.

Sailing Beyond the Sea

CHAPTER 2

From Terrace to Tintagel or North to Alaska, Almost

I must have inherited nomadic tendencies from my parents. Every few years, we developed the urge to make a move. In the spring of 1961, I applied to write the veterinary board exam for the province of British Columbia, Canada. The call of the wild was ringing in my ears. I had graduated from college four years before, and reasoned that I had better write any other board exams needed before I got any dumber.

When I phoned the board examiners' office in Vancouver, they informed me the test for that year was scheduled to be held in three days, so I would have no time to prepare.

"You'd better wait until next year and try again," the administrator advised.

My friend and colleague, Dr. Mick Glasgow, visiting us in Newport, reminded me that I had pretty well bluffed my way through six years of university, so a little thing like no time to study shouldn't bother me now.

With those encouraging words, we once again contacted the board administrator.

He replied in a strong cockney accent, "My dear lad, it is highly irregular to apply three days before the test, but, oh well, let's give it a try."

The next day, I boarded a plane for Vancouver with a load of books under my arm and promptly used the same escape mechanism that I used in all emergencies (like when Carole was delivering one of our six babies), I went to sleep. The following morning, well rested, I wrestled with the board exam, one of the most difficult I had ever encountered. Completely drained, I returned home to Newport, wondering if by any chance I could have beaten that thing.

Two weeks later, one of the board members from Vancouver stopped by our home in Newport to inform me, indeed, I had passed! A candidate from California, who had written the exam with me, had failed. Would I like to move 600 miles north to Smithers, B.C., Canada, and assume the practice that had been arranged for him? The government of B.C. was offering a subsidy of $3000 per year just to have a veterinarian start a practice there. In those days $3000 was quite a substantial boost; a years wages for some. What a neat sounding idea; a "neat idea" to everyone except Carole's parents, who were not impressed with nomadism or wilderness.

Without hesitation, I located another veterinarian to cover the Newport practice, loaded the car with one wife, four kids, the family pet which was a large Akita dog named Butch, and Carole's eighty pound Golden Retriever Guide Dog, Wick. A good friend, Ray Foley, loaded up all our worldly possessions in his truck, and soon we were motoring our way to that big foreign country to the north. This would be a bit of a challenge for the average wife, I'm sure. To a blind girl, it must have been a little frightening.

We moved into a rustic, two room cabin on Lake Kathrine, on the outskirts of Smithers. Smithers was like home in Montana for me. Large and small farms dotted the many pillow-like, rolling hills in this cozy vale known as the Bulkley Valley. The Creator garnished this work of art with a background of sky high mountains, giant blue tinted glaciers, and year-round, snow capped peaks

The temperature registered minus eighteen degrees when we arrived that November day and a foot of snow covered the valley. The cabin, however, was not without "some" amenities. For instance, there was running water. Even though it was "cold" water and out-of-doors, it wasn't too far away. The property was complimented with a really romantic outdoor toilet which rendered a delightful view of the lake through the wide cracks in the door. The one room kitchen, dining, living room, and bedroom combo, was provided with a unique, antique, wood-burning, cook stove. It could also heat water to bathe four kids, including one fairly new baby, Shannon, who didn't use much water.

From Terrace to Tintagel or North to Alaska, Almost

I could tell all this was beginning to rankle Carole a little one day, when she burned a spot on her hand that had been burned twice before. Raising high an 'unbreakable' Melmac plate, she slammed it to the floor causing a crescendo of hundreds of shattered bits of unbreakable Melmac flying about the room.

She never was much good at swearing, but as I recall, she let out something like, "Darn it all anyway!"

Once My sister, Margaret, asked Carole why she didn't leave me. Carole thoughtfully replied, "I would, but I'm afraid I might miss something."

The official government subsidy area extended from Terrace on the west, 200 miles east, to the tiny rail stop of Tintagel. The villages of Smithers, Burns Lake, Houston and Hazelton were all within my practice area located in the Bulkley River valley and beyond, all suitable for agriculture.

The actual area covered was much larger. It extended from Ketchican, Alaska, in the north, to Ocean Falls, B.C., in the south; from the Queen Charlotte Islands in the west, to Burns Lake and Tintagel in the east. This is an area of some 90,000 square miles, boasting a population of one person per three square miles. The animal patients were located a long distance from each other. Most of the small animals were concentrated in a half-dozen small towns. My mandate called for stamping out animal disease in that vast territory.

This challenge developed into the most exciting life I had ever experienced. To the west lay the Pacific Ocean, with it's myriad wilderness islands and inlets. Valleys stretched inland, seemingly without end, punctuated with innumerable lakes. Moose roamed everywhere. Rivers and streams teemed with salmon in the summer, and lakes with trout the year round. European visitors compared the area to the Swiss Alps or fjords of Norway.

The other half of B.C., north of us, remained pretty much an uninhabited wilderness. The region under my care became one of the largest veterinary practices in North America; ideal for a family fascinated by untamed frontier. Bush planes connected many communities such as the Queen Charlotte Islands, Hyder, Alaska, and Stewart, B.C.. We traveled by freighter to Ocean Falls, one-hundred and seventy miles south of Prince Rupert, and by power boat to Kemano, located on an inlet sixty miles inland from the open sea.

The scourge of white muscle disease became the major animal health problem and the prime reason for the need of a veterinarian in the area. This is an acute muscular dystrophy-like condition. The cause was unknown to the farmers in the Bulkley Valley and resulted in serious financial loss. The disease attacks newborn calves, generally the best and most rapid growing individuals. They would become unable to walk due to hind leg muscle deterioration and eventually die. Often, it would attack the heart muscle first, causing instant death from heart failure.

Cattle in northern Idaho and eastern Washington, where I had started practice, were afflicted with the same condition. One spring, a former client in Idaho lost fifty of his fifty-two calves. He soon changed to the grocery business. The cause there had recently been uncovered. Animals in Montana, afflicted with another disease resulting from surplus selenium in their diet, would never contract white muscle disease. After some clever investigation, it was discovered that white muscle disease resulted from a deficiency of selenium and vitamin E in the diet. Soon, an injectable form of selenium was developed and the effects were magical. If any life at all remained in a calf, it would recover rapidly after a single treatment of selenium, or the mother cow could be inoculated before giving birth. This would prevent the calf from developing white muscle disease.

Armed with this bit of knowledge (and some other lucky breaks), the first veterinarian soon became appreciated throughout the area.

There were a few exceptions. Some anti-American sentiment prevailed. I will always remember the dear, sweet old lady, Aunt Mary Shelford, aunt of Cyril Shelford, MLA for the Bulkley Valley-Burns Lake district. After inoculating her calves against brucellosis, she invited me in for tea.

She asked, with her quaint English accent, "And from what country do you come?"

I answered, "Montana, originally, and Washington State, recently."

There was a lengthy pause. "Oh, then you are an American?"

"Yes" I replied.

From Terrace to Tintagel or North to Alaska, Almost

Then, with her usual sweet, but partially forced smile, she sighed, "Oh well, we all have to come from somewhere, don't we?"

Bob Titmus was an intriguing individual who appeared in the Smithers veterinary office one day with deep concern in his manner. He lived, at that time, on the rugged, west coast on Swindle Island, one hundred miles south of Prince Rupert. He had spent a good many years of his life chasing the elusive "sasquatch". I had never before heard of the sasquatch and was abruptly chastised when I used the term "legend" in questioning him about the beast. His closest friend, a large Weimaraner dog named Gretchen, had run a sharp stick into her abdomen while running through the forest. When he entered the office, he laid a ominous looking 357 magnum pistol on the desk and stated in a slow serious drawl, "I wouldn't want anything to happen to my dog while she is here!" I managed the best serene guise I could muster and examined the dog. Bob had paddled by canoe for thirty miles, walked several miles, and arrived in Kitimat by boat eight days after the injury. Fortunately for both the dog and I, her wound had already healed by itself. An x ray revealed no serious complications. Bob and I became close friends after the incident. His adventures would make an interesting book.

Most of the farmers were a delightful collection of rare characters, and frontier pioneers turning a small part of the wilderness into viable farms.

My eldest son, Jim Jr., is an intensive reader. After reading the book *All Creatures Great And Small,* he speculated, "Hey Dad, you could have written this book."

That statement is probably true of a lot of veterinarians, especially those in practice areas like that one in northern B.C..

To service the land-based communities, we purchased a fifty-passenger Greyhound-style

Veterinary Clinic

11

bus. We removed all seats and turned the front portion into a reception area. The center became a surgery and examination room, while the rear served as comfortable living quarters. I was "King of the Road." It was a lot of fun, but entirely practical. Heavy snows were frequent, and a bus functions like a giant Volkswagen with a rear mounted engine, most reliable in winter conditions. With this unique mobile hospital, we traveled to Burns Lake, Smithers, Terrace, Kitimat, and Prince Rupert, as well as anywhere else that looked like an adventure. Assembly line surgery and treatments became a routine and an exciting way to practice veterinary medicine.

Besides the animal health business, I had always been afflicted with a yen to own real estate, and I began to accumulate several choice pieces of land.

In fact, the kids used to cup their hands beside my eyes when we drove by for-sale signs. "Don't let Dad see that sign!"

We owned 170 acres on the edge of Smithers, and 200 acres adjoining the city limits of Terrace. Located on the property in Terrace was an antique squared-timber log home which was the oldest home in Terrace. It had been constructed by a pioneer, Mr. Ted Johnston, around the turn of the century. (He was later killed by a grizzly bear when he jumped off a log and unfortunately landed directly on top of the sleeping griz.) After living in Smithers for six years, we moved to Terrace and lived in that great old home for the next six years. Often, we would find moose in our yard, and a colony of rare, pure white Kermody bears took up residency on our spread.

Meanwhile, we began to subdivide the property into two and five acre parcels. On some we built homes. The Smithers project was a special challenge since it consisted of a seventy-acre mosquito swamp. I traded my Rambler station wagon for that swamp on the outskirts of Smithers, and was able to purchase the adjoining hundred acres for $11,000. No one else wanted one-hundred and seventy acres of mosquito bog. Using blasting powder and the services of a buddy, Berney Champoux, who was an artist with a backhoe, we ditched the entire property and turned it into high and dry, fertile little farms.

Now, we were well on our way to being entrepreneurs. Land was cheap here and no one seemed to realize that condition wouldn't last, and it didn't!

CHAPTER 3

An Attention Getting Device

Most North Americans who like myself, have a strong worldly influence in our lives, find it difficult to be great parents, which should have been the number one priority in my life. Luckily, our children had a more dedicated mother.

Carole performed most of the kids rearing and accomplished a remarkable job. Often, two kids were in diapers simultaneously. I can recall the sight of only her head barely visible over a mountain of diapers on the coffee table. Until about the third or fourth child, she felt obliged to iron and fold all diapers, and insisted we had to be able to see ourselves in her waxed floor or it wasn't suitable.

Carole is a convert to the Catholic faith and, like most converts, is a far better Christian than many "cradle Catholics." When people suggested she be prayed over for a healing, or go to Lourdes France where hundreds of miraculous cures have occurred, she usually conceded that she felt God had more use for her blind than sighted. This is obviously true, her attitude toward life influences many. It is difficult to concentrate on "poor me" when exposed to people like her. She has remarked though, that sight certainly would come in handy.

Both Carole and I were raised with good moral and family values. I took leave of those values during the early days. Parties became a priority. Like my Dad though, as life unfolded, circumstances gave evidence that somebody out there was trying to attract my attention.

I dedicated myself to building a veterinary practice and building a fortune in the real estate game rather than combining a life of faith with work and play.

Scripture says you should have only one master. If you love one, you despise the other. I somehow didn't hear that message and chose masters other than the one recommended. The pursuit of wealth with a great retirement and parties became our other deities. Sometimes, this resulted in harmless humor; other times, it helped build my school of hard knocks.

We thought the Greyhound bus clinic was quite innovative. It served the purpose well and business flourished. Often, there were as many as fifty appointments in one day, including surgery; whereas fifteen appointments is a good day for most single doctor clinics. The bus doubled as a roomy family camper and became one of the better party wagons ever devised.

One evening, in Prince Rupert after a busy day of surgery, a resounding party evolved on board the bus parked on the main street of town. Someone obviously registered a complaint, evidenced by the arrival of a police car, red lights flashing.

"Oh! Oh! We could be in trouble." Luck was on our side. Two police officers were already attending the party. These two departed to negotiate with the men in the car. They returned after a half hour, accompanied by the occupants of the police car now off duty. The bus moved to a more discrete part of town with all police joining a more dignified party.

Since I was the first resident veterinarian to practice in the Smithers area, it qualified me for a certain degree of prestige. While enjoying a position at that level, there is an obligation to present a good example to the community. My example was a mixed bag.

I am not proud to relate one incident, but it demonstrates an example of a device to capture my attention, and may have been the beginning of results of my faithful mother's continual prayers for her own six children.

Carole and I were invited to attend the Bulkley Valley Cattlemen's Banquet celebrated in Telkwa, a short distance east of Smithers. This is a gala affair with lots of good food, drinks and dancing. We lived it up in the usual manner and I consumed my usual share of scotch. During the evening, I was invited to dance with one of the most charming ladies in the area. She was doing a dance with me that was anything but edifying, in full view of everyone. This was great for the ego since she was such a beauty and

An Attention Getting Device

my inhibitions had been washed away with scotch. Fortunately for me, my blind wife could not fully appreciate the performance. After the dance, I sat down with "the boys", enjoying a hearty laugh over the incident. Suddenly, out of nowhere, marched a little lady holding a large glass of whiskey and ice in her hand. She promptly and willfully dumped the whisky over my head. (Luckily, one important value had stayed with me. It is not acceptable to hit a lady.)

As I was recovering from the shock, plucking the ice cubes from my pocket, she spoke in a loud clear voice. I thought the entire world must have heard. "So you call yourself a Catholic!"

It would have been kinder to hit me over the head with a two-by-four. At the time, I feigned a laugh, but the incident means more and more to me as I "grow up", and I see how poor examples multiply to the bane of many. I often wondered if that lady was a real person or could she have been an angel?

In July of 1967, we embarked on the move from Smithers to Terrace, 100 miles west, to experience more significant events. The government subsidy had ended, since my monthly reports indicated that income was no longer a problem. The business was increasing rapidly in the larger towns of Prince Rupert, Terrace and Kitimat. This involved working more with small animals such as dogs and cats in a nice warm clinic as opposed to stripping down to the waist in minus twenty degree weather for a calf or foal delivery, or to remove the rotten afterbirth from a cow. Not to say that isn't an exciting form of medical practice, but it does get old after several years. The monetary returns of city practice were considerably more attractive as well. We kept the mobile hospital busy running between the three towns until business warranted a permanent building in each town. We then sold the bus to a Jehovah Witness missionary who planned to evangelize Canada.

Jim Callanan, a friend and Oblate religious brother residing in Terrace, provided the next attention getting device. He decided that Carole and I needed a Marriage Encounter. This is a spiritual exercise designed to make good marriages better. He signed us up for the Marriage Encounter without our knowledge, and then later convinced us we should attend. This Jim was a "Spiritual Con Man." Even though we were certain this sort of thing was not necessary in our lives, we would attend anyway, to better inform others who "re-

15

ally needed" Marriage Encounter. Not too long into the weekend, it became vividly clear that we needed it more than anyone present. Everyone knows big boys and cowboys don't cry. During a period close to the finish, the others were sniffling and wiping away their tears, but not this cowboy! I hadn't cried since I was twelve and I wasn't about to start now. A few moments later, when we returned to the privacy of our room, I put my head on Carole's shoulder and sobbed uncontrollably for fifteen minutes. It seemed like a ton of troubles had been removed from our lives; not all but a good start.

I know there are amazing coincidences, but sometimes the evidence leans far beyond coincidence. Many stories tell of close calls in peoples lives; times when they would not have survived had they followed a different path or if something unusual hadn't interrupted a series of events.

Dad once described to me one of those instances in his early Montana days. While traveling cross country, he came upon a lake. It would have been a long trip around the lake, so he decided to swim across. He misjudged the distance and discovered, too late and halfway across, that he was too exhausted to carry on.

He thought to himself, "I guess this is it; I'm going to drown."

Down went his feet, but "What is this?" His feet landed on something solid. He couldn't believe it! He stood there on the support for some time until well rested and able to complete the crossing. When he informed his friends of the experience, all agreed it was a deep lake and no one had ever reported a rock in the lake. They borrowed a boat and spent the next day dragging the lake, but never discovered what had, fortunately, spared his life.

One of many close calls particularly captured my attention toward the end of our tenure in the north country. Having someone pour ice cubes down your neck can be irritating, but several hundred tons of ice thundering down a mountain side can ruin your whole day.

Highway 16 runs between Prince Rupert and Terrace. The ninety mile trip between those two towns was, and still is, a hazardous journey. Nearly vertical mountains ascend from one side of

An Attention Getting Device

the highway, while the wild Skeena River flows and sometimes rages close along the opposite side. Over the years several cars have plunged into the river. Often, snow will pile up five to ten feet from a single storm, producing the all too common threat of avalanche. I traveled that route over 1000 times during our twelve year term in the north. The routine schedule was twice a week, Wednesday and Saturday. All those years, I arrived in Prince Rupert faithfully in time to open the Veterinary Clinic at nine o'clock. Nearly every trip, I would visit the North Route Service and Restaurant, on the way, at eight o'clock for coffee, gas, or just to visit the Dumonts, my friends who owned the business. The Dumonts raised eight children, so we held some common interests. Due to the rugged terrain, theirs was the only place of business on that long wilderness stretch. One morning, in the winter of 1973, my rather new Datsun station wagon refused to start. I drained the battery completely by trying. I weighed my options. There had been a heavy snow fall the day before. Town was a three mile hike through knee-deep snow to a car rental agency. We had plans to leave the area on a sailing adventure in another year. To heck with it; I would fail the pet owners in Prince Rupert this one time. I contacted the Prince Rupert nurse, asked her to cancel the appointments, and happily returned to the warm comfort of our bed.

When I awoke again at 10 o'clock, I turned on the radio and could scarcely believe the incredible news broadcast. At 8:15 that morning, a giant avalanche had swept down the mountain slope completely demolishing North Route Service. The entire area was buried in tons of snow and forest debris. All buildings exploded into oblivion. The lives of eight people inside came to an abrupt and violent end at precisely the time I would normally have been in that same building, myself, if my car would have started.

The mail truck driver, standing under an archway in the building, somehow survived. When they dug him out with a backhoe, it became necessary for his rescuers to bind him to the stretcher. He had lost his mind and went into a violent rage. The shock of the tragedy was reinforced when the emergency crew delivered the frozen body of Dumont's little bull dog for me to bury.

That same afternoon, the car came alive at the first turn of the ignition key.

17

Since that time, I have pondered over that "coincidence", along with other similar experiences. I am kind of thick-headed, and it seems to take a few years for the meaning of these things to sink in. The question arose, if the Creator was preserving such an undeserving individual as I, what on earth for? Why were all those innocent children and their father killed while the undeserving one survived? Was I supposed to be doing something different with my life from the present worldly behavior? So far, the Kingdom of God had received very little, and only half-hearted, attention from me.

CHAPTER 4

Running Away

All six children turned out to be exceptional people, but somehow I short changed them by not providing a solid faith. Too late, I realize that should be every parents foremost act of love. That omission left a vacuum to be filled by worldly philosophies. I am continually reminded, with deep regret, that a large portion of the responsibility for their eternity is resting on my shoulders. Now, there is nothing I can do to change that but pray. Children often follow the interests and behavior of their parents. Even though there was no lack of love, how could I expect our children to believe in Christian values when my Christian life was, at best, half-hearted and hypocritical.

I'm envious of friends, who unlike myself, live lives close to the gospel and teachings of the Church during the early years of their children. Many of their children are now growing up close to their Creator and their faith. We attended weekly Mass, but did not live exemplary Christian lives. Our kids learned to spot hypocrisy early in life.

In those days, many of the kids' peers were beginning to experiment with drugs and premarital sex. Since the advent of artificial contraception, all at once, for the first time since the days of the Roman Empire, promiscuity became acceptable. A paradox arose. Teenage pregnancies became rampant, in spite of the availability and promotion of contraceptives. The arrogance of technology was hard at work. This is exactly as Pope Paul VI had predicted at the beginning of that era when he wrote the epistle on Human Life in July, 1968.

That epistle reads. "Artificial contraception leads to many vicious wrongs in society; it facilitates the sexual revolution which leads to much unwanted pregnancy and abortion. It has made women much more open to sexual exploitation by men. In fact, a general lowering of morality should be expected if artificial contraception becomes widely available." (Humanae Vitae.)

Just this week, we listened to a doctor on TV pondering the problem.

In confused wonder, he said, "I can't understand what is happening. We have filled the airways, the nations books, and schools with information about sex, and yet unplanned pregnancies and venereal diseases are spreading more rapidly than ever."

We watched as the world compounded the problem for the innocent mother by offering the false, even more devastating, solution of abortion. We worried whether the values our children received from us would be strong enough to counteract those fallacies? Our kids would be leaving home soon. During the zenith of my empire building sojourn, Bobby our middle boy, asked his mother, "Mommy, why doesn't Daddy live at our house anymore?" That question rang a loud alarm bell within. Maybe an answer would be to bundle up the kids and run away from the world before it was too late.

Carole and I had long dreamed of someday owning a sailboat and slipping away to the South Pacific. All those mounting potential problems added fervor to what might have sounded like a hairbrained scheme at another time. In a sailboat, we could run away from the world. If it looked like the kids might be misled by wrongminded peers, we could pull anchor and move to another island, or even another country.

What's more, by that time we had lived in Terrace for seven years. We were getting into a rut and losing our gift from the nomads. Up to that time, six years was the longest we had ever settled in one place. We'd better get a move on.

Our subdivisions were completed. Lot and house sales were beginning to transpire. Bank mortgages were on the decline. Only one obstacle remained, the veterinary practice. I returned to my old alma mater, Washington State University, where I interviewed several newly graduating veterinarians. Two ideal candidates pre-

Running Away

sented themselves; Dr. Lou Elorza and Dr. Les Hays. They were a pushover to convince, as they too, were full of adventure and well motivated to experience the wilds of the north country. Directly after graduation, they moved to Terrace and joined me in a partnership. After a year, they were ready to take over. The budding sailors were unleashed from the shackles of land.

Shopping for a boat was nearly as exciting for us as sailing. However, not everyone is as equally enamored with sailing as we. A simple experiment has been developed to help discover if sailing is the answer for you. Anyone can test themselves by following these five simple steps in the privacy of their own bathroom.

1) Put on your very best and most expensive suit.
2) Step into the shower room.
3) Turn on the cold water.
4) Now proceed to tear up $100 bills while standing under the cold water. wearing your most valuable suit.
5) If this gives you any kind of thrill or enjoyment, then sailing may be for you.

Unaware of the test, we dove headlong into the sailing scene. We read periodicals and books, talked to other sailors and traveled as far as California to study boat design. We finally agreed beyond any doubt, that the absolutely perfect style boat for our purposes was a fifty-one foot Gardin designed ketch known as the Force 50. It was fifty-one feet long, and could sleep eleven people. It was well built, extremely strong, and seaworthy. The interior, floors, walls, furniture, and two spiral stairways were all covered with teak from one end to the other;. (I think the teak spiral stairways were the feature that turned Carole's crank.) Force-50s are built to resemble an ancient sailing craft, with turned up bow and lines molded in the fiberglass sides to give the appearance of a wooden hull. Ample teak trim and decks on the outside increased the wooden-boat effect. The boat came equipped with a powerful and reliable four cylinder Perkins diesel engine hidden beneath the floor. We found a Force 50 in Seattle to probe and discovered they were built only in Taiwan. The builder was contacted and soon construction began on hull No. 14.

A year of total frustration followed. Months passed by after the estimated completion date and still no boat. Many complications arise when boats are built far away. Some are never started or delivered even though paid for. We listened to horror stories from others who contracted foreign-built boats. Were we also victims of a terrible hoax? Finally, on February 3, 1973, our boat actually arrived. Looking back on our naive expectancies, we were extremely fortunate to have received an exceptionally well built boat.

A huge Japanese freighter made the delivery to a loading dock in the Green River estuary near Seattle. After waiting over a year, we were ecstatic! We rushed to Seattle barely able to control our hyped up emotions. As we stood on the wharf, we could see our boat majestically poised atop the freighter, five stories up. Most astounding to behold was to watch Carole scramble up the side of that ship, over freight boxes, and up floppy rope ladders. I could barely keep up with her as I shouted ahead the directions for her to go. This was my blind "handicapped" girl?

Our next surprise was the tremendous size of a fifty-one foot boat! It weighed 57,000 pounds and was actually fifty-seven feet long considering the bow sprit and other accessories. The keel contains six tons of iron ballast, equivalent to the weight of six automobiles.

When a boat is delivered by a builder, it arrives only partially fitted. Masts and rigging are lying on the deck and most metal fittings are packed away inside. To our dismay and eventual panic, several rather important components, normally installed by the builder, were not in their place. Professional boat fitters joined us to help unload the boat and prepare for sailing. Facilities for boarding the sailboat were unavailable once afloat in the water. Thus, it became necessary for us to climb aboard before it was unloaded from the freighter. We were lifted high into the air by a giant crane and then lowered into the river. It was a fingernail biting thrill to be suspended by a cable, eighty feet above the water, swinging precariously to and fro.

Carole giggled, "This is great!" I always wondered if she would be as brave if she could see?

The crane lowered the boat into the flowing river and once the engine started, the longshoremen let go the lines. We had motored only a few hundred feet when water was discovered spewing into the bilge at a frightening rate from several formerly unnoticed openings in the hull. At the same time, the poorly installed drive line broke loose from the engine, leaving us without power.

At the mercy of the river, we drifted swiftly downstream in the current, out of control, with the water level in the bilge rising rapidly. The foreboding word "sink" began to take on real meaning.

Pushing aside all feelings of doom, we managed, somehow, to guide the boat to drift alongside and grab a hold of another large freighter anchored in the river. There, we tied a line to rings on the side of its hull. The hull of this freighter slanted outward and upward hiding us under this vast wall of steel. We were out of sight and hearing for any assistance from its crew. Many "Our Fathers" and "Hail Marys" were breathed as we rushed to plug the fountains of water pouring into the bilge.

This did not resemble the happy sailboat venture we had dreamed of. Once the final hole was plugged, we went to work on the drive line and manned the pumps to remove a foot of river water now in the bilge. Darkness was rapidly descending as we gratefully limped into our destination at Des Moines, a few miles south of Seattle.

It was interesting that our spirits were only lightly dampened by that harrowing near-disaster. We had survived our first debacle and felt confident we could handle even greater tests.

We left the boat in Des Moines, securely tied to the dock, while it was made ready for the sail to Victoria. We returned to Terrace long enough for the kids to complete the school year and for us to clear up loose ends. Moving onto a boat was an excellent method to reduce excess worldly goods otherwise difficult to part with while living in a roomy home on land.

Our new boat required a name. We didn't want to call it "the boat" for sixteen years like we did with our dog, "Puppy". He was called Puppy all sixteen years of his life because we could never agree on a proper name. Dad came to the rescue with a very oriental-sounding name for the boat. Our three daughters are Marggie, Carita and Shannon. Using their names, Dad created the name "MARITASHAN," which we considered pure genius since it also had a proper oriental ring to it. Puppy remained Puppy.

Two months after her arrival in Seattle, Maritashan was rigged well enough to sail north to Victoria, or so we thought. Two other budding sailors, Roy and Kathy Brown from Terrace, joined our voyage. Just as we entered the Straits of Juan de Fuca, catastrophe struck again. A storm blew up, and at the same moment the chain link steering mechanism collapsed. With our tails between our legs, we limped into Port Townsend, the nearest safe refuge. If that weren't enough, on entering the marina, the drive line separated once again. With no power and no steering, this time we were at the mercy of the wind. We watched helplessly as we drifted into disaster, the nearest fishboat! The bow sprit on a Force-50 protrudes forward from the bow an additional six feet. With this powerful ramrod, we skewered ourselves a fishboat and wiped out its entire fishing apparatus and cabin window.

The port captain approached, surveyed the mess, and stated coldly, "I wouldn't want to be you people. The owner of that fishboat is a hippie and he looks real mean."

Reluctantly, we contacted the owner, and with rising trepidation, awaited his arrival. He sauntered down the dock. Our heads hung low as he started to speak. He must have possessed a big heart under his hostile appearance, after all.

He spoke only one line, "Boy, am I glad I wasn't on board when you hit. My friend here thinks he can repair everything for fifty dollars."

I couldn't believe my ears!

In Victoria, we located some very proficient boat fitters. Together, we examined and corrected every function on the ship. Hopefully, we would never experience a repeat of the earlier calamities.

We installed every emergency and safety device available. During our days in Terrace, we had owned an ancient thirty-five foot power boat which we purchased for $700. Then I acquired a lifeboat to go along with it. I complained to Dad that the lifeboat cost more than our original power boat.

True to his predictable philosophy, Dad thoughtfully proclaimed, "Look at it this way Jim, if you save just one thousand kids worth a dollar each, you will have paid for the lifeboat." We followed that philosophy in preparing the Maritashan.

Running Away

When school ended in June, we piled five of our kids, one dog, two cats, and the necessities of life into our VW van and headed for Victoria. Young Jim remained in Terrace to work and joined us later. I watched the people hurrying along the sidewalks of Terrace as we drove through the town for the last time.

I thought to myself, "You poor unfortunate souls; you have to remain here and endure this boring life."

Our seventy pound part-German Shepherd dog, the one known as Puppy, and the cats, Frisky and Stinker, became part of the crew. Cruising advice recommends no dogs at sea, especially big ones. However the kids considered Puppy a fundamental component of the family. "Where we go, Puppy goes." After finding quantities of kitty litter in the bilge, we gifted the two cats to my ever patient father. Kitty litter plugs the valves in a bilge pump.

Many sailboats ply the Seven Seas. Some are famous for being the swiftest, some the smallest, others for the skipper surviving single-handed across stormy seas. Some find fame traveling the farthest or surviving the wildest storm. Our claim to fame was a great pile of kids from one family at sea. Our six were the crew, with various additions and subtractions along the way.

Two of my nephews, Joe and Ted Revlock from Philadelphia, joined us for portions of the trip to California. They had planned to travel by bike, but Joe was injured in a severe fall and was forced to give up the bike adventure. The bike's loss became our gain.

Jim Jr. was seventeen when we set out. He spent a lot of time reading and thinking. Forever inquisitive, he was never satisfied *that* things worked...he had to know *why* they worked. His grandmother once commented, "If you ask Jimmy for the time of day, you will likely receive an explanation on how to build a watch." Jim was trying to find himself and didn't want to remain forever naive like his parents.

Marggie was the next oldest at sixteen. Her most serious dilemma was leaving a pet calf, Bollo, and cat, Frisky, behind, as well as many school friends. A great deal of effort was required to wind down all her pending social engagements.

The vice principal's advice was, "If they give you any static, just tie the teenagers to the mast and go!"

Poor Marggie resented my pulling her away, so I bought her a diary and suggested she keep track of how much she resented me.

Carita, at fifteen, was also reluctant to part with friends, but with no alternative offered, accepted the challenge in her usual enthusiastic mode. After all, she was weary of feeding her horse anyway.

Motivation to excel was a tradition at Veritas Catholic school, the smallest school in Terrace. A city-wide marathon race found the Veritas students winning the first nineteen places. To our surprise, Carita took first place. After careful reflection, it became less of a surprise. While preparing for school, she regularly procrastinated and generally missed her bus. Most mornings, she was obliged to run three miles to make school on time. Three years of this routine molded her into an Olympic level contender for any race.

One time at sea, her brother, Jim, was taking pride in what a charming person his sister was. Just at that moment, bare handed, she dragged sixty feet of half inch anchor chain onto the boat, and with one hand, slung the seventy-five pound anchor on deck. He thought, "Well, so much for charm."

Shannon, thirteen, like the other two younger members of the crew, always seemed happy, gentle and everybody's friend. Bobby and she were inseparable pals.

Bobby was twelve. He's just a neat guy. My sisters called him the S.O.B., "Sweet Ol Bob." He spent a lot of time on the boat reading everything he could lay his hands on.

It seems younger children find less difficulty leaving home. Mark was the youngest at nine. He was always ready for anything, happy to be part of the gang, and continually preparing or manufacturing something. We became accustomed to his resourcefulness.

Before leaving Washington State, we were moored in Bellingham near a boat belonging to a contractor who had been employed by Evel Knevil, the dare devil stunt man. He constructed Evel's stunt props. Recently, he had built a ramp so Evel could attempt a jump across Idaho's Snake River in a speeding convertible car. (Evel failed this attempt and ended up in the river.) While we visited, the contractor watched Mark with a keen interest. Mark launched our dingy, loaded it with crab traps, paddled out into the bay, caught himself several choice crabs, then returned to the boat. He cranked up the Coleman stove and cooked a gourmet meal with salad and all the trimmings. The contractor marveled and exclaimed to the proud parents, "I'd like to see that kid when he grows up. He's going to be something."

And then there was Puppy, deliriously content to be anywhere with his kids. He was sold to this veterinarian as a tan colored, purebred German Shepherd. Each month, as he matured, evidence of his breed purity diminished further. One ear hung straight down and the other stood erect, giving him a hint of at least minimal Aryan ancestry. He may not have been pure, but neither was he just another "cocker scandal". Puppy did not appreciate being left behind. One time, he was told to stay home. Fifty miles away from home, we heard muffled snoring and discovered a large stowaway beneath the car seat. His surreptitious plot to deceive was unveiled in the ecstasy of sleep.

Anticipating dangers that might lay beyond in foreign lands, we encouraged all six to enroll in Judo lessons. Even if self-defense never became necessary, the experience and self-confidence they gained from judo was well worth the effort.

Jim was a late-comer in tasting Judo victory, but finally advanced to the winning circle. Marggie and Carita were more or less equal champions in their weight class. When they fought each other, we had to cheer for both. It probably sounded strange to hear us shouting, "Come on Carita, that a girl Marggie!" Likewise, Bob and Shannon made nearly an equal match.

Mark, the little guy, continually came out on the bottom in every duel, until one day he tired of that status and announced in a determined voice, "I'm sick and tired of losing all the time."

With new found determination, he threw the next opponent over his shoulder and promptly pinned him to the mat.

These kids held an advantage over other contenders. They had been vigorously battling each other, tooth and nail, all of their conscious lives. Friends would marvel as they watched them bleed and giggle simultaneously, rarely showing any sign of anger.

Before the northwest divisional tournament, I was doing my often, "non-present parenting".

The coach, in an effort to remedy my shortcoming, advised, "You had better come to the big tournament. One of your children could be Olympic potential."

"Which one?" I queried.

"If you really want to know, come to the tournament," he replied.

To our complete amazement, he was referring to our cute little innocent-appearing Shannon. With her long blond curls hanging down, at age nine, defeated all contenders, both boys and girls her age and two years beyond. It was sad to watch the little eleven-year-old former boy's champion cry after sailing over the head of the determined little blond. Contestants are required to ritually bow, then seat themselves at the edge of the mat. Shannon, in her exuberance, couldn't contain herself.

She ran up into the bleachers and plunked herself on my lap chirping, "How'd I do, Daddy?".

Daddy, and her granddad next to me, both had to turn our heads to hide the tears of pride.

The referee stopped me at the exit and remarked with a grin, "You better talk to that girl when she turns seventeen, she may never get a date if she keeps this up."

The crew became the envy of other skippers. Many boaters along the way offered to trade crews when they witnessed how jovially they behaved, yet how efficiently they handled the big ship. Fortunately, others seldom noticed their maniac behavior on board or the mischief they unearthed on shore. Members of a family stay in harmony on a long ocean crossing, whereas mixed crews often develop serious conflicts.

I informed the crew that I was to be addressed as "Captain Wonderful" for the duration of the voyage. This command was ignored totally, except when, with sarcasm, they found a crying need to irritate me. They

The Admiral

embroidered the words Captain Wonderful across the front of a sweater which they presented to me accompanied by pretentious, yet pompous ceremony.

There is a certain level of prestige that should go along with being the captain of a boat. I tried to impress Carole by gloating over my new title. She boldly announced, "OK, you go ahead and be Captain Wonderful. I'm the Admiral!"

After two months of practice sailing in the San Juan Islands, we were ready for the plunge to California. A serious legal problem arose when I tried to obtain radio equipment for the trip. It would be foolhardy to go off-shore with six children on board and no emergency radio equipment. We could not have a Canadian radio license since I was a U.S. citizen. This problem changed to hair-pulling frustration when we were told the boat was a Canadian registered boat, so it could not have a U.S. radio license. Bureaucracy and red tape are so special!

I conveyed the problem to a naval officer in Seattle.

He agreed. "You have a serious problem. You better phone the department of transport office in Washington, DC."

He gave us the number, and at four p.m., without thinking about the time difference in Washington, DC, I phoned. A man answered who was obviously one of the head honchos, if not "the" honcho. He informed me it was seven p.m. there, and the office was closed, but he was working overtime on an unusual situation. I poured out my sad predicament and he listened with a genuine sympathetic ear.

"Boy, you do have a problem. You cannot go out into the ocean without emergency radios! Listen, you don't know me and I don't know you. I'll tell you what you'd better do. Load that ship with everything you need to be safe. The worst thing that can happen is you could go to jail, but jail is a heck of a lot better than drowning. Good luck."

His advice made a lot of sense, so we immediately installed all three VHF, AM and single side band radios.

With apprehensions at a peak, we set out that September down the rough weather coast of Washington and Oregon for five long days. With continual rain, fog, and high seas, it was not a pleasant trip. Most of the crew became seasick. One morning, I entered the main cabin to behold a great pathetic pile of bodies on the cabin floor...a huge mixture of six kids, books, laundry, bedding, and everything that had fallen from shelves in the rough seas. Atop this great heap was one big puppy, like a cherry on an ice cream sundae, all cuddled together for consolation.

When we reached Crescent City, California, Puppy, with a pained, yet determined expression on his face, leaped to the wharf when we were still ten feet away. He had not relieved his bladder in a Guinness-record book of five days, and me without a catheter. His front end made the distance, but the rear dangled down over the wharf. He whined, struggled, and finally managed a rear foot on top. Then, with great effort, climbed onto the wharf and ran to the nearest bush. His relief procedure lasted for several long minutes. Many dogs are able to show a sort of smile. However, there was a genuine heartfelt glow of ecstasy radiating from Puppy. That job completed, he continued his joy spree leaping about the beach, grasping whatever came in sight into his mouth, and flinging it into the air while he bounded after the next object. After that uncomfortable experience, we taught him to use a canvas on the forward deck, the so-called "poop deck".

During a storm while making the next passage along the California coast, the boat exceeded its hull speed, sliding down an extremely large wave. The boat spun sideways and the sail jibed, causing the sixteen-foot main boom to break in two. We learned from that to always tie the boom forward when surfing downwind on heavy seas. We crawled into San Francisco Bay where the boom was repaired. We prayed that would be the end of major breakdowns on the voyage.

In Los Angeles, we were greeted by my sister Margaret Duran, her husband David, and their family of four. We spent three enjoyable months in California, then continued on to Mexico for another three and a half months.

Our eldest boy, Jim Jr., left the ship in California and entered journalism school at Pasadena Junior College. This was the most painful moment of our otherwise happy adventure. Jim was eighteen and our communication left a lot to be desired. I mistakenly thought he hated me bitterly; he may have felt the same about me. It broke our hearts to see Jim standing alone on the wharf as we sailed away. Why couldn't things work out different? Why couldn't we just go on forever being a happy family? I was left with the feeling that my calling to be a dad had failed miserably. We were not ready for our nest to empty, especially the first born.

Brother Jim Callanan joined us in L.A. for the trip through Mexico. Jim was the Oblate brother from Terrace, who had conned us into the Marriage Encounter and performed the task of school athletic coach for the kids. He took a three-month sabbatical leave to join us. Brother Jim consoled us after the departure of our boy and gave the other kids a feeling of being at home.

The three and a half months in Mexico were filled with fun, excitement, adventure and misadventure. We tried every form of Mexican food, camped in the Mexican wilderness, and attended Mass in their spectacular ancient churches. While attending a bull fight one day, the crew became part of the contest when the barriers broke down three different times and the rampaging bulls sent us all scrambling for high ground. We even prospected for copper and gold with our mining enthusiast friends, Lefty and Billy Gardner from Smithers. Each year, the Gardiners prospected the hills of Alamos while avoiding winters in the north. The kids found companions wherever we roamed, either on boats or on land. They thrived on Mexican culture as if it were their native land.

While residing in Alamos, some of the less desirable Mexican lads became overly enamored with our daughters. Lefty alerted us to the fact, and on his sage advice, we returned to the boat, pulled anchor, and left the Casanovas behind to conquer the maidens from some other crew.

We plied the waters in the Sea of Cortez for several weeks, living a rather carefree Mexican life punctuated with little surprises. On one occasion, I failed to check the level of diesel and halfway across the Sea of Cortez, the diesel tanks ran dry. At the same moment, the wind began to wane. There we sat, becalmed, until four in the morning when a sixty knot wind returned with a vengeance. Carita was alone at the wheel while the boat lunged from one giant wave to another.

When asked if she was scared, "No, I was mad!" she retorted. "Why me?"

A half-hour later, we narrowly missed losing the boat and bringing our entire adventure to an untimely end. We dropped the anchor in a sand bottom near the village of Loredo where we hoped to refuel with diesel. We intended to avoid that town because rumor had it that the port captain was insane. (It was said he liked to tear up passports and shoot his revolver into the air to emphasize his point). While arranging to go ashore in the dingy, the anchor pulled loose in the unstable sand. Maritashan drifted to shallow waters and shuddered as it bounced along the bottom in the angry swells. I raced to the cook stove. One quart of fuel remained in its tank. Somehow, the engine restarted in the nick of time. A few seconds more and the boat would have floundered over on its side and wrecked in the violent swells. Not far away, we found a better bottom ground in which to anchor.

A second mishap visited us in the calmer waters of Mazatland Bay. On most days in Mazatland, we attended the downtown celebrations. We returned one evening, puzzled, to discover our boat no longer in its place. While searching in a panic, a young man from Chili approached to report what had taken place. His wife noticed our boat had drug anchor and was drifting toward the exit of the harbor. Once free of that bay, it would be well on its nonstop way to South America. The Chilean couple tried to board, but Puppy would have none of that and kept them at bay with his fierce beast act. Frustrated with the dilemma, they noticed his tail wagging as vigorous as his bark. It was then they decided he was a fraud, called his bluff, made friends, and were able to come aboard. On retrieving the anchor, they found it covered in garbage; a rotted cable wound round and a rusty old bucket over the end.

We discovered the harbor at Mazatland doubled as a sewage dump. The odor was sometimes rank, so we carefully avoided contact with the water at all cost. The kids reluctantly transported Puppy to and from shore in the dingy, at least twice each day, to take care of his toilet needs. On one of Carita's turns, Puppy's footing became off balance. In panic, he jumped from side to side. Each time he jumped, the dingy rolled further over. Finally, over it went, all the way, dumping Carita and Puppy into the putrid water. Her wonderful siblings were terribly amused. Holding their sides, they rolled around the deck in uncontrolled fits of laughter while poor little Carita treaded in the mire with a countenance of disgust, until she rescued herself in the refloated dingy.

CHAPTER 5

Mexican Jail

The three and a half months in Mexico were punctuated with excitement, adventure and misadventure. La Paz, Mexico was a "fun place". An assortment of interesting sailing families congregated there in the bay. But, here also, we encountered our greatest fiasco. When entering a foreign port, most countries require that all sailors report to the port captain first and foremost. A good deal of time and effort was expended with the La Paz port captain, satisfying the customs requirements. Mexican officials love red tape. Five copies of a two page crew identification were required, together with copies of all ship's papers, birth certificates, passports, registration of firearms, supplies, and Puppy's medical history, etc., etc. I struggled through my newly acquired Spanish language for nearly an hour as he patiently listened and prompted. I never realized he was "pulling my leg" all the while. Later that evening, we ran across the same official in a downtown restaurant.

In broken English, he labored, "How you Spanish come?"

"OK," I replied.

Then in eloquent college English he quipped, "Well keep it up Mac, you're doing real fine."

"Of all the...!"

The spectacular misadventure occurred later that same evening. Carole and I were living-it-up downtown; the kids asleep on the boat. The Mexican celebration preparing for the season of Lent was in full swing and we joined with enthusiasm. Now, the toilets in La Paz were overcrowded due to the holiday season, and impossible for the staff to maintain. Carole was not comfortable using the Braille system to explore an overused Mexican public toilet, so we decided to take advantage of the privacy provided under the ferry landing. All of a sudden, eight military officers in white uniforms appeared on the scene brandishing submachine guns. It would be reasonable to state that they caught Carole with her pants down.

"That will be forty pesos fine," ordered the officer in charge.

Earlier in the evening, we had downed several glasses of tequila courage. I told the officer I did not believe in paying bribes. This was the second big-mouth mistake of the evening. The first was not yet apparent.

I took Carole's arm and uttered. "Let's get out of here." Third big mistake.

The barrel of a machine gun was placed securely against my abdomen. Within three minutes, the paddy wagon arrived on the scene.

Demonstrating heartfelt repentance and humility, I lamented, "about that forty pesos, I have it right here."

The officer grunted, "No morbido." (No Bribes.) "You will now get into the police wagon."

Abandoning all further protest, we promptly obeyed and were whisked away to the La Paz Mexican jail. I agonized when it was obvious they had escorted Carole away, I knew not where. All sailors were well versed in horror stories of Mexican jails.

The thought came to me, " If I ever get out of this place, never will I so much as look at tequila again."

The police escorted me to a large, dimly lit cell containing twenty other prisoners. The foreboding rear of the cell, without any light, loomed a gloomy black and gave the appearance of an unending abyss. The only furniture consisted of hard wooden benches fastened to the gray smoke stained walls all around the perimeter. These served as seats by day and beds at night.

One young American befriended me and became my personal guide and informant for the duration of my incarceration. I shared the concern for Carole and the ominous tales we had heard of Mexican jails with this new found confidant.

He reassured me, "You should not worry. All of us are in this jail because we belong here. We broke the law. You will probably be released in the morning."

"Mexican jail stories are often exaggerated," he explained.

At least no one had reported any mistreatment here. In Canada and the U.S., you pay a clever lawyer to talk your way out of jail. In La Paz, you pay directly for your crime in one way or another. Carole and I would be released when the police changed shifts. It would not look good to the arresting officers if we were freed while they were still on duty.

I became cautiously relieved. His confident reassurance seemed genuine and he apparently understood Mexican law. Later, I discovered Carole had idled away the night drinking coffee and eating cookies with a prostitute who failed to pay her license fee.

The parade of events which began to unfold in our cell then became so fascinating that I dared not sleep for fear of missing the action.

Across the hall in another cell, we observed a scene of luxury and creature comfort, not what I expected in a house of detention. The crude floor was buried under a luxurious Persian rug and the room was adorned with ornate furniture. Four, apparently contented, gentlemen were seated around a large oak table in the center of the cell. They seemed to be enjoying a friendly game of cards. A bottle of wine and four crystal glasses shared the center of the table. My advisor informed me these people were in the drug trade and managed business from the jail. He speculated the system evolved into a sort of a cat and mouse game. The police felt better able to keep an eye on the entire network by allowing them to operate from prison rather than somewhere in hiding. Prisoners could have any comforts within limits they could afford; from all appearances some could afford quite a bit.

Excitement began to blossom when, at first, we could hear vigorous scuffling down the hall, accompanied by a violent exchange of opinions. The iron gates opened and a new prisoner was hurled into our cell with enough thrust to skid him a good distance across the floor.

He was yelling, "You cannot do this to me. I am Mexican law student, I go to the Mexican university. I am Mexican citizen."

My guide reassured him, "Hey, don't sweat it, Mac. This guy next to me is a doctor."

He soon settled down and issued no further comments. Shortly thereafter, another prisoner sailed through the gate in similar fashion. He screamed and carried on like the first, but the minute the jailer disappeared, he rose and brushed off his clothes.

Grinning, he unscrewed the heel of his shoe, removed some sort of drug from a compartment in the heel, and announced an invitation, "Come on boys, let's have a party!" Most of the cell mates joined him and, together, they disappeared into the darkened depths of the cell. My guide returned with a puzzled look on his face.

"Aren't you joining us?" he asked.

"Sorry, I'm trying to get out of here, not qualify for permanent residence."

By this time, I was more at ease. The intriguing pageant continued. I was told you could set your watch by the entrance of a great heard of rats in the night. That parade invariably commenced at two o'clock sharp. The rats failed to show that night, and my cell mates were notably disappointed as they seemed quite proud of the event they wanted to display. I was assured their failure was quite unusual. Perhaps, they were shy from all the activity that particular evening.

The next event was heralded by the emergence of a frail and elderly man out from the deep inner sanctum of the cell. He staggered toward the gate. Until then, his presence had remained unnoticed.

My guide coached excitedly, "Watch this guy, he is really good!"

With his back to the gate, the old fellow slid heavily to the floor. Then, with a loud scream, he was overcome with violent convulsive seizures. He banged his head against the gate, screaming pathetically in a raspy voice. I leapt to his side with the intention of cushioning his head! My guide grabbed my shirt sleeve and pulled me back.

"Hey, don't screw it up," he pleaded. "Just watch. This guy knows what he's doing."

Sure enough, in a few minutes, the jailer arrived with an eight ounce bottle of tequila in his hand. He passed the bottle through the bars, then lo and behold, miraculously at the mere sight of the bottle, the convulsion ceased as quickly as it had begun. The jailer strolled calmly away, as if it were part of his routine. The old man sat up, smiled, and with a look of triumph, imbibed in a healthy swig from the bottle of medication. Without a word, he disappeared into the gloomy depths from whence he had emerged.

I never slept that night. At four in the morning, they offered freedom upon payment of a $50 fine, $45 more than I had.

The thought dawned, "Why didn't I agree to the forty peso offer the night before?"

Leaving Carole behind for security, I was allowed to return to the boats where I was able to borrow fifty dollars for Carole's bail. She seemed to be unruffled by the experience and offered that the prostitute was a delightful conversationalist.

As we parted, my guide and other cell mates presented a list of requests.

First, "Please don't call our folks back home. It's better they know not where we are!"

Next, they requested a large supply of vitamins. They feared their diet might be lacking? I returned to the jail with an armload of vitamins and sundry supplies.

The jailer sternly rebuked me, "Vitamins are not allowed."

"Why not," I asked.

"The prisoners grind and smoke them for kicks."

Embarrassed, I departed from the jail scene never to return.

Like the other inmates, I knew this event was not the type of adventure my mother or Carole's mother would be proud to learn. The episode was omitted from our letters home. We experienced many adventures in Mexico, but this provided the greatest measure of education.

Later that same day, we discovered the nature of our first big mistake. One should not go potty under the ferry landing when the president of Mexico is due on the ferry the very next morning. Here was the reason for the militia guarding the ferry landing, and consequently, the cause of our free lodging for the night.

Sailing Beyond the Sea

CHAPTER 6

On to the South Pacific

A nagging question lingered from the onset of this voyage...we prayed and wondered, "Does this family have what it takes, including luck, to survive an ocean crossing to the South Pacific?" Our ship was one of the largest and most complicated in the area. Total experience at sea consisted of seven months along the shore. Most other boaters we met appeared as mature and seasoned sailors. The majority of our crew members were between the age of nine and seventeen. Our first mate had a vision problem.

Standing on the beach, looking out across the largest body of water in the world, was a humbling experience. We chalked up some good experience, but by most standards, would still be considered pretty green.

Many mornings I woke at four AM with sweaty palms and thought, "Are we terribly foolish? Who are we to challenge that giant ocean with our funny little crew?"

I kept the apprehensions to myself. Carole and the kids had no such fear. They kept urging, "Lets get on with it." They weren't aware I was stalling, hoping courage would somehow reach out and grab me.

"Lets go to the South Pacific, Daddy," pleaded Marggie, the girl who was so difficult to extract from her friends at home. "*Everybody* goes back to California."

The worst fear stemmed from the responsibility of seven other peoples' lives. Not only were they our beloved children, they were other peoples' grandchildren. What if even one was injured or killed? Peter Gonzales, our new crew member, was ready anytime. Peter, who joined us in California, was Dave Duran's nephew, another to be responsible for.

Earlier I mentioned, if the kids got involved in any trouble, we could always raise the anchor and move to another country. Guess that should hold true for delinquent parents as well. Two weeks after our jail term, we made the decision. "Let's go for it!"

Once the decision was made, an endless list of essential preparations developed. You can't just *go*. Maritashan seemed better prepared with equipment and emergency supplies than most boats, a slight thread of consolation. A world traveling sailor friend of my sister Lois, met us in Mexico. He relayed to the folks back home his opinion that we didn't look very competent. His observation was probably pretty accurate, but my mother didn't need to hear that opinion.

A single side band radio we had purchased in Washington failed to function properly. Three weeks went by waiting for the radio to be repaired and sent back from Washington to Cabo. Guess we would be waiting for it yet if not for our hero Dave Duran, who in the midst of his busy life, dropped everything, and personally delivered the radio to Cabo.

One good thing developed out of La Paz, Mexico. We had the good fortune to make the acquaintances of Wayne and Bridged Walters, a couple from Vancouver, sailing on a Trimiran, the Gaviota II. Gaviota is the Spanish word for seagull. They became our siblings of the sea, searching for the same courage to cross the big pond. Our common interests drew us together, and we soon enjoyed a congenial friendship. It was reassuring to have another captain to share concerns.

In mid-April of 1975, we weighed anchor at Cabo San Lucas with 400 gallons of water, 360 gallons of diesel, and a half ton of groceries stowed in the hold. Hopefully, that would sustain the colossal-eating-five for a while. The village of Nuku Hiva in the Marquesas Islands lay 2550 miles southwest of our Mexican anchorage, across the equator and a vast expanse of wild ocean water.

Gaviota in front, we rounded the giant rocks protecting Cabo San Lucas from the ravages of the sea. Immediately, heavy seas confronted our vessel. The wind was whining through the shrouds at 35 knots. (I hate it when it makes that sound.) In the Northwest, this is gale warning stuff. In Mexico, it means fishing will be a little rough that day. Typically, the Sea of Cortez has gale force winds every other day this time of year. Gaviota decided to turn back until the weather improved. We followed and spent the remainder of the day picnicking and throwing Frisbees on the beach to divert our thoughts from the concern that lay ahead.

The following day, we ventured out to sea once again. With winds reduced to twenty knots, the sea was still menacing, but considerably improved. Gaviota glided along a quarter-mile away, over our starboard quarter. She would completely disappear from sight when descending between swells. For long periods, we could only catch glimpses of her mast tip. It was strange to note that apprehensions and fears seemed to vanish as the sight of land disappeared. We were now committed. (Or should we have *been* committed.)

Trimirans are triple hulled boats, and under most circumstances, faster and more comfortable to sail than traditional mono-hulled boats. Their single drawback is their reputation for turning turtle; that is, turning upside down in severe weather. They are said to be more stable upside down than upright. Many reports tell of sailors surviving on an upside-down trimiran hull, cutting through the bottom to reach the stores in the hull.

We expected Gaviota would leave us behind, but to our surprise, we traveled faster, at least on some points of sail, due to our longer water line length. Visual contact disappeared after the first day at sea. That was a little disconcerting save for the fact both ships carried AM and VHF radio equipment, good up to 300 miles, so hoped to keep in touch. We agreed to make radio contact each day at 0800, 1400, and 2000 hours.

We devised a plan, which would be an exciting challenge in celestial navigation, to rendezvous at Clarion island and then again in mid-ocean near the equator and toast our genius with a martini. The meeting place would be 1200 miles from Mexico and 1300 miles to the Marquesas Islands (only a mile to the land below).

Never before had celestial navigation been essential, although we had practiced a bit when we knew our location. A boring, ho-hum exercise then, but now had become a serious exercise in survival. The sextant may have smoked a little from overuse those first few days.

According to ocean charts, Clarion is a tiny island that should be 400 miles southwest of Cabo San Lucas, Mexico. Locating it would be a good test of our ability to navigate. It was small and not visible on my chart. Wayne had to point it out to me on the chart as I had inadvertently buried the island under the fine pencil line charting our course. If that little Island could be located, we could find *anything* in the South Pacific. If not, and celestial navigation wasn't "as advertised," we could always turn due east, and eventually bump into land, either North or South America.

Feverishly, I checked and rechecked the charts all through the night as we neared the vicinity where the island was supposed to be. Over and over I plotted the sun shots recorded the day before, and experimented with star shots for the first time. My plotting chart looked like a wild chicken yard with lines and scratches running in every direction.

We reduced our speed during the night by dropping all but two sails, in case the island showed up before the calculated time. Colliding with a solid rock wall in the dark of night became a real concern. Bobby and Peter were manning the helm for the early morning shift. I was resting in the cabin, trying to squeeze my eyeballs back into their sockets after searching the dark throughout the long night.

Peter managed to show less emotion than anyone I have ever known. I never heard him say anything as ecstatic as "oh gee". Early that morning, from the cabin, I heard him mumble something under his breath. Because my nerves were on edge, I sat upright and shouted, "What did you say?"

"There's the island," he calmly proclaimed.

Would you believe it was there, exactly where our plotting said it should be, ten degrees off the starboard bow, fifteen miles SW! We exploded with excitement! Celestial navigation works! Gaviota checked in at 0800. With ecstasy impossible to hide, we announced our arrival and reported our imminent anchorage in a small bay in the lee of Clarion island.

Exaltation at finding the island was humbled a dash when we encountered a tiny sailboat leaving the anchorage on its way to Hawaii. We weren't the only sailors who could find an island in mid-ocean. The couple on board directed our way to avoid an encounter with a huge coral reef in the bay. It was reassuring to see humanoids again. As we entered, a large American fish boat cruised by several miles to the south, the last sight of humans for many days.

Clarion Island was a delight to explore. Exotic birds, lizards, and tracks of giant turtles were everywhere. Clarion originated from a long ago, burnt-out volcano, and many lava tide pools dotted the beach. A closer exploration found them teeming with life. Schools of the most beautiful tropical fish we ever observed banded together in the coral branches for safety...orange with blue trim, white with black stripes, green with purple trim, and jet black. Countless species of little marine critters darted about the pools. Hundreds of brightly colored crabs swarmed across the rocks as we approached. Octopus and giant snails occupied the shoals, but were not much into "swarming".

Coral piles galore, two feet high, lined the beaches in every direction. In California, coral sold for 50 cents per piece. At that rate, we tramped over several million dollars worth of coral. Thousands of pucca shells were strewn all about. These were even more valuable back home. We didn't collect any puccas; certain that unlimited amounts would turn up along the way. Those were the last we ever saw outside of jewelry stores.

Two whales engaged in a colossal free diving exhibition in our bay, one with a large bite ripped out of his tail. We speculated on the story that must have produced that enormous wound.

Maritashan and Gaviota anchored in the shelter of the uninhabited island for two nights, then set off on the long stretch to Nuku Hiva, 2,150 miles beyond.

The seas grew more turbulent as the security of Clarion's bay disappeared over the horizon to the north. Half the crew was seasick during that first week. Carole, Mark and Shannon suffered the most. Seasickness is a terrible malady...tired and can't sleep, sick and can't die, hugging the toilet bowl, the last solitary friend in a topsy-turvy world. About the third morning out of Clarion, the crew was eating very little. I found Mark in the galley, literally stuffing himself with corn flakes and milk.

"Why are you eating like that?" I asked. " I thought you were sick?", "

"I am," he pitifully moaned, "But when I throw up, I want something to come out."

After seven days, the crew recovered. They started to talk about ice cream and hot dogs. Whenever the conversation turned to food, we knew their stomachs would soon be happy once again. Eventually, they were reading books and managed some school work.

Two crew members stood on watch at all times. Our family size was perfect for three teams of two crew each. Each team took the wheel for three hours; Dad and Shan, Peter and Bob, Marg and Carita. Mark took turns on all shifts. Night and day, each team took their turn at the wheel. It was tough, especially for little guys, to wake up and take charge at 2 o'clock or 5 o'clock A.M.. They complained very little and only at the start. Really, there was no alternative. Heading back now would be more difficult than to carry on and there was no place to park that thing in mid-ocean. All kids, reluctant at first, decided after Clarion Island, that sailing was a pretty neat adventure after all.

As Maritashan plunged southward through the rollers, nature furnished a perpetual real-life video for the kids. Two days out of Clarion, those on the early morning shift spied two giant turtles lumbering by. Schools of flying fish continually entertained the crew. Inherently corny, Carole inquired, "Are they schools of flying fish or flocks?" From a tiny half-inch to about twelve inches in length, they took off from the water when startled by the boat, or a "bigger fish in the sea" desired them for lunch. They fly as far as several hundred yards at a time. Actually they leap into the air, then glide with the aid of trade winds until a return to the sea is safe. This was exciting to watch, but after you see thousands, it's like everything else. "Oh, (ho hum) there goes another flock of flying fish."

Bobby and Mark holding flying fish that landed on deck.

On to the South Pacific

Shannon was sleeping in her bag on the cabin deck one night. I stood at the wheel nearby and heard a muffled muttering and wiggling from inside her bag. "What's the matter, Shan?" "Yikes," she cried, "there's a flying fish in my sleeping bag." She gently dropped the eight inch fish back into the Pacific and curled up once again to sleep.

Nearly every morning, we found flying fish on deck along with squid that the waves had tossed aboard. One day, a fish flew through the hatch and landed on the rug in front of the stove. What service! Shannon refused to allow their consumption; they were "too cute". Each, in turn, was returned to the sea. Good thing we had good food stored; it's difficult to survive on "cute".

On several occasions, we discovered huge dorsal fins cutting the surf along side; no swimming for us out there in the deep. Porpoises joined us in our journey nearly every day, showing off their act, playing "chicken" as they dove under the bow. Sometimes, they actually collided with the boat. A resounding thud sent vibrations through the length of the hull. Sound travels well through fiberglass. It was fascinating to lay in the bow and eavesdrop while porpoises babbled and gossiped to one another.

Marggie and Carita were steering one day, and shouted below, "We are passing a big green box floating in the ocean and there's a giant turtle tied to it!"

The turtle was at least three feet long, they claimed. We arrived on deck too late to observe the event. Later that day, when we talked with Gaviota, the girls, without thinking how vast was the ocean, asked Wayne if he might have seen a giant turtle tied to a green box.

They were mortified to the degree only teenagers can when Wayne replied with a wee touch of sarcasm, "Oh sure, we see lots of big green boxes tied to turtles. They are all over the place. Sure!"

Never was our world without birds; several species we'd never viewed before. Albatross often appeared, presenting their twelve-foot wing span, as they glided in the heavens above. In their abundant spare time, the kids speculated on topics like "where do birds nest 1,000 miles from the nearest land? Do they lay floating eggs, or very light eggs that will float in the clouds?" When bored with that line of thinking, they would sometimes compose trivial little songs on such topics as sickness or other equally heartening themes. Further south, the weather began to change. Cloudy skies, and sticky, damp air signaled the start of the doldrums. The doldrums are a weird place with tremendous cloud formations resulting from the meeting of northern and southern weather patterns. Cloud bursts drenched us regularly. Lightning and thunderstorms were frequent. Looking around the horizon, a dozen separate storms could be seen, known to sailors as tiger squalls. Meanwhile, the sun would maintain its brilliance in the sky up above. The squalls were identified by a black cloud over each. Doldrum seas were often mixed up, but not too rough. The wind seemed to come from several directions at the same time.

One night, Carita and I received a wild reception while on deck to reduce sails during a storm. Just as I touched the main mast, the entire length of the halyard rope extending parallel up along the mast, burst into brilliant blue flame with a resounding crackling and popping. After the shock subsided, we realized it was St. Elmo's fire, a harmless electrical phenomena that occurs during tropical storms at sea. As a makeshift lightning rod during storms, we kept a half inch copper cable dragging in the water attached to the metal shrouds.

Gaviota remained in regular contact and reported she was positioned about 200 miles to the north. Realizing the increasing clouds would make celestial navigation impossible, we decided we had better try soon to rendezvous. We agreed to aim for a point six degrees north latitude and 127 degrees longitude. By reducing sails for two days, and then changing to a northerly course, our paths should meet. That should occur around 10 p.m. Darkness descended. Radio contact became loud and clear, indicating Gaviota was near, but nowhere in sight. After a few hours of search, we decided to postpone and try again another day.

Three more days and the doldrums hung on. The days continued hot, sticky, and weird. Lying on the deck at night, wearing nothing but shorts, was even too warm for comfort.

Bad news hit that evening. We discovered diesel had somehow contaminated our water supply. A chemical called Bio Bar was added to the diesel to prevent the growth of filter clogging algae which thrives on diesel in the tropics. This toxic chemical rendered the

On to the South Pacific

water undrinkable. Nuku Hiva was at least another ten to twenty days away, and no drinkable water available! Now what?

We chased down a tiger squall. By lowering the sail part way, a sort of trough formed in the sail and we collected twenty gallons of rainwater from the squall. Providing the winds cooperated, rationing water, the twenty gallons could last. My mother taught me to pray every day. Why do I always wait till there is a crisis to start?

At latitude four degrees north this time of year, the southeast trade winds should have started to blow. Officially, that was the end of the doldrums, but nobody informed the wind. We decided to have a picnic with popcorn, pickle and pop, to give our spirits a boost.

Emergency supplies contained a plastic floating solar still which supposedly produces one quart of pure water in a day from salt water. It didn't work. It produced salt water from salt water! Tremendous! We then constructed a still from fifteen feet of copper tubing, coiled into a water bucket. One end connected to the pressure cooker, the other to a collecting bottle. We placed the pressure cooker on the Coleman stove and sat back. After about thirty minutes, drops of water started to ooze, then a steady dribble, and finally, a substantial stream. The first few spoons were terribly bitter from the tubing. As the mechanism proceeded to perk a generous production of clear, clean water, distilled from the sea flowed at the rate of one quart per hour, more than sufficient for eight sailors. Jubilant at our success, we then went to work on the 200 gallons of polluted water in the port tank with renewed vigor and confidence. Thick layers of medical cotton served as a filter. Lo and behold, the water came out clear and tasteless, good enough for cleaning. At the same time, the southeast trades commenced to blow. Boy, were we ever wealthy!

Boat speed had been increased those last few days, and we even motored one day to reach Nuku Hiva before the water supply ran dry. This left Gaviota far behind on the trail. Their wind was not as steady. With new confidence and plentiful water, we reduced our speed to attempt another rendezvous. Both ships were on a heading of 190 degrees. Gaviota's crew could not see sun or stars due to heavy clouds. We were under clear skies and knew our position from the stars. Gaviota estimated their position and continued in our direction. Maritashan turned about and headed northeast. Using the AM Radio, we counted, sang, babbled trivia, and joked over the radio while Gaviota tuned in with their radio direction finder. I hoped no other ships could hear those crazy kids. They would be convinced our crew had been in the hot sun too long and lost it for sure. As dusk began to descend, we motored two more hours, heading ten degrees at eight knots. Gaviota proceeded for two hours at six knots, heading 190 degrees. Our best guess showed us to be twenty five miles apart and we should meet if our calculations were true.

Searching the horizon, Gaviota was nowhere in sight. The radio direction finder indicated the positions were correct, but that gives a choice of two directions, 180 degrees apart. We were unable to learn if the beam is behind or in front, unless you have a pretty good idea to start. Could Gaviota have passed us by? If so, we would now be moving away from each other.

Wayne suggested we wait until dark and signal with a flare. Maritashan Shan hoved-to and feasted on a dinner of fish called Wahoo. (They say they call them Wahoo because that is what you shout when you hook onto one, "Wahoooo!") This was a three-footer which the Gaviota neighbors gifted us during the rendezvous at Clarion. Wayne apparently could catch fish wherever he went.

At 1730, the dishes finished, we prepared to launch a flare, when all of a sudden, the radio crackled alive, "This is Gaviota to Maritashan Shan; Gaviota to Maritashan; we see sails two miles dead ahead. Is it you?"

"I don't think there is anyone else out here," we hurried to reply.

Fifteen minutes after starting up the engine, Maritashan and Gaviota were happily circling each other in mid-ocean. Mexico lay 1300 miles behind and Nuku Hiva, 1200 miles ahead. Several minutes were used cheering and congratulating ourselves for our remarkable navigation skills. The plan had been to tie the boats together and celebrate, but seas were far too rough. Both ships would be damaged had we tried. After several minutes of cheering and compliments, ad nauseam, we downed our promised martinis. At the same moment, the sky broke loose with another, now familiar, doldrums downpour, as if to say, "can the ego trip you guys, lets get on with it." The crew closed down the hatches, raised the sails, and the two ships turned south in search of a new world beyond.

CHAPTER 7

Equator

On the following day, the Pacific Ocean stretched out before us calm as a lake. Southeast trade winds appeared softly on the scene and a gentle sea started at noon. It was the most pleasant sailing we had ever experienced, carried over long easy swells. Soon the winds increased to fifteen, then twenty knots just off our port quarter. We moved along at a steady eight knots of speed.

The long days were all much the same; smooth sailing became the norm. We took advantage of the ship's automatic pilot allowing more time for school. The kids managed four hours of schoolwork each day. No more excuses to postpone the lessons. Two terms would be too long for the kids to go without school, so we had enrolled them in correspondence school from Victoria before leaving Canadian shores. Carole used the excuse she was blind and I reasoned I was too busy managing the boat. The kids tackled the work on their own. Mark was a little young to be on his own, so Marggie took on the task of his dedicated tutor. They progressed remarkably well, in spite of milking the seasick alibi every chance they found. Each time we arrived in a port, they mailed the finished work to Victoria and notified the school when and where to forward their corrected tests and new lessons.

Bobby's science course contained a chemistry set. Trying to perform experiments on a rolling, tossing boat proved an arduous task. Returned papers were often badly wrinkled and blotched from sea water stains. One essay Bobby wrote described his home that floated on the sea, but didn't have any trees in the yard like his former home. The teacher correcting the lessons was highly impressed. The vice principal back in Terrace was right; what they discovered about the world couldn't be learned from a book or a school.

A typical day at sea consisted of steering, cooking, eating (a lot), studying, and mostly goofing around. Cooking on a rough sea was an adventure in itself. Carole performed most of the culinary art. Often, the entire meal spewed across the room in rough weather. If Carole wasn't alert, she wore it.

Carole and the girls learned from others, but developed many reputable survival recipes on their own. One popular treat was sea water bread. It consisted simply of sea water, flour and yeast. "Wednesday Night Surprise" was a semi-delightful "goulash" made from a combination of canned green beans, wax beans, kidney beans, and tomatoes folded meticulously in with a can of corn-beef (or canned roast beef on very special occasions), delightfully seasoned with exotic flavor-enhancing pepper and salt.

Three cases of oranges purchased in Mexico survived exactly two days after discovery by the voracious five. Ten pounds of turtle meat acquired in Mexico seemed to last forever.

Four of the crew in mid-Pacific

Chicken noodle soup was a favorite, made by the gallon using canned whole chicken and Mexican noodles. Various salads were concocted using cabbage, the only green food on board that would keep. Twenty heads of cabbage survived just under three weeks.

Carole and I guarded a secret stash of rare delicacies such as nuts, antipasto, red wine, and junk snacks hidden under our bed. These would have vanished in seconds, like dust in a vacuum cleaner, had the crew ever discovered them. Our berth, located in the stern, provided an escape to maintain sanity when the juvenile crew turned on their animal act.

On a few occasions, alone at night with the kids sound asleep below, Carole would join me on deck. The sky, full of stars, clear to the horizon in every direction, provided a most romantic setting. With warm tropical winds flowing by and the moon lighting the way, we realized the nearest other people were a thousand miles away. Memories like those will not be easily forgotten.

Rarely was it possible to stroll around the deck without hanging on to something rigid. Sitting usually wasn't a problem, but sleeping became a learned art on a rolling sea. We learned to lie diagonally across the bed, otherwise every time the boat yawed we would roll over and wake up. The kids' berths were built on a slant so they were kind of wedged in. Often they slept on the floor. To this day, none of them have difficulty sleeping wherever they are.

Boredom often becomes a major problem at sea. We watched, with interest, as the crew developed projects to entertain and stave off monotony. Bobby was always the comedian and would keep the others entertained for hours. His precise portrayal of a seagull landing was the performance of most renown. He would receive repeated encores until the seagull became so fatigued, it could land no more.

Mark was the most enthusiastic sailor on board. Up at daylight, he wanted to be involved in whatever projects the others found, either work or play. He tried his hand at celestial navigation and eventually accomplished the knack! He could produce a line of position as close as anyone. Not bad for a ten year old. Marggie also became an accomplished navigator.

The girls learned a hot secret tip from a California hairdresser, never before disclosed until this writing. She used Palmolive dish detergent and sea water to wash some of her clients' hair. People came from far and near to receive this secret hair treatment. Washing each others hair over the side of the boat, using this formula, became not only a game, but a required routine for teenagers. They used a canvas bucket on a rope to scoop water. One morning, Marggie was rinsing Carita's hair over the side. The boat lurched causing Carita to lose her balance. Marggie caught her seconds before she would have become a mid-Pacific floating object, difficult to retrieve in huge swells at ten knots of speed.

Saltwater baths on deck were a welcome relief from the sticky humid heat of the tropics. The ocean water temperature generally remained near eighty degrees. It is difficult to imagine how eighty degree water could actually feel cool. When the air temperature hovers over one hundred degrees, cool becomes a relative sense.

For electrical needs, we installed an alternator in California, powered by the freewheeling propeller when sailing. This produced electricity at the rate of six amps, far more than needed to keep three bus-size batteries well charged.

May 4th 1975 was a memorable day. At 15:30 hours, the momentous equator crossing would occur. Due to strong steady winds, we arrived a half hour early, longitude 128 degrees 40 minutes, latitude 0 degrees.

The crew was ready for a celebration with New Years noise makers, balloons, peanuts, popcorn, canned milk shakes and miscellaneous junk food. We hailed Gaviota on the radio so they could join in our celebration. The revelers launched fifty balloons into the sea, the ship's bell rang loud and long and the kids cut loose of any relationship to sanity. They shouted and cheered like maniacs.

We thought it unfortunate; there were no signs or flags on the road telling us this was the equator...a most important landmark (seamark) on the surface of the earth. Steak, baked potatoes with sour cream, and wine was the carte du jour. We really had it tough. The celebrants exhausted, we sailed on into the night at a steady eight knots. My admiration for this crew continued to grow. They roused each other in the middle of night, took their shift without a complaint, and maintained a nearly perfect course, no matter who was at the wheel. Who needs Captain Wonderful?

One evening, I felt a little dumb after executing a celestial star shot. The easily located star, Arcturus, viewed through the sextant, seemed to shine with an extra brilliance and appeared to be moving. I removed the sextant from my eye just in time to see what I deemed to be Arcturus disappear over the horizon. My Arcturus turned out to be a roving satellite, circling the world. The north star was lost from sight near the equator and the southern cross came into view.

Gaviota caught fish nearly every day, so why couldn't we? We put out the lines and, sure enough, hooked a big one which we towed for half a mile. As the furious denizen of the deep approached our craft, a vigorous leap broke both the line and the pole. We learned from that experience to use a rubber bungy and 200 pound test line rather than a pole and fifty pound test. There were some good ol big ones out there. We read ocean crossing reports claiming that fish were unavailable in mid ocean. Gaviota disproved this by catching fish nearly every day with the exception of the doldrums. Even we, who were not great catchers of fish, managed to capture several tuna after learning the art.

Some days the winds grew stronger and waves rose higher. When storms came up and ominous sounds pierced the night like something about to break, I became inspired to pray once again, with a grand new fervor. We reduced sail often during those past few days when our speed rose well over nine knots, the intended hull speed for Maritashan. Faster than hull speed results in difficult steering and can lead to most undesirable events at sea.

Sailing Beyond the Sea

CHAPTER 8

Paradise is Many Islands

I once read that sailors could smell land long before it appeared on the horizon. There it was, the unmistakable tropical perfume, sweet essence of coconut wafting over the sea, two days before we were to arrive at our first South Pacific landfall. The fragrance created a thrill of anticipation. The night of May 10th seemed to pass slower than the entire eighteen days at sea. Again, if celestial navigation is 'for real' and not just science fiction, Ua Huka Island, our first sight of land south of the equator, should come into view just off the port bow, twenty miles south. Daylight finally appeared at 0600 hours. A great dark cloud covered the horizon, obscuring any hope of sighting land; kind of an ugly old cloud that shouldn't have been right there. At 0630, the sun rose over the cloud and it quickly melted away. The stunning scene that unfolded before our eyes was breathtaking, the fabulous steep slopes of a huge green jungle resting in the sea and rising to the sky. Only one word could do justice to the sight, "Wow!"

Marggie's celestial navigation was bang on. Marggie, Carita, and I were on duty, and quickly shook the crew out of their deep slumber to share the grateful news. Land was in sight, banishing all fears that the sea had no end; what a remarkable occasion and incredible thrill for eight ocean-weary mariners to experience.

Nuku Hiva, our first landfall, lay due west, another thirty miles. A large smudge of cloud veiled this island, too. It didn't take shape for over an hour. Maritashan began to tug at her reins and her speed increased to ten knots. Could she smell the land? Caution thrown to the wind, we turned her loose and let her fly. Soon, we were close by the shore and peering up into the rocky crags of that second wondrous mountain rising out of the sea.

Nuku Hiva is larger and higher than Ua Huka. The east shore first came into view. The high cliffs gave the appearance of six giant apes standing on guard. Two tiny rock islets marked the entrance to Nuku Hiva Bay, our destination. Inside this bay, we discovered a quaint little village nestled among luxuriant banana and coconut trees. The jungle-covered volcanic mountain formed a perfect backdrop for this breathtaking sight.

Eleven other sailboats anchored in the bay. Maritashan was not alone in the world, after all. Two were from Germany, three from France, one from England, two from U.S., one from Panama, and two others unknown. The Gaviota joined us in Nuka Hiva and often sailed alongside in many areas of French Polynesia. The sailing families and the natives welcomed us with enthusiasm. The first landfall became the most memorable and most fascinating of all the islands visited. The people of French Polynesia were the friendliest people we had yet come to know.

It is customary, and sometimes mandatory, when sailing in foreign waters to fly that country's flag aloft. We had no way of obtaining the different flags before entering each country on our route, so clever Carole and girls manufactured flags out of colored clothing on board. The French flag was fabricated from the leg of Carole's blue slacks and red blouse and my last white shirt, recently relegated to the rag bag. They fashioned a yellow quarantine flag by using powdered mustard and the final remnants of my white shirt.

The Gendarmerie or port officials gave us no hassle (unlike some of those in Mexico). Many animals meandered carefree through the town, so why not garner a little political favoritism by offering free veterinary services? Twice I learned to regret that offer.

We had mastered the Spanish language in Mexico well enough to stumble through a simple conversation. Now we faced the new challenge to communicate in either French or Polynesian. Since there are only about 250 words in the Marquesian dialect, we soon managed a survival vocabulary in that tongue. Their second language is French, and here, I ran into trouble. The kids, who had studied French in Canadian schools, breezed by with ease. The natives preferred, and we gained a lot more mileage out of conversing in Marquesian rather than French. It was a new experience to encounter a people who resented the French rather than the U.S.

Nearly all locals attended the open air Sunday Mass in the spacious church, together with many of the island's birds and lizards. We recorded on tape the beautiful chanting by hundreds of uninhibited Polynesians, who had preserved 2000 years of original Christian musical tradition. It was interesting to observe an area yet uncomplicated by the confusion of newly invented philosophies, religions, and politically correct language. Indelibly printed in my mind was the elegant life-sized figure of the mother of Jesus carved in rosewood standing beside the sanctuary. I knew that the word Catholic meant universal, but roving in the hidden corners of the world revealed a whole new meaning to the word. Everywhere we roamed, we found tireless missionaries and faithful lay people preserving the original faith. At this stage of my life, church and God had only a passing appeal. Attending Mass in these primitive countries, free from controversy, opened new avenues of thought. My shallow bank of faith acquired definite new deposits.

On the secular side of life, we learned that hooking onto a 100 to 400 pound fish was not uncommon around Nuka Hiva. Interest in fishing back home might become difficult after being spoiled in Polynesia. In one village, we wormed through an excited crowd to view a victorious fisherman displaying his 1200 pound Sword Fish. A trolling speed of seven to eight knots is recommended in those waters. When trolling at that speed, no doubt remains when a big one is hooked.

Life was so enchanting, our time was totally consumed exploring this new world. Goat hunting was available in the next bay to the west, since early explorers like Captain Cook planted domestic goats along his route. They adapted readily to the lush mountain growth. Coconuts, bread fruit, and bananas were plentiful and free.

The Marquesians became skilled wood carvers, especially replicas of an ancient revered, big-eyed, pot-bellied king known as Tiki. We became very fond of one little artist who was badly deformed, but recovered from leprosy. Most of his fingers, parts of his face, and the greater part of his ears were missing. His cheerful attitude and contagious sense of humor seemed to disguise all of those defects. He developed an unquenchable yearning to become the owner of a chain saw we carried on board. Regardless of the fact that he could never operate the saw with his crippled hands, he would be the sole, proud owner of a chain saw in the islands! We agreed on a trade: one chain saw for three large, pot-bellied Tiki carvings. Both of us were delighted with the deal. I'm not sure why we carried a chain saw on board. Trading stock I suppose.

The Governess of the Marquesas Islands was an exception to the amiable people in this land. Her chickens were rapidly diminishing from an outbreak of disease. Six mortalities resulted in a fifty percent reduction of her flock. The Gendarmerie reported a doctor of veterinary medicine was among the sailors in their bay. A command performance was issued in the hopes I might bring the epidemic under control. I invited a bilingual skipper from a French boat to act as interpreter. We hiked three miles to the Governess' mansion...a remarkable little shack, about 5000 square feet of early European architecture, in contrast to the grass huts of the commoners.

The Governess greeted us graciously. Carefully, through the interpreter, we collected all the data, symptoms, and history of her declining flock. I questioned her in English; she replied in French. The interpreter translated for each of us, in turn. I explained that the extremely hot weather made an autopsy impossible, since the birds were well into decay within an hour of death.

In an attempt to match her elitist attitude, I pronounced the diagnosis in the most professional manner I could muster. "It is obvious that your chickens are afflicted with infectious coryza, a common, serious, and contagious malady of chickens." She would have to send to Tahiti, or possibly France, to acquire the prescription of sulfa needed for treatment. In her political position, that should not be a serious concern.

The diagnosis and prescription, translated between French and English, took over an hour. We then engaged in a half-hour social, sipping ginger ale and beer. During this social, the Governess addressed only the interpreter. I was ignored. When the time came to part company, for the first time, she turned directly to me, and in flawless Oxford English, intoned, "You really should learn to speak French, you know."

My nose was definitely rendered out of joint as we proceeded down the trail to the boats.

Paradise is Many Islands

There was another purpose for inviting that particular interpreter. A strange story circulated among the sailors, of an incident during his voyage in the Atlantic that I wanted to learn more about first hand.

En route to the royal mansion, I inquired, "What is this we hear about you and your fellow crewman shooting down an airplane in the Atlantic with a *banana*?"

"Oh, that was very strange." he answered. With arms and hands forming images in the air, he proceeded to relate the story. (My new friend proved the old adage. If you tie the hands of a Frenchman behind his back, he becomes unable to speak.)

"We sail from France, where I was the school teacher. My shipmate, he is run from the law. The trip, she was no problem until one day this airplane she fly over our little bateau. Then, she turn around and give us the buzz. She dive at us and turn around and she dive again. My partner, always he acts like the clown. He tear off the banana and point at the plane. 'Rat-a-tat, rat-a-tat.' And you know what? The plane she crash into the sea! We are full of the fear! We do not know what is happen, or what we should do. Was the sun on us too long? Did we have the problem in the head? Was it all a bad dream? Is it possible the banana is really the gun? We become very concerned.

"We sail to the splash one mile away and you know what? There we find two American pilots in the water. We are surprised! We pull them onto our little bateau. "Sirs, we are so sorry. We not know the banana is loaded! We mean no harm." The pilots, they calm us down. They explain they headed for Florida and run out of the fuel, so buzz us so we see them go down. That problem finish, we have another. There is not room for four people on the little bateau. We sail to the island which is belong to the Dutch. The Dutch, he not let the Americans leave our bateau because there is no passport. One American he say, "Darn, that is the thing we forget as we watch our plane sink to the bottom." Finally, we convince the Dutch that we could not leave with the pilots on board, and they agree the pilots could stay.

"Several weeks after their arrival at Nuku Hiva, these two were on a short cruise with others when a plane flew by. My friend grabbed his shipmate and shouted, "Don't let him touch the banana, he cause too much trouble."

One day, the kids and I were washing clothes in a communal pond with the natives. This clown partner suddenly came flying over our heads, landed with a grandiose splash in the middle of the pond, and proceeded to vigorously scrub himself, all for the sake of comedy. The native women stood for a moment in shock, but soon saw the joke and began to giggle. The last comedy production we witnessed took place near the beach. He was descending into the water while holding one end of a loop of old hose in his ear and the other end in his mouth.

"What are you doing now?" My interpreter friend shouted to him.

Just before his head went under, he shouted back, "I don't like it here. I'm leaving for France."

The original boom on their boat had broken in a storm similar to the experience of our break down in California. They replaced the boom somewhere in Central America with a notably crooked apple tree. It was functioning quit well for two-thousand miles, so no need to change, odd though it may look.

One adventure follows another in those islands. Dangers stalk the unwary in the South Pacific as they do anywhere. In Canada and the United States, poison mushrooms and poison shell fish are plentiful at certain times of the year. The shallow waters off these islands abound with stonefish covered in sharp spines. We paid little attention to these mysterious looking fish until we learned how serious, and some claim even deadly, a puncture from those spines could be.

Certain species of coral fish in the tropics become poisonous when feeding on toxic coral. We were enjoying one of our many leisurely days in the sun, when a Gendarmerie approached in his boat. He excitedly explained that the entire crew of six from an American boat had succumbed to toxic coral fish poisoning.

"The medical team is away from the islands for a week. You are a veterinary doctor. Will you visit the patients at Nuku Hiva Hospital?"

This caused some serious mental consternation. In North America, at that time, the question was being argued; if an off-duty doctor became involved in an emergency and complications came about, who was liable? What was my position, here in a foreign country? Veterinarians have many skills that can be used for human medicine, but I was without a license to practice even veterinary medicine in this French territory. If I refused, what other kind of trouble would I be in?

I asked Bridgid from the Gaviota to come along. As a licensed lab technician, the two of us could, at least, give each other moral support! Feeling very disturbed under the circumstances, we arrived at the hospital and proceeded to interview the patients. Sailing directions recommend that visitors to the islands seek out "local knowledge" as to when and what fish can safely be consumed. Had they not taken advantage of that local knowledge?

"We *did,* " the boat skipper-patient replied, "but everyone on that island is sick, including the chief who provided the feast where we ate the fish."

So much for local knowledge.

After interviewing the patients, it was obvious they were each showing good signs of improvement with no treatment other than rest. Bridgid and I agreed that the best therapy was no therapy, and that seemed to please the people in charge. We left the hospital immensely relieved.

In Tiepi Vi, we met a young Polynesian, Pierre, who developed a keen interest in our daughters. Pierre, unlike some others we met, was every bit the gentleman. He may have been bragging for Carita and Marggie's sake when he described his two occupations. Typing for the government was one, and diving outside the reef at night for lobster was the other.

We had been sternly warned never to swim outside the reefs, especially at night, for fear of the plentiful sharks. We voiced this concern to Pierre.

He scratched his head before his thoughtful reply, "Well, that's okay. But, what *I* don't understand is how anyone can live in a country like Canada where there are bears and cougars running around on the ground?"

The native islanders loved to show off their island. Pierre and friends introduced us to Daniel's Bay on the west end. There they led us to a jewel-like pond formed in front of a cave. A breath taking waterfall careened down the face of a cliff from high above. The natives boasted this to be the second highest waterfall in the world, second only to Victoria Falls in Africa. The waterfall plunged through the roof of the great lava tube cave into a larger pool within. Following Pierre, we swam the length of the first pond through an opening into the pond inside the cave. There, in the larger pool, the roar of the falls echoed like thunder. I shuddered as I watched Pierre wielding my new $300 camera over his head with one hand, while casually swimming with the other. The camera survived, but regrettably, none of the pictures of that fabulous water display turned out. The crew cavorted for hours in the splash of this most unusual aquatic wonderland.

On another occasion, the crews of the Gaviota and Maritashan embarked on a banana harvest expedition. We returned with a generous supply suspended on a long pole. Wayne and I carried the pole on our shoulders, like unto Tarzan and Boy in the popular movie. As we approached the village, we came upon a horse tethered near the trail who convinced us he originated directly from hell. Like a screaming banshee, he thundered toward us with lips curled back displaying a fierce set of glistening white incisors. Rearing up on hind legs, he flayed the air violently, dangerously close to our heads with his front hoofs. We instinctively dropped the bananas and retreated beyond reach of that demonic beast. With an instant personality change and smile of triumph, he calmly sauntered over and proceeded to munch on our bananas. Humiliated at being outsmarted by a miserable swaybacked nag, we quickly called his bluff with a barrage of rocks. He clenched his teeth as he backed off, spread open his lips in a sardonic grin, and whinnied. He left us with the impression he thoroughly enjoyed the exchange.

We visited a bay on the east end of Nuku Hiva, where we encountered Madam Clark, a native widow lady who had once been married to a French sailor. She owned this obviously fertile valley and appeared to be its benevolent dictator. Madam greeted us cordially and led us on a personally guided tour. Ancient ruins were everywhere, some with a history of terror, some with stories of renown. She showed us many house-size platforms made of lava blocks from long past generations. One bigger than the rest and guarded by a larger-than-life statue of the ancient King Tiki, featured a deep pit in its floor. "There," Madam explained, "once upon a time, the warriors threw the heads of their enemies after the chiefs had eaten the eyeballs." She didn't comment on who got the residuum and none of us felt like digging to confirm the story.

As we continued the tour, Madam introduced us to a young surrogate mother who happened by on horseback. Madam explained that she had already borne many children for her relatives who were barren. She peered with a look of disdain at Roslyn, a twenty-five year old teacher from California who accompanied our crew. Roslyn was near the same age, but had not yet borne any children.

While visiting, Madam Clark asked if we could supply her with a quantity of aspirin. We unwittingly obliged and later learned of our mistake. She liked to consume large quantities of wine and aspirin together. Whatever that did for her, couldn't have been good for her health.

Before we left the bay, Madam's townspeople loaded the kids up with a generous supply of bananas, bread fruit, papayas, fifty soccerball size grapefruit, and a fruit known as sour sop. We sincerely appreciated her hospitality; however, the sour sop tasted too much like unto sour goat stomach. It was too dreadful to eat, so was discreetly given a burial at sea.

After one month, we reluctantly departed from Nuku Hiva, where we had made so many kind friends. One day and night's travel south of the Marquesas lay the Tuamotu Islands, also known as the Dangerous Archipelago. These islands were formed over coral reef beds, and lay low in the water. Some of the reefs are covered by water and are impossible to see. The calm and gentle waters are deceptive. Many boats have been lost when holed by one of those beautiful, yet deadly, hidden snags.

Pitcairn Island, made famous in *Mutiny on the Bounty*, is located at the eastern extremity of the Tuamotu chain. We anchored first at Manahee, a pleasant little atoll situated at the western extreme. Atolls are coral islands that develop, more or less, in the shape of a horse shoe. A singular narrow entrance opens into a large central bay protected on all sides by land covered in trees. They provide an excellent natural anchorage. They are flat, only a few feet above sea level. Fortunately, the tide change ranges only one or two feet. The last hurricane had been seventy years before. A mixture of soft, white sand and colorful coral flank most of the island shores. The picturesque islands are covered in palm and coconut trees, continually swaying in the tropical breeze.

Most of the houses blend well into the picture. Generally they are constructed from thatched vegetation and roofed over with either palm leaves or tin. Tin roofs are essential as the solitary source of water supply. They collect the rains which drain into a storage barrel at the corner of each home.

A lad called Tefanui warmly greeted us immediately on our arrival in Manahee. He was a handsome, bronze-complected young man with curly hair, bleached blond by the continual sun. Tefanui was "gifted" with exceptional enthusiasm. He guided us safely around coral reefs to our anchorage, entertained us with his friends playing their ukuleles, and then became "smitten" with our seventeen year old daughter, Marggie.

My forty-second birthday was celebrated here on the beach in a cozy little hut with fanfare befitting that of a native king. Gaviota joined in the feast where music was provided late into the tropical night by Tefanui and his musical entourage. As long as Tefanui's hands were kept busy on the ukulele, my daughter should be safe.

While we were tied up at the village wharf, on one of the area's 365 beautiful days of the year, we were surprised by the arrival of two Canadian sailboats from Vancouver, B.C. The three young sailors were delighted at our invitation to come aboard and indulge in a cold beer. Maritashan was equipped with refrigeration, a luxury few other boats enjoyed. In that weather, anything cold was bliss.

During the conversation, they questioned, "Have you ever heard of a Canadian boat by the name of Gaviota?"

They had met the owners in Mexico and had hoped to meet again. It was great fun to report, "Gaviota is anchored just around the corner, behind those palm trees," in this, indeed, small world.

One of the boats we met in Nuka Hiva moved on to Ahe, the next island west. They radioed back to the remainder of the fleet that Ahe was a most delightful place to be, and the native people were overjoyed with their presence.

It soon became overwhelmingly obvious that Tefanoi's intentions were other than honorable. Marggie had discovered this for herself. She appeared frightened and interest in him rapidly faded after they returned from a walk together. We were becoming more concerned with his intense, unrelenting interest in her, and kept in mind the anchor-pulling option. I believed the only thing Tefanui understood about the ten commandments was "thou shalt."

As Tefanui became even more bold, we decided to slip away to join our friends on the island of Ahe. The word "Ahe" is translated 'paradise' in the Tuamotu dialect. And paradise it definitely was.

By this time, we were beginning to accumulate quite a few boats in our awesome armada. The fleet was composed of the original Gaviota and the Amazing Grace, crewed by our new friends, Tim and Dave. She was a twenty-four foot, converted lifeboat from the Canadian naval vessel, Bonaventure. Tim, from the Amazing Grace played a bagpipe, and we often enjoyed the strains, "Amazing Grace," drifting across the waves as we sailed together through those enchanted islands. I never really appreciated that song until then.

Another boat was the Lori-Sue, a thirty-five footer with a Vancouver couple and their two young children on board. The Larky was skippered by a couple and their young daughter from Seattle. These children were the first of many sailor friends our kids accumulated in the Southern Islands. Jim, a young man from Calgary single-handed his boat, the Alkanoos.

Among the sailing crowd, rarely is anyone addressed using their last name. Sailors are affectionately known by their given first name and the boat they are from, such as "Wayne off the Gaviota, or Jim from the Maritashan." The natives knew us by some description of the boat we were on, or other obvious characteristic. I was known as "Le Capitan De Gran Bateau." This was a big ego thing with the natives, but a source of amusement among our friends.

During their Marquisas passage, the three single boys found themselves on an island occupied by twenty-one single girls and no other men. At the start they, thought they had died and gone to heaven. One day, their attention was distracted during a volleyball game with the girls when Amazing Grace drug anchor. It went aground and a large hole was torn in its side by a jagged coral reef and Amazing Grace nearly met with her Waterloo. Jim's boat, the Alkanoos, later did sink near the Cook Islands, when holed by a reef.

There were six boats in our little fleet. Traveling through some of the more dangerous passages the Maritashan took on the appearance of a mother duck. The smaller boats trailed behind, taking advantage of Maritashan's radar. Radar increased the odds of surviving the passage through areas festooned with low islands and their nearby coral reefs.

As we were setting our anchor in the bay at Ahe, a canoe full of excited native youngsters came alongside. They invited us to a party in the town hall. We warned them that many children were aboard the six boats, especially our own. That only served to enhance their enthusiasm. That evening, the villagers displayed their generous hospitality by an entire night of feast and dance. We were welcome!

The following evening. We decided to reciprocate with the boaters hosting a party. Bobby, Mark, Shannon, and their friends produced a huge five-gallon tub of popcorn. The islanders had obviously never experienced that delicacy before. The first time around, the villagers gingerly picked out one kernel each. On succeeding passages, they dove in enthusiastically, with both hands.

The day after we anchored in Ahe, who should arrive on the deck of the Alkanoos with an ear to ear grin beaming across his impetuous mug, but that pesky Tefanui. Marggie cried, "Daddy, don't let him come over here," and dove for cover. I played the stern and dotting father, and finally discouraged this latest Casanova, whose sole cranial content appeared to be hormonal. He sailed back to Manahee, presumably brokenhearted. (We were saving Marrgie for a guy named Doug back home, who as yet was undiscovered.)

Our crew and the native kids became instant friends and joined Ahe's daily volleyball games. Shannon became close friends with Laureen and Susan from the boat, Lauree Sue. Susan and her father challenged Shan and me to a sailing dinghy race around the bay. We won the race in our Boston Whaler sailing dinghy, and to this day, hold the one-and-only coveted "Ahe Cup."

Marggie became special friends with Mama Fanna, the very robust, jolly mayor of Ahe. Neither spoke the other's language, but would sit for hours sipping tea, smiling, and laughing. Finally, Mama helped Marggie compose a short Tahitian dictionary which improved their dialogue considerably, as well as our own. Many tears were shed by both when, once again, it became time to raise the anchor and move on to every sailor's ultimate destination, the "big apple" of the South Pacific, Papeete, Tahiti.

CHAPTER 9

Tahiti

Gaviota and Maritashan sailed side by side as the high volcanic mountains of Tahiti first signaled their welcome. We raised all sails and raced Gaviota for the last ten miles to the harbor entrance at Papeete.

Papeete, Tahiti, is the center for the French government, and the largest town in French Polynesia. Tahiti belongs to the group known as the Society Islands. In contrast to the Tuomotus, but like the Marquesas, the Society Islands are high mountainous volcanic eruptions, blanketed to the top by rich, green jungle growth.

Most sailors arrange to arrive in Tahiti for the celebration of Bastille Day. This is the French national holiday commemorating the destruction of the Bastille prison in France, 14 July, 1789. We discovered much of the story of the Bastille was propaganda. When the Bastille was captured, there was only one solitary old prisoner remaining in captivity. He had been institutionalized and even reluctant to leave. It gave the revolutionaries a cause to promote a war, but in Tahiti, it was a cause for a month long celebration. And what a celebration! Here, an unprecedented education lay in wait for our traveling students during their colossal field trip, and a great opportunity to acquire even more interesting new friends.

This small history lesson regarding the Bastille was just the beginning for the young ones. They soon took part in an exercise of current affairs. During our stay in Tahiti, the Russians and Americans collaborated in a joint space capsule expedition. The recovery ship, Vanguard, tied up in Tahiti, not far from our moorage. For the first time in history, the public was allowed to come aboard. The ship resembled a floating Houston Space center, with 'acres' of high-tech, scientific instrumentation. We met the captain, and were surprised to learn he employed daily readings with the ancient sextant identical to ours, in spite of access to millions of dollars worth of the latest high-tech navigation equipment.

Early in our visit to Tahiti, I felt this insatiable urge to return home to be with my dad one more time, in case it might be the last. We last saw him shortly before departure from Washington State. He looked so frail! I was deeply torn at the thought of leaving the family tied up to a quay in a foreign country, six thousand miles away, but all agreed it would be best that I go.

Flying over waters in one day that had taken six weeks to cross in a boat, was kind of an anticlimax. I went immediately to the ranch. It was so great to be with Dad one more time! Even though not many words were spoken, we had an intimate and loving visitation. Before returning to Tahiti, I flew to Terrace to check on how the veterinary practice had survived. The two doctors were managing very nicely in my absence. This did not sadden me in the least. Cheerfully, I returned to paradise.

Our stay in Tahiti lasted longer than any other anchorage, June to September. There was so much to see and do. We swam ,we snorkeled, we hiked, and like every landing, we sampled all food offered in the country! Here, we attended Mass celebrated in French and Latin in their great cathedral. Most Polynesian people are Catholic with some others attending a branch of a Mormon church. We enjoyed visits with international airline travelers, sailors, and Tahitians.

Polynesians and Mexicans love kids and voiced their approval of our large family. This was in stark contrast to affluent Canadian and American tourists lolling about in their various international condominiums or yachts.

One such questioned Carole haughtily, "Are all those your children?"

"Yes," was Carole's pert reply, but they are not *all of* my children."

"I'll bet the world hates you," The lady retorted.

"Not the real world," Carole countered.

Carita, Shan and Marggie found four girls their own ages; Monica, Leslie, and Karen, on a California boat, Aegir; and Joanne, Shannon's age from the ferro cement boat, Babalatchi. Babalatchi was a Canadian boat from Gibson, B.C. The girls became inseparable during their stay in Tahiti, and dubbed themselves the "secret seven." It was uncommon to find a spoiled child among the inconveniences of sailing. All kids were generally well-behaved, with one notable exception. We were mortified parents years later when the girls confessed to an evening in Tahiti when this naive secret-seven were chased and nearly caught by a pimp. They had followed some prostitutes and tried to spy through their window. They were lucky we didn't learn at the time. They would have been immediately sentenced to the brig or worse.

One night in Tahiti, Puppy turned up missing. After two days of searching, panic ensued. Earlier, the kids were aghast to discover butchered dogs, skinned and hung to age behind a delicatessen store. (Dog is a delicacy in Polynesia.) We had visions of him roasted and stuffed with an apple in his mouth. Many joined in the search, day and night. Great was our relief when he finally reappeared on the third day, his tail between his legs, but with a guilty smirk painted across his face. True facts of the three-day frolic were never revealed to the rest of the crew.

In Tahiti, we met the Kitchings, Bill and Dawn, and their precocious seven year old, Simon. We soon became lasting friends. They lived on the forty-foot Meridian II from Auckland, New Zealand. Bob and Mark loved to engage Simon in conversation; his accent was so cute and his behavior so clever.

Once, while observing the big dog, Puppy, he asked, "And why is it that you call him Pup, when he's not a pup atoll."

Simon watched us popping corn, something he had never witnessed before.

The seven year old declared, "In New Zealand, popcorn is virtually unheard of."

Life must be pretty dull not to have kids to watch. While tied to the quay in downtown Papeete, Mark gathered several pieces of junk and fashioned a fish spear gun, a quality replica of the local native spear guns. Several adult natives were quite impressed with his project and came aboard to observe and to coach him through the final stages of his endeavor.

Next in line, the island of Moorea beckoned to us. It is only a short hop and within sight of Tahiti. There, we anchored under the cone-shaped mountain, Bali Hi, after which the movie *Bali Hi* was named. We will always remember this island for its giant plants, flowers as big as dinner plates, and spiders of equal size. When Carole was caught in a monsoon rain storm, I picked a three foot philodendron leaf for her, which adequately served as an umbrella.

An umbrella for the Admiral on the island of Moorea

It is impossible to describe the beauty and the exhilaration of visiting all these fantastic little Edens, especially by boat. Airline tourists never see the real outback culture of the islanders. Forty miles west of Morrea lay the island of Huahini, the next objective. One thing that kept us moving was the excitement awaiting beyond each successive new horizon, and never were we disappointed. Each landfall revealed a whole new world.

While anchored in Huahini, we received a call on the AM radio. An urgent message was waiting for me at the Gendarme's office in Bora Bora. Unable to learn the contents, we set sail for Bora Bora, a one day passage. The message; Dad had passed away.

No one in Washington knew where we were. My brother, Dave, located a ham operator in Spokane who transmitted the call on what is known as the "pacific net," centered in the New Hebrides Islands. The message was sent from there in every direction across the Pacific, and relayed to me through the Gendarmerie in Bora Bora.

This was a sad day, but somehow not so unbearable as I had thought it would be. I recalled the vision-like experience Dad had recounted to me, and how fascinated he was to discover that there really is a God and that afterlife is not just a ferry tale. I gave thanks that I had given in, less than a month before, to that overwhelming desire to return and be with him one more time. The government officials, who always seemed so cold and callused toward sailors, were ever so sympathetic. They led us to a concealed World War Two submarine bunker where we could secure the Maritashan. There, in that concrete barricaded refuge, I could rest assured the family and boat would be safe, even in the event of a hurricane.

The Gendarmes, with attentive care, organized flights from Bora Bora to Tahiti so that I could connect with a flight to Spokane. Mark joined me for moral support. He was Granddad's special buddy. Everything progressed like clockwork so that we arrived in time for the funeral. It was good to be there. I managed to hide my ecstasy at having Jim Jr. join us after so long apart. I didn't want to embarrass the teenager. During the funeral, they played a tape of Amazing Grace on bagpipes. That hit a tender spot, with the gang 6000 miles distant and our friends with the bagpipe on the boat, Amazing Grace, standing by.

I was asked to say a few words at the funeral. I related Dad's profound spiritual experience to those present. Most had never heard of the event and assumed he still maintained his unbelief. I broke down after that, reading aloud a most meaningful poem that Dad was reading the night he entered eternity. Now, he could enjoy fully that great loving vision he couldn't find words to describe.

Sailing Beyond the Sea

CHAPTER 10

Return Toward Solid Ground

Many tales could be told of the Maritashan's South Pacific passage. Many volumes could be filled with adventures and anecdotes. As August, 1975 was coming to a close we felt the time had come to head toward home. We couldn't be bums all our lives; or could we? Carole was not at all ready to return and the kids were becoming content with their vagabond life. Wayne and Bridgid stayed on and worked in Tahiti for a time and many of our other friends sailed on to the Cook Islands and New Zealand. Bill, Dawn and Simon on Meridian 2 eventually joined us in the North Pacific. Economically, we would have done equally as well to stay, but something was drawing me to return. Adventures lay beyond that brought definite changes to our lives and to our way of thinking.

In my early years, reading material consisted of science and medicine. On the sailing trip I read only two small pocket books. The first one "Life After Life", was written by a doctor, Raymond A. Moody, MD, who interviewed a number of people injured in severe accidents or affected by a life-threatening illness. At one point they were pronounced dead. Later they were revived to tell of fantastic supernatural sights they had witnessed. This sort of story would not ordinarily interest me, but for the fact these people described exactly the same scenes Dad had related to me when I was seventeen. Dad was not prone to wild claims or fantasies and was known as a stable and knowledgeable person.

My first thought was "Gee, too bad Dad couldn't be alive to read this." Then something dawned on me and I had another thought.

I laughed at myself: "Hey, he's there, he doesn't need a book!"

The other book was written by Malcolm Muggeridge a famous non-believing writer who wrote about Mother Teresa of Calcutta.

Here is a lady who is accepted and revered by the whole world, when in fact, she is practicing exactly what the world is telling us is ridiculous and foolish. She was dedicating her entire life, every moment of her life, to the poorest of the poor for the love of her Creator. She called herself a fanatic. Malcolm changed his philosophy and was converted from just being in her presence. Even religious educators and leaders were telling us we must have a "balance", don't go overboard on this religious stuff. Mother Teresa meanwhile, like St. Francis was bubbling over with a joy unequaled by anyone seeking the pleasures offered by the world. St. Francis was considered a nut by the world's standards.

One quote from Malcolm Muggeridge haunted me, "Anything that is not about eternity, is eternally worthless."

My Mother, the one person who made the greatest impact on my life explained to us when we were young, "In the end nothing else matters but the condition of your soul. The way you behave now will determine your eternity. This life is just a blip: eternity is forever."

One great advantage of sailing is the time it affords for deep reflection, free from influence by people's hidden agendas, new conflicting philosophies, skeptics and materialism.

Before turning the rudder toward North America and home, we returned to Tahiti and the Warehouse Store for supplies. Enough food was stored to last for our next and longest crossing, Tahiti to Hilo, Hawaii, 3000 miles north. We made one last visit to Robinson's Bay on the island of Moorea. This was such a magnificent little jungle, we wanted to remember the South Pacific just that way!

Seventy year old Kermit Parker anchored his boat Patience near by. Kermit was a boat broker from California. He and his quaint little wife of equal vintage had attempted the crossing to California several days before. They were intercepted by a violent storm and his wife thrown across the galley. Several ribs were fractured when she collided with the kerosene cook stove. The poor dear lady had to abandon her dream adventure and fly to California for recovery. Three young experienced racing sailors flew to Tahiti to help bring Patience home. Kermit was a rare character, in excellent physical condition for his seventy years and a lot of fun to be around. Kermit and I swapped views and stories over a beer at a sidewalk restaurant in Papeette one afternoon.

"You know," he said," I shouldn't be sitting here drinking like this. Drinking has caused the death of most of my relatives. Mom and Dad, and Uncle George all died from drinking. Aunt Helen and Aunt Martha, they both died from drinking. Granddad too, he died that way. They all lived to be over ninety five but damned if drinking didn't finally get every one of them in the end!"

Kermit departed two days ahead of us for Hilo. As we parted, I said something that somehow must have offended him.

Innocently I joked. "Well Kermit, we will wave when we pass you by."

He turned on me like an angry cat; the first time I ever saw him act other than jovial.

He was obviously insulted and barked in no uncertain terms, "You do not pass a forty-five foot Herschoff Racing sloop with more sail area and half the weight of your Force 50 dog. To say nothing of my professional crew. Your crew are nothing but kids."

"I'm sorry, Kermit, I was only joking," I mumbled with great humility. Guess he had a bad night or maybe it was the stress of undertaking the long crossing to California.

On the passage north we listened regularly to the single side band radio conversations. Every night Kermit's loving little wife would contact Patience from California.

It was really cute to hear her squeaky voice end the conversation each evening with, "Good night Kermit, I love you."

Each time she called, Kermit would report his latitude and longitude allowing her to map the progress of Patience. When we reached the equator, five hundred miles along the way, the readings showed Maritashan had passed the Herschoff sloop and was already 100 miles ahead. The kids, elated after the chastising Kermit laid on me, gave everything they had to maintain top speed.

Sailing directions recommend that when making the passage from Tahiti to Hawaii, first travel in an easterly direction for several days before turning north. This would allow the winds and sail set to line up for a good sail to Hawaii. Before leaving Moorea we talked to people who had recently made that passage. They convinced us to forget those directions and head straight north to Hilo.

The winds were exactly right. We followed their advice, and the winds were perfect. That was the major reason we were able to overtake poor Kermit.

The trip was an exciting one. The winds blew twenty-five knots continually, right on our beam. That is the most efficient wind direction for sailing with the greatest speed possible. Often the speedometer would read twelve knots for long periods as we surfed down giant waves. Some days we averaged ten knots per hour for twenty four hours. At times it felt like Maritashan had sprouted wings and was flying over the sea. With that angle of wind the boat was well heeled over, and the deck continually wet from huge waves boiling over. Several times freak waves would sneak up behind and dump a great slosh into the cabin. One of those sloshed through an open port and destroyed our ham radio set, newly purchased in Tahiti.

On those long passages boredom remained the most difficult obstacle to overcome. Mark always showed the most ingenuity by inventing projects to busy himself as well as the others. Midway on the passage he had persuaded us to help clear the walk-ways on both sides of the deck. He wanted to jog and stay in shape, this ten year old! The deck was fifty feet long. So all things considered, if he ran around the entire deck 52.8 times he would chalk up a mile. This was great sport for all especially on a pitching and bounding boat. The kids developed another popular sport swinging out over the water on a halyard strung from the tip of the sixty foot mast. This trapeze performance caused the parents to shudder at times; best their mother couldn't see.

Any boredom we might have felt completely disappeared one afternoon when disaster struck. Shannon was steering on one of those high speed, big wave days with a wet and slippery deck. Puppy used to hear things inaudible to us, like when the dolphins would chatter below the bow. That day the seventy pound dog raced around the stern deck for some urgent, unknown destination. He collided with Shannon's legs flipping her upside down. Her head hit first and slammed on the hard deck with a resounding thud. No one could possibly hit that hard without incurring a brain concussion or worse. I still cringe when I think back on those moments. We were a thousand miles and ten days from the nearest hospital.

Return Toward Solid Ground

Shannon lay motionless. Then a whimper, a muffled cry, and then, by some miracle, held her head, regained her footing, and took hold of the wheel ready to steer again. With astounded relief and prayers of thanks, we happily gave her a vacation from the helm. I immediately fastened a foot brace to the deck to prevent a repeat of that potentially fatal disaster.

As an interesting diversion on that long journey, we decided to visit the uninhabited island of Palmyra, a little over half-way to Hilo from Tahiti. Carole was our radio monitoring specialist, and was receiving some ominous reports of an incident on that island.

A couple had sailed to Palmyra from Hawaii. Each day they contacted their friends in Honolulu by radio. During their conversations they had described some unsavory characters on the only other boat anchored in the bay who made them quite uncomfortable. In spite of the uneasy feeling, they had accepted an invitation to join the unsavory couple for dinner. That was the last radio message the friends in Honolulu ever received from their sailing friends.

Carole is an accomplished snoop and daily communicated blow by blow reports of the scenario from radio broadcasts. Under those circumstances, Palmyra did not seem as romantic as we had first believed. The reports removed any desire to stop. We sailed on past the very place where a heinous crime may have been perpetrated.

After continuous pleading by the friends of the missing couple, the Hawaiian Coastguard made a flight to Palmyra, but found no trace of either boat. Weeks later, back in Honolulu, the missing boat arrived at the very berth in the marina where it belonged, only with a new couple on board. Although painted a different color, the neighbors recognized the boat and immediately notified authorities. When the police arrived, the new occupants of the boat engraved suspicion on their guilt by their actions. One dove into the water and the other attempted a retreat in the dinghy; both were quickly apprehended.

The trial continued long after we returned home because no victims could be found. Several years later, people on a visiting yacht discovered the bones of the murdered owners washed up on the beach at Palmyra. Originally the bodies had been placed in a metal box and sent to the bottom of the sea. The trial was consequently able to close and a conviction made. Seventeen years later we watched a made-for-TV movie retelling the entire incident.

Thus we continued north. A strange phenomenon puzzled us as we approached Hilo on the big island of Hawaii. Hilo is the highest island in the Pacific Ocean. The big Island came into view 250 miles away. Charts and experts claim a sighting is impossible at that distance. But there it was. Then when we arrived within ten miles it disappeared! Nor could we find a trace of the island when our charts showed it only five miles distant.

The kids used the opportunity to make cute, encouraging little remarks like "Nice going, Dad, here we are in the middle of the Pacific and you are loosing it. Somebody bring me an airplane!"

The last vestige of daylight remained and we could hear the bell buoys on shore, but no island showed. Then all of a sudden at four miles distant, it suddenly exploded into existence. A colossal giant sprang up in the middle of the sea, orchestrating a grandiose entry solely for our benefit. Captain Wonderful was once again exonerated. No one has ever given a reasonable explanation for that strange illusion.

Darkness set in before we neared the bay at Hilo. We opted to drift at sea until daylight rather than hazard an unfamiliar channel in the dark.

We had grown unaccustomed to the kind of landfall that awaited us. We tied up to a wharf and were able to walk off the boat to shore; like downtown Tahiti but unlike most places in the south where the shore could only be reached by dingy. Carole and I were treated to the coldest beer in the history of the world at a little restaurant near the wharf. We all stared in awe at the rows of fresh fruits and vegetables in the supermarkets as though we had never experienced anything like it before.

The Patience, Kermit and his crew crept into the wharf four days following our arrival in Hilo. They avoided us like the plague and refrained from speaking for several days.

Finally one of the young professional crew members sauntered over and said." O K, how'd you do it?"

Again I shouldn't have, but the "devil made me say it." With a kind of phony bewildered look I answered. "All I can say is, good boat -good crew."

The sailor swore under his breath and stalked away. Time heals all and after several days they became cautious friends again. A good-guy skipper would have told the truth about sailing directly north, but we preferred to bask in the glory. We might never have another chance to win a race.

A short time after our departure from Hilo, an earthquake and resulting tidal wave destroyed several boats tied up at the marina. The bay emptied of water causing the boats to fall over on their side. The most severe damage resulted from the raging torrent as the returning mountain of water refilled the bay.

Sailing Beyond the Sea

CHAPTER 11

Intrigue Continues in the North Pacific

The entire voyage was so incredible. How could we ever describe it to the folks back home? One way would be to invite our mothers to join us on the final leg of the journey. At their age, would they dare consider the risk? My mother, Adelaide Proctor, to whom I owed so much, was eighty four years old, and Carole's mother, Elsie Schell, ever loving, but who often questioned our sanity was sixty-one. Once we mentioned the idea, we couldn't have kept them away with an army! Elated with the invitation, they both scrambled to catch a plane for a happy reunion with grandchildren about whom they once wondered, "Would we ever see them again?" Neither mother had been to the Pacific Islands, nor had they been on a sailing voyage. It was an opportunity to show them we cared. Mom was in excellent condition for eighty four years and ready for anything. Mom had thirty-six grandchildren and loved them all immensely and equally.

The seas between the Hawaiian Islands are unusually steep and rough, and waves close together. Many times the Maritashan groaned and creaked under the strain of heavy twisting seas, unlike any sounds we had experienced before, even in the middle of the sea. I noticed the mothers looked a little concerned.

They must have questioned, at times, if the trip was really that good of an idea.

Further north, the seas became more calm, and the "old girls" had a ball. We felt gratified to be able to share our sensational adventure with them.

Many places we visited bore reminders that the renowned explorer, Captain Cook, had preceded us. Here, on the Big Island of Hawaii, he met his end. The misbehavior of some crew members raised the wrath of the local natives and they put him to death. (Let that be a lesson to the Maritashan crew.)

With the mothers anxiously taking in each new scene, we moved north to the island of Maui, a Mecca of opulence. In a rental car, we drove to the highest peak. There, snow and freezing weather shocked our tropic adapted systems. Since all of us were clad in beach attire, retreat followed quickly after arrival.

The Kitchings from Meridian II caught up with us near Maui. The three of them came aboard and joined us for a picnic and a day on the beach at Lanai. The Dole Pineapple Island of Lanai is only an hour sail from Maui. Little did we realize that this innocent trip would lead to another brush with the sinister side of life. Because the wind had died half-way across, we were traveling under engine power. The crew on another sailboat, becalmed and floundering along the way, waved and shouted to attract our attention. When we motored over to investigate, they reported their battery was dead. Would we loan them our spare? None of us will ever forget the little "lady" spokesman. Her stature was small, but the cigar in her mouth was big. She wore a black beret topping off a total masculine attire, including combat boots. Most unforgettable was her language. She poured out a string of four letter words we weren't aware had yet been coined. They accepted our battery and resumed their travel to Maui. We thought no more of the exchange for the moment.

The Dole Company provided a picturesque little campsite among the coconut trees on Lanai. Large waves continually broke on the beach however, providing a most difficult approach. The crew and grandparents made an acceptable landing some distance from the park. I chose the direct approach and braved the waves. My timing turned out remarkably poor. The dinghy flipped upside down and flew high into the air casting poor Captain Wonderful into the sea. The dinghy then descended down on his head, an undignified arrival for Le Capitan de Gran Bateau.

There in the park we enjoyed a relaxing picnic followed by an "unlaxing" wrestling match, as the crew attacked the already wounded Capitan.

Intrigue Continues in the North Pacific

When we returned to the bay at Lahina, the people on the disabled boat had anchored out from the beach a fair distance. We drafted Bobby and Shannon to retrieve the borrowed battery in our dingy. I still shudder when I think about sending them on that errand after the reports we subsequently received.

After our return to North America at the end of the voyage, Bill Kitching wrote often keeping us informed of events in Hawaii. In the first letter, he described his trip to Honolulu. The same little "lady" from the becalmed vessel, requested passage to Honolulu on Bill's boat. "Her behavior was surprisingly quite pleasant," he continued. Apparently he had learned to disregard her four letter vocabulary.

The next letter carried a far different tone.

"Dear Jim;

Do you remember the lady to whom you loaned the battery, and later I transported to Honolulu? Well, they recently discovered her body riddled with five bullet holes, washed up on the beach in a burlap bag. There were several rocks in the bag with her, but evidently not enough, because she drifted to shore. No evidence or motive has yet been found."

Sailing Beyond the Sea

CHAPTER 12
Attempt at Becoming Land Lubbers

North to the island of Oahu and the big city of Honolulu, became the final crossing in our dream-like venture. During the night, as we sailed by, we could just make out the silhouette of Molokai in the moonlight, the island made famous by the leper colony located there. I explained to the children the story of how those doomed lepers were exiled so society could pretend they no longer existed. I recalled the incredible story of Father Damian, the selfless priest from Belgium who came to live with the lepers. He became one with the outcasts to confer on them a shred of dignity. He labored for years to bring joy, some of them health, and finally, some of them rights. After years of sharing their life, Father Damian himself succumbed to leprosy and died in 1885. Unselfishly, he sacrificed his entire life for his brothers and sisters. Why would a man leave wealth and a comfortable life in Belgium to live and die among the most depressed and miserable people in the world? *"No greater love has a man who will lay down his life for his brother."* *"Whatever you do to the least of my brothers, you do to me."* This was a sobering thought for a family on a fifty-foot yacht with all the amenities life could offer. (Another nudge from above?) I thought to myself, why does the media so love to concentrate on the few priests who commit scandal, while the majority of the 400,000 priests in the world more closely resemble Father Damian, the stories about whom we rarely see in the press. They seem to forget that 8.4% of the first twelve priests, hand picked by Christ himself, also blew their calling (Judas).

I began to pray, "God, You have given me more breaks than anyone deserves, the most precious wife a man could have, and six fantastic healthy children. You have preserved my life over and again. Yet, what have I done in return? Show me what You want from me and I will try to understand."

Several last carefree days were spent on the beaches of Oahu. Carole's mother returned to Washington and my mother happily became an integral part of the crew. Now came the sad ending of our wonderful escapade. It was time to quit the roving life that had become so comfortable and return to earth.

October arrived and sailing directions warn that fall is not a good season to sail a small boat to Canada. New Zealanders play and sail in weather where others head for shelter. Bill Kitching thought it would be jolly good sport to sail our boat back to Washington for us. That way our kids would not be at risk in treacherous waters. Bill located three vigorous young American boys who felt the need for a challenging experience, and they agreed to help bring the Maritashan home. That was the first time we ever watched Maritashan sail over the horizon with another crew at the wheel. We felt like mourners gathering for a funeral.

The five kids boarded a jet headed for Spokane to be reunited with their grandmothers and many relatives. Carole, Puppy, and I flew to Los Angeles where we had stored our VW van with my sister, Margaret. As we flew, I pondered...the rest of life could be a drag. " Was the time I have left on earth going to be a total bore? Had we done it all? Was there nothing remaining in life that could be fulfilling?"

Our flight to Los Angeles lasted four hours. When Puppy was emancipated from the shipping crate, you would have thought he had been imprisoned for four years. He went into orbit, knocking Carole to the pavement on her back. He then, trounced over her entire helpless frame. With both feet on her chest, holding her down, he gifted her with a total face wash. Some passersby first thought they were witnessing a mad dog attack until they discovered the give-a-way vigorous wagging tail.

We returned to Terrace, waiting in anticipation and growing concern during the next three weeks for word of the Maritashan and her new-found crew. We became extremely uneasy when Mom, who was listening regularly to U.S. weather forecasts, relayed foreboding news. Hurricane force winds up to 100 knots were reported

Attempt at Becoming Land Lubbers

off the coast of Washington. Semi-panic replaced worry when, a week after their estimated time of arrival in Juan de Fuca Strait, and no word had been received from the Maritashan. One evening, we were having dinner with friends, the Sariches in Terrace. We decided the time had come to sound the alarm and contact the coast guard to initiate a search. The crew was the priority; our Maritashan may have to be forgotten. That evening was our lowest moment. We hid behind smiling masks.

In the middle of the dinner, the phone rang. It was Bill!

"That was a jolly interesting ride we had, Old Buddy, "he chirped in that most welcome New Zealand voice, "but I don't think we would care to try it again."

The Maritashan and crew arrived safe in Neah Bay. Safe, but not so sound. The news from Bill confirmed that our worries had been justified. The weather deteriorated rapidly after they left Honolulu and winds grew more menacing each passing day. The heavily constructed turnbuckles on two shrouds supporting the mast had broken loose. The pulpit and several stanchions had been transformed into wrinkled scrap metal by the flaying half inch steal cables. Since sailing was impossible, the diesel in the tanks, enough for 1500 miles under normal conditions, was rapidly consumed by the hungry Perkins engine battling an angry sea. Without power and under bare poles, they often averaged 300 miles a day adrift, faster than we had ever traveled with all fifteen hundred feet of sail raised. They dragged two large truck tires and an anchor to slow the ship down and keep the bow pointed toward home. Due to heavy cloud cover, they could not use the sun for navigation. Dead reckoning presumed the ship's location somewhere near three hundred miles off the coast of Washington State. They were in big trouble!

Radio instructions generally inform sailors in distress to use the code word "pan" to signify help needed. This they tried many times, but received no response, and concluded that the radio had packed it in. Finally, in desperation, one of the boys went to the radio and screamed "May-day! May-day!" In radio language, this means: "we are in serious trouble, in danger of sinking!"

Immediately, the U. S. Coast Guard replied. (They were later informed the Coast Guard only answers may-day calls.) A rescue ship was dispatched posthaste. The Coast Guard confessed they had never before been called to venture into a storm so severe. Battling its way to the Maritashan, the rescue ship itself overturned in the storm. Although these ships are constructed to survive a roll, the maneuver completely disabled the rescue boat's electronics. For a while, the question was raised; who would tow who back to port? Eventually the rescue ship was repaired, and Maritashan traveled the remainder of the journey under tow. After that performance, we developed a genuine affection for the U.S. Coast Guard.

Bureaucracy is a many-splendored concept. We met it head-on when we returned to B.C. I drove Bill to the Vancouver airport for his return flight to Hawaii. When traveling on a sailboat, a visa is not required to enter or leave the U. S. or Canada. A passport only is required. When Bill applied for a plane ticket to Hawaii, a frustrating dialogue developed between him and the agent.

He was told, "Sorry, you need a visa to enter the U.S."

"I don't have a visa because on a sailboat, it is not required."

"Then you will have to enter the U. S. on your sailboat."

"I can't. My sailboat is already in the U.S. in Hawaii, 2500 miles away."

"Then you will have to apply for a visa to enter the U.S. from Canada."

"That will take several weeks. Besides, it has to be applied for in New Zealand, in person, and I have no means or money to reach New Zealand."

"I'm sorry, there is nothing we can do."

"But my wife and seven year old child are alone on our boat anchored in Hawaii, and we are well overdue." " I ' m sorry, our hands are tied. There is nothing we can do. We will have to close now for the weekend."

End of discussion.

After traveling in four different countries, dealing with every kind of bureaucracy, we had learned the art of survival. We purchased two bottles of liquor, placed them on the rear seat of my car, then drove to the border crossing. When asked by customs, we told the truth. We were headed for a party in Seattle.

"No problem, have a good day." We drove straight to Sea Tac Airport where Bill did not require a visa because he was headed for a U. S. destination from a U.S. departure. He returned to his anxiously waiting little family with no further complications. Later, I sponsored Bill to become a landed immigrant in Canada. The following spring, he sailed to Canada and settled in Sidney, B. C.

The crew, for our part, moved to Spokane nearer to our extended family. We purchased a home on Lake Spokane and I applied for a real estate license, something I have always carried a yen to try. The kids entered regular school. Although correspondence school did not hold a high priority on the cruise, we were proud of our gang when it was discovered they fit into the local school's curriculum with no difficulty. They had pretty well managed one year of schooling on their own.

The crew of the Maritashan after the return

Once accustomed to a wanderers lifestyle, it is difficult to settle down to a normal life pattern. I was continually searching for new adventure while playing the real estate game, ever searching for that ultimate answer to what life is all about. The answer evaded me, just out of reach.

Not long after our arrival in Spokane, a geologist from northern B.C. phoned. He told of a large, sixty mile tract of gold mining claims on the Liard River in the Yukon Territory. Historical records reported story after story of rich gold discoveries, murder, and conspiracy in the area. Maybe I had found *the* adventure. We raised $200,000 for exploration, and I became president of Sayya Creek Mining Company. We leased fifty square miles of placer claims along the Liard River, built sixty miles of road over the tundra, and a quality air landing strip in the middle of the Yukon wilderness. I commuted between real estate in Spokane and mining in the Yukon.

My parents, the church, and nuns in my early life, had taught that lying, cheating, and stealing under any form were unacceptable. It became obvious that to make a success of this mining venture, those methods would have to be employed. The good ladies had thoroughly ingrained positive values into my brain. When the inevitable became the obvious, I had no choice, but to drop the mining venture like the proverbial hot potato. Several, especially myself, lost a good deal of money in the process. Although it seemed eclipsed, the roots of the early Christian training my mother had tried so hard to imbue actually took hold.

During this pursuit of adventure and materialism, the Creator found another way to attract my attention. My brother's family persuaded us to join them at prayer meetings in a place known as Tum Tum. My worldly mind was quite uncomfortable with charismatic prayer meetings. They seemed a little silly. Besides, I had seen and heard some questionable goings on in the past. Every movement has its damaging problem people, who can make the entire movement look bad. I remained cautiously reserved. While attending one of these sessions, a German lady, who once performed as a professional opera singer, began "singing in tongues." Charismatics speak or sing in unknown tongues, and other gifted persons are supposed to interpret a message from this. This is all biblical, but as St Paul advised, don't scare people out of the church by displaying gifts they don't understand. It all seemed a little ridiculous to me, but I went along with everything, just in case. I was half-asleep in my chair (which I quite often was during church services), when this enchanting Polynesian melody sifted through the room. I remember hearing "hoy," the word for love in the Marquesian dialect. Since I was daydreaming at the time, it didn't register that Polynesian singing was a little unusual in a back woods Washington church. Very few outsiders ever reach the Marquesas Islands. The prayer meeting over, we piled into the van for the drive home.

Our twelve year old, Shannon, piped up, "did you here that lady singing in Marquesian language!"

"Yes, I heard that too," Carole agreed and then quoted the Marquesian word for friend, and other words she had recognized along with that definite unforgettable Marquesian, Polynesian beat.

Several weeks later, without giving a clue as to what had transpired, I inquired of the German lady, "have you ever heard of the Marquesas Islands or spoken any Polynesian?"

"No, I've never heard of the Marquesas Islands, and certainly don't know the language," she replied.

Opera was her style. She was as curious as we when I explained the reason for my questions. I filed this episode away at the back of my brain for future reference. The lesson there must have been, "Don't be so smug; you don't have *all* the answers."

We settled into the home on Spokane Lake at Nine Mile so we could be near the water. We all agreed this was the nicest home we had ever occupied, but something was missing. The sea, the islands, and the good ship Maritashan were calling. We learned how a fish must feel when trying to survive on the land.

Sailing Beyond the Sea

CHAPTER 13

Vancouver Island

Some sailing adventures end in success, others in disaster. Those with unhappy memories generally move to the land and never care to set eyes on the sea again. Those who, like ourselves, have a memorable experience, become attached to the sea. We were torn between the desire to live near the family in Spokane and our yearning to be by the sea. After a year, the real estate business had lost its charm.

While traveling, we discussed, "where would be the best choice in the world for a family like ours to settle?"

Having experienced a good share of the Pacific, all things considered, Vancouver Island seemed to be the best choice. The advantages were many; numerous uninhabited islands, protected waters, uncrowded, good weather, and just plain beautiful. There sat Maritashan, tied up alone in a Victoria marina.

After fourteen months in Spokane, we decided to take a short leave and visit old friends in Terrace. As we sailed north, we ventured into the seaport of Comox, one-hundred and twenty miles north of the U.S. border on Vancouver Island. There we met the Wearns, former cattle rancher friends from Smithers. Greg introduced us to the local veterinarian, Dr. Azelstine, affectionately known as Dr. A. Several months later, after we had returned to Spokane, he invited me to fill in for a month while his assistants were away.

That kind of settled it for us. I returned to Spokane, collected our belongings, moved to Victoria and took up residence on the Maritashan. I inquired at the first clinic that came into sight, Cranston Animal Hospital, and went to work the following day.

That was a comfortable and easy way of life, working for someone else, without any worries. Living on the boat, it was no problem to let the shorelines go and take to the sea for as many days as we had off, or just play around in Victoria.

Many sailboats and sailors reside near Victoria, so it was like old home week, spinning yarns and retelling ocean adventures. The Maritashan, with its caved in bow pulpit and broken stanchions, created a lot of attention and was the talk of the town for many months. After a reporter from the Victoria Times Colonist interviewed us, a full page picture of the weather-beaten boat, and a story showed up on the front page. The most important story they found to report was our jail term in Mexico! *We* thought the six kid crew would be a much greater scoop.

We are not real high-tech sailors; more "raise the sails, fill them with wind, and go type." We didn't keep abreast of all the latest sailboat jargon or knowledge. In Victoria, there are many knowledgeable crews that are "someday" going to go offshore. For some, Victoria is the end of the line. We were big time offshore adventurers, and some sought us out for experience on how to survive the awesome sea. One evening, while visiting with a large group of sailors at a local pub, someone mentioned a fixture on a boat that was unfamiliar to me. It was something on the mast, as I recall, and evidently a well known component, as I soon learned.

"What's that thing you guys are talking about?" I innocently inquired.

Instantly, I was overcome with self-conscious embarrassment when all eyes focused on me in disbelief. In one voice they chorused, *"You* don't know what *that* is?" My fame as a worthy seaman vanished into thin air.

When we moved to the island, our eldest daughter, Marggie, newly graduated from high school, remained in Spokane. Turning our first daughter loose into a world that was so rapidly dropping morals and values was terribly disturbing. It felt like we were releasing her into a den of hungry vipers and there was nothing we could do about it. Carita stayed, as well, to finish her last year. The sad feelings were the same with her. Bob, Mark and Shannon joined us in Victoria, where they soon settled and found new friends.

All the while, I was having difficulties over philosophy of medicine at the hospital where I worked and found it necessary to leave. The poor kids. Maybe we move more often than is healthy. I was in deep deliberation over these conflicts when the phone rang. Dr. A's assistants in Comox had moved (Dr. Jack and Dr. Jill had gone and moved up the hill), so he wondered if I would consider working full time with him. It's always amazing how developments occur automatically in our lives.

The ever gentle and mild mannered Dr. A apologized for suggesting we move. "I realize how difficult it is to pack and uproot, but I surely could use your help."

"Moving is not a real problem," I replied. "All that's required is to unplug the telephone, release two ropes, and raise the sails."

That we did, and in less than a week were moored in Comox, working at the Comox Valley Animal Hospital. Poor little Shannon cried at leaving what she hoped were some permanent friends. The nomadic spirit was alive and well. Or was our life being arranged for us?

Comox became our home for two full years, and after six months, we even purchased a house and moved onto the land. This, too, was a fascinating practice dealing with "all creatures great and small." For instance, I treated an injured seal in our swimming pool for a time. That didn't go over too well with some because seals don't toilet train, nor pool train for that matter. Neither do they cooperate at feeding time. A stomach tube was required. He was pretty cute. Nonetheless, we were happy to turn him back to mother once he recovered.

Another amusing event in Comox raised some curious questions once again. A government experimental farm is located North of Comox where Dr. A and I were often called to maintain the health of a large Holstein cow herd. On one occasion, he was called to care for a cow which was unable to stand or eat. Before he could leave the hospital, Diane, a worker at the farm, called to report that the cow was well and his help was no longer required.

When I asked Dr. A what happened, he replied, "She wouldn't tell me."

A few weeks later, he was called for another case. While there, he pressed Diane for information on the recovered cow.

"She got well," Diane replied.
"How did she get well?" asked Dr. A.
"You don't want to know."
"Yes I do," he insisted. "That's my job."
"I'd rather not say."
"Come on Diane, I have to know," he insisted again. "It's my job."
"OK, but you have to promise not to laugh."
Dr. A promised. Then Diane sheepishly uttered, "We prayed over the cow and she got up and started eating."
Dr. A replied with his usual wry sense of humor. "You know people like you could run veterinarians out of business."
That was not the end of events with Diane. I remained dubious about that sort of incident so once again, filed it away.

Our family nest was now half empty. Carita had returned after Graduation but was considering a career as a travel agent. Our primary reason for existence, the family, was rapidly diminishing.

This produced a large hole in our hearts and once again we asked, "Is this it? Why are we here? Is there any purpose or value in our lives?"

At times like that, I would often contemplate Dad's spiritual experience, and the notable change it made in his way of thinking. I recalled the many events, including the "avalanche coincidence" that saved my neck. Was that, and the many others, mere coincidence or was someone trying to tell me something? I had read more about the thoughts of Mother Teresa and St. Francis of Assisi.

Cardinal Ratzinger spoke some words of wisdom that tugged at my conscience. "Concentrating on materialistic activities of the world is like shuffling the deck furniture on board the Titanic."

Somehow, I was hearing all this phenomenal wisdom, but not listening. Like most, I was listening *instead* to the message of the media and the world, especially that of TV. "Work harder and make more deals and more money, and arrange a good retirement because in the end, the guy with the most toys, wins." And get as much pleasure out of life as you can in the short time provided.

Quality of life is the number one goal. Right?" I wrestled with these two opposing philosophies.

Real estate deals came naturally to me, and I began to accumulate and trade property, once again, until I had amassed several million dollars worth of real estate. We had done it before, and would have been really well off by now if I had stuck with developing, rather than "blowing it all" by running away from the world with our kids.

It was about that time my sister, Margaret, sent me a copy of a letter Dad had written years before. The letter described in detail the incident he had related to me personally, and which had such a profound impact on his view of life. I didn't realize he had put the story in writing. As I said before, Dad was a dedicated atheist. We could not talk about God, prayer or church in his presence without upsetting him. My older sisters spoke of how they used to make their way to catechism classes by way of back alleys in order to avoid his knowing. It's interesting, in most families now, the situation is reversed. The parents can't discuss spiritual matters without the children becoming upset.

Dad was a good and kindly man, however, and everyone loved and respected him. We prayed for him constantly (when he wasn't around). My mother prayed for him for thirty years. Then, in 1950, her prayers were answered rather abruptly when Dad was struck with the vision. Many others have reported the identical experience.

After reading and searching and praying and getting over being seventeen, I began to understand. Now, I was in the process of making a large scale attitude adjustment, myself.

Following is a copy of Dad's letter to my sister Margaret Duran in 1950. Our parents had six children and thirty-six grandchildren. This letter has done more for their spiritual growth and that of many others, than any of his condemnations ever did to turn people away from God.

He wrote:

> *Marggie, I had the dream* of a lifetime not long ago. Words are a very feeble means of trying to describe what I saw. What I told you of the marvels of the Northern Lights*

---

*   When he described the vision to me, he said he was not assleep but very alert and awake.

would amount to less than one percent of the vision seen in sleep. Two thousand artists, painting two thousand years, could not produce all I saw in that brief instant of a dream. Not being an architect, not being religious, where originated the picture? Briefly, I was standing with several on the edge of a gently sloping draw when thunder began to roll and lights flashed across the sky, to be replaced by a scene not bending around as the earth does, but in the opposite, always sloping upward higher and higher of magnificence, splendor, color, architecture, nature, spires, domes, cathedrals, steps, arches, trellises, flowers, shrubs, foliage in beautiful colors, quiet and peaceful, like an old oil painting. Before us, as far ahead and as far behind, we could see was a line three and four deep of boys and girls, all approximately about twenty years old; all smiling and tripping happily along, singing a most beautiful tune I had never heard. I cannot produce the notes nor the words, except one line, "Come on with us to Zion."** They beckoned to me to join them, and all who could see the vision, told me that this was the end, to leave all my worries and troubles behind. Seemed like Mother, David and Jim had been with me, and I wanted them to go along too, but was told we would all meet ahead, except those who had not seen the vision would have to remain behind for further trial.

It was about then that I woke up.* Most vividly was the picture impressed in my memory, more marvelous than man or words could do justice to. Had I been a religious fanatic or a visionary architect, there might be some reason for seeing what I did. No, I have not slipped no worse than usual—tish—tish."

(The letter continues with news about the farm).

I often offer a copy of this letter to friends who have recently lost a loved one; it does a lot to provide the consolation needed in this unbelieving world.

** Zion: Dad had to ask my Baptist Aunt what Zion meant because he wasn't familiar with the term.

Later, when we began to pray the scriptural rosary, something about one of the bible quotations used in the rosary tickled my memory. I had heard it somewhere before. (Rev. 11,19 and Rev.12,1) *"And the sanctuary of God in heaven opened. Then came flashes of lightning and peals of thunder. Now, a great sign appeared in heaven: a woman, adorned with the sun. She was standing on the moon, with the twelve stars on her head for a crown."*

I'm a little slow, but it finally dawned on me that it was in Dad's letter where I had seen it before. Dad wrote, "I was standing with several on the edge of a gently sloping draw when thunder began to roll and lights flashed across the sky." The way it sounded to me, when the woman appeared to the kids at Fatima, Lourdes and many other places, the sanctuary of God in heaven opened and they were able to see someone from heaven. They stated that her clothing was brighter than the sun, but didn't hurt their eyes. ("A woman adorned with the sun, with the twelve stars on her head for a crown"). In Dad's story, thunder began to roll and lightning flashed across the sky, then he was able to see into the sanctuary of God and experience all the beautiful scenes he described to me. This letter fed the fire smoldering inside of me.

Sailing Beyond the Sea

CHAPTER 14

Campbell River

After working in Comox for two years, I purchased the Campbell River portion of the practice from Dr. A. in the summer of 1978. Here, I constructed the tenth animal hospital of my career.

I purchased a romantic old cedar cabin on the beach at Willow Point, only two blocks north of the veterinary hospital, and twenty-five feet from the ocean shore. We raised the cabin and built another floor below to accommodate our dwindling family. Carole was reluctant to move, especially since Bobby wanted to finish school in Comox. She and the kids moved back onto the boat. I moved to the house in Campbell River, feeling rejected and abandoned since no one was anxious to join me. Could it be they were tired of moving, or were they tired of me? Frequently, whenever the occasion arose, I used the expression, "my bachelor pad in Campbell River," hoping to cajole Carole into joining me. Eventually, they came along, except for Bobbie who we farmed out to another family in Comox. Carole preferred to be near the water in a boat, but became quite enamored with the new home, since she could at least *listen* to her scenery. The wilder the waves the more thrilled she became with her scenery, even when at times during storms, the more adventuresome waves frolicked boldly on our front window panes. Here, we lived for eleven years in the same home. (Prying her out of that home could eventually become an even bigger problem.)

The view from the porch was spectacular. Killer whales romped in the surf. Otters played tag amidst the piles of driftwood. Eagles, herons, and innumerable species of waterfowl, rode the waves or ducked for food. More wildlife appeared on the edge of that city than we ever found in the wilderness. Beyond the bird-haven view, were the rugged, snow covered mountains of the Coastal Range. Below them, and across Georgia Strait, tree covered islands freckled the waters of Georgia Straight.

The home crew had now been reduced to three children; Shannon, Bobby and Mark. Bobby remained in Comox long enough to finish high school. He then entered college and started the long ten year climb to a Ph.D. in plant pathology. Mark graduated in Campbell River, moved to Long Island, New York and took up architecture and carpentry. Shannon became an animal health technician and worked in the animal hospital for several years. Then moved into art and carpentry. Carita went to school in Spokane to become a travel agent. Marggie went into training to become a nurse. Almost unbelievable to me, Jimmy entered medical school.

Most children leave home when its time to sprout their wings. Seems like we moved out from under ours. We shed kids all over North America. Shannon was quite proud to be first to actually leave home rather than be left. Originally, we decided to raise a family while we were relatively young so we would still have a few miles remaining on our bones after the children vacated the nest.

Carole handled her handicap better than she could handle the empty nest, and better than anyone I knew, although there were times when the burden showed through. Some people are uncomfortable when they encounter blind people, almost as if they fear blindness might be contagious...maybe, if you come too close, you might go blind!

During our early years at a New Year's Eve party, we asked a girl at our table to guide Carole to the restroom. The girl appeared as though she were going into shock. All she could mutter was, "No-no-no I can't." The reason was obvious, and Carole was so hurt we had to leave the party, Carole in tears. She had formed some solid friendships in the past, but often with difficulty. Tears were shed when she felt people avoiding her. She found this especially true as a teenager when she first lost her sight, and some of her closest friends abandoned her. She was one gorgeous looking dish, and a lot of men want to be her friend for the wrong motives. We usually joined a Catholic parish wherever we lived and this became a reliable source of friends.

In 1981, two friends, Joe and John, invited me to make a Cursillo, or more accurately, conned me into a Cursillo in Campbell River. Cursillo is a difficult movement to describe as it is best understood by experience; like Dad relating his vision experience, said words could not describe what he saw. Cursillo is Spanish for "short course," but it is far more than that. The originators of the movement in Spain uncovered what is missing in the world and in most of our practice of religion." With these discoveries for a guide, leaders share their experiences openly. These experiences include their change from a worldly sense of values to values more worthwhile. In the process, they become extremely close friends with large numbers of people who are searching and making the same discovery. Friends don't become intimate until they know each others deep feelings and faith. Those who have made Cursillos (Cursillistas) now number in the millions and are in every country of the world.

Up to that time, not all, but many friends were "party friends," or only casual acquaintances. Carole complained that if it weren't for parties, she would have only a few close friends. Since she made her Cursillo, I have to stand in line to receive a hug! Now, she has dear friends everywhere in countless numbers. We cherish not only our Cursillo friends, but through it, we learned how to make deeper friendships outside. After she made her Cursillo, she told me she had more fun that weekend than she ever had, with or without me. Since my experience preceded hers, I was only lightly devastated.

During this same period, I received the honor of appointment to the Bishop's council for the Diocese of Victoria. Bishop Remi De Roo is the Bishop of that diocese. It was there I first learned that there are two tremendously different and opposing philosophies present in the church. More accurately, some are attempting to form another parallel church alongside of the original to replace it, somewhat like another new Protesting religion forming within. It is difficult to describe and quite astonishing to most of us who weren't aware of its presence. The two philosophies overlap a great deal, making it difficult to detect without serious study.

The first philosophy is the "orthodox Catholic faith." Here it is believed that Christ, who is God, knowing that he would be put to death, appointed twelve apostles and declared Peter to be the leader of the twelve and the church when he said, *"and so I say to you,*

you are Peter, and upon this rock I will build my church, and the gates of the nether world shall not prevail against it. I will give you the Keys to the Kingdom of Heaven. (The old testament describes what a monumental presentation the Keys of the Kingdom involves. Isaiah 22:22) *Whatever you bind on earth shall be bound also in heaven; and whatever you loose on earth shall be loosed in heaven."* (Mat. 16:16). This statement is about as straightforward as any scripture, and was accepted without question for fifteen hundred years of church history. Authority had to be possessed before it could be transferred. After Peter died, this position was passed on to the second pope, St. Linus, in the year 67, by election among the remaining apostles and other first bishops. This succession has continued in various ways until today, with John Paul II, the 266th pope, elected in the same manner and continuing to hold the "Keys of the Kingdom." Orthodox followers believe Christ gave Peter a mandate to observe everything taught by scripture and oral tradition (2 Thes 2:15), and all popes must adhere to this, regardless of how much pressure is applied, even death. A few whose personal lives left much to be desired, miraculously maintained the unchanging faith in spite of their weakness. Many popes lost their lives for remaining faithful to this teaching, including the first thirty popes. This philosophy requires loyalty to scripture, the pope, and the magisterium, or teaching authority of the church. This is the reason the church has held together for 2000 years rather than continually fragmenting like the newer ones.

Then as Peter himself predicted, speaking of Paul's letters and other scripture, *"in them there are some things hard to understand that the ignorant and unstable distort to their own destruction, just as they do the other scriptures."*

The present pope, John Paul II, has come out stronger than anyone, defending the scripture, church teachings and especially Vatican 2 documents, to prevent their manipulation by those who would twist them to promote their own particular agenda.

The second or modernist philosophy believes the church beliefs should be improved upon, should be modernized, that the scripture is not necessarily accurate, or can be interpreted correctly by anyone, even if they come to different conclusions. Proponents of this philosophy, like the reformers, feel that the guidance of the Holy

Spirit in teachings of the church is not restricted to the successors of the apostles. This new system within the Catholic church has many and varied allies and ideologies which more or less network loosely together. They believe liberation from doctrine promotes freedom, and exist under names such as progressives, modernists, liberation theologists, radical feminists, Marxists, Catholics for free choice, new age philosophy, and gay liberationists, etc. They feel that in order to establish this newer, more correct philosophy, a revolution is necessary, and they are busy promoting this agenda at the present time. A parallel magisterium is being generated and promoted by dissenting theologians. The secular media and present governments are quite helpful to this cause. Pope Paul reasoned that there are signs that this phenomena could be what St. Paul predicted and termed the great apostasy presaging the great tribulation. Jesus asked if there would be any true faith left when he returns. It is an interesting paradox that while most non-Catholic religions are beginning to understand and accept the truth of Catholic teaching, the modernist element within the church is promoting a revolution against the traditional teachings, sort of "theological hippies."

I thoroughly enjoyed the opportunity to spend five years on the council, especially for the education I gained. I felt obligated to choose the orthodox view which, even to this day, results in a degree of conflict between me and those holding the modernist view.

In 1984, Pope John Paul 2 made a pilgrimage across Canada. Ten people from each Diocese of British Columbia were invited and honored to receive Holy Eucharist from the Pope when he visited the city of Vancouver. Carole and I were struck speechless when the Bishop's office invited us to re-

Pope John Paul II in Canada

ceive Communion from the Pope. Carole is a softy. She was in continual bouts of tears from the moment the Pope's helicopter landed until some time after the reception of Communion. A native lady, a complete stranger to Carole, stood beside her. The two of them spent a long time hugging and crying on each other's shoulder.

We were all impressed by the awe-inspiring power of the presence of the man. Hare Krishnas and even pagans, who had come to the celebration for another purpose, were struck with awe and tears by his presence and words. It reminded me of the story of Peter in the Acts of the Apostles; wherever he walked, people crowded near so that even his shadow might pass over them and make them well.

One of my greatest friends and an employee at the veterinary hospital, (whose name, coincidentally, is Brian Pope) was as impressed with the honor we received as ourselves. He glued himself to the TV that day hoping to watch us receive Communion from John Paul. He was disappointed that we never showed up on the screen. Some months later, an acquaintance of Brian's from Vancouver who had organized the pope's visit, happened to be in Campbell River. He stopped by to renew old times. Brian asked if there were any pictures taken of the event. He answered that yes, there were a few.

Without our knowledge, Shannon confiscated pictures of Carole and me from our album. Brian forwarded these to his friend in Vancouver, who painstakingly searched the photo file of the Pope's visit. At Christmas time, Brian handed me a gift-wrapped package. When I opened the box, I was dumbfounded. I was holding the most beautiful photograph of Pope John Paul II placing the Host on my tongue with Carole at my side. The spectacular, snow-capped mountains of B.C. loomed in the background. For the longest time, I stared in disbelief. Brian said he wished he had a camera to capture the look on my face as I stood there in disbelief. Then came the tears.

One of the most curious experiences of my veterinary career happened through Diane...she of the prayer-cured cow from the experimental farm. Diane is friends with a semi retired priest from Comox, Father Joe. She asks Father Joe to bless *everything* that isn't normal and healthy. This is a regular part of farming in Europe, but a forgotten practice in North America. Father, on the other hand, a shy and humble man who doesn't appreciate publicity, is definitely not into miracles. Diane has a way of asking that makes it difficult to refuse, so Father Joe prays whenever she asks, even if it hurts. If the fruit trees aren't bearing the way they should, then Father Joe is summoned to bring down the full force of God's mercy.

At one point, the herd of cows at the experimental farm were beset with various complications to their health. Father Joe was sweet-talked into blessing the entire herd. Diane asked Carole, my Mother, and me to be on hand to lend support. Apparently, Father felt that if the veterinarian were involved, it wouldn't look quite so weird.

Father arranged the blessing for the noon hour to reduce the chance of "pagans" being present. The four of us then accompanied Father to the barn yard for the blessing. That blessing proceeded with great haste; some seventy cows were covered in a period just short of ten minutes. Diane reported that the herd health seemed to improve.

Sometime after this, I was in my office feverishly trying to revive a semi-comatose Siamese cat. This cat was in a serious condition from a disease known as feline urinary syndrome or FUS. This condition is essentially due to a plugged urinary bladder. Certain male cats have difficulty with the metabolism of magnesium, one of the elements. This results in crystals forming in the bladder which pile up in the urethra, the tube leading from the bladder out through the remainder of the urinary tract. Eventually, enough crystals accumulate so that the bladder is entirely blocked. Urine over-fills the bladder; urea and other toxins back up into the blood stream, resulting in uremic poisoning. Once the animal becomes comatose, the prognosis is poor. If the condition is not relieved, usually within 24 hours of complete blockage, the cat proceeds to sustain irreversible damage to heart, kidney and other vital organs. This was the case with Elsie and Bob's cat. It was comatose. I had managed to free the crystals from the urethra and was proceeding with intravenous fluids in an attempt to flush the cats system of the toxic chemicals in its body. With large volumes of intravenous fluid-flushing and rigorous therapy, some animals, even though comatose, will respond after a period of several days. At that moment, who should arrive on the scene but Diane and Father Joe, just popping in to say a hello. Diane is an animal husbandry major and ever curious of medical theory. After explaining to her the physiological basis of FUS, she hurried into the next room to collar Father Joe.

"You've got to come help Jim. He has a serious problem with a patient," Diane pleaded.

Poor Father Joe. You could see the agonized expression on his face that clearly betrayed his thoughts..."All those nurses present are probably non-believers; what will they think?"

If only there had been a video camera available to capture the moment. Father Joe glanced over both shoulders, hoping against hope that none of the unbelievers would notice. I watched as I witnessed what possibly may have been the smallest and speediest sign of the cross ever in the history of Christianity. Less than three seconds elapsed during the blessing of the recumbent cat. Father Joe then did an abrupt about face, marched quickly out of the door, retreated to the car, and sat waiting the return of Diane.

Diane sighed, "Well, I guess I better go," and followed him to the car.

Now the strangest of all, the cat which lay flat out on his side, immediately rolled over on its chest, stood up, arched his back, stretched, and began to purr. He then meandered over to my side of the table and proceeded to bestow on me an affectionate rub. For my part, I just stood there rather dazed. What is going on here? Never had I witnessed anything quite like that. Then a perplexing question came to me. If this sort of thing is real, and if supernatural things do happen, why on earth would God ever use one of his most humble priests to save the life of a *cat*?

The next day, the cat remained in a normal, healthy condition, eating and being a typical nose-in-the-air Siamese. I contacted Elsie, the owner, to inform her that her cat had recovered and could be discharged. I felt a little awkward after explaining earlier how serious the cat's condition was, the guarded prognosis, and the long recovery expected. Elsie and her husband, Bob, came to retrieve the patient. Since she was a fellow parishioner at St. Patrick's church, I couldn't help but let it all out; what had taken place. Bob managed to look off into space as if I weren't talking. What I didn't know then was that Bob didn't believe in anything. Nor did I know that their marriage was in the process of coming apart at the seams with a permanent separation. For my part, I was exuberant over the cat's remarkable recovery.

Diane giggled with delight when I explained the scenario to her over the phone and she relayed the story to Father Joe. He made it clear that he wanted to hear nothing more of the event. Curiosity, though, doesn't only catch the cat; it sometimes catches up with the odd priest.

Two months later, Father Joe phoned to inquire, "did that cat really get well the way Diane described?"

"Yes," I said. "I have never seen any thing like it. Would you mind coming to work full time in this office, Father Joe?"

He laughed and good naturedly declined.

"But I wouldn't mind seeing that cat again," he ventured, "just to relieve my curiosity."

"Okay," I agreed. "I'll line up a visit for you with the owners. They are extremely anxious to meet you."

I contacted Elsie and arranged a meeting. The three of them enjoyed a long, friendly visit. They discovered that they had mutual acquaintances in Edmonton, Alberta, where Bob had formerly been in the oil drilling business. Father Joe had been a math teacher in Edmonton for several years. They struck up a lasting friendship and over time, Father was able to convince the couple that divorce was not a good or necessary answer to their problems. From then on, the marriage, with counseling, improved each day.

A few months passed and it was announced that a Marriage Encounter would be held in Campbell River. Now a Marriage Encounter is a weekend event which is a further development of the Cursillo. It is not meant for marriages in trouble, but is a movement to make good marriages better and to prevent future difficulties. One of the objectives is the development of communication between a couple. The lack of communication is often the start of the disastrous road to divorce.

Elsie intercepted me leaving Mass one morning, "Jim, you have made a Marriage Encounter before; could you come to our home and convince Bob to attend a Marriage Encounter with me?"

"Sure, no problem," I assured her with unbridled confidence. However, I quickly discovered Bob was no push-over. He was like my kids. One word about spiritual things and the door slams shut. To reduce the clumsiness of the visit, we switched the conversation to the more acceptable level of well drilling and Bob's occupation of game fishing guide.

Having achieved a colossal failure, I rose to leave.

Elsie groped in desperation, "Jim, didn't you make a Marriage Encounter once?"

With obvious uneasiness in my voice, all I could think to say was, "Yes, I did, but if you guys are thinking about it, be careful, you might fall in love all over again."

I departed from their home depressed. I felt I had let Elsie down. The Marriage Encounter could have been a real boost to their recovering marriage. I had not yet discovered that prayer is the best solution to every problem. I prayed only at the brink of disaster or impending death. Directly without reasoning why, I went home and knelt down next to our bed. Dejected, I prayed for Elsie and Bob what could have been the most sincere pleading rosary of my career. Just as I finished the last *Glory Be,* the phone rang. Carole answered. It was Elsie, elated, calling to tell us Bob had invited her to attend the Marriage Encounter with him! I knew that cowboys shouldn't cry, but this cowboy turned into mush.

Elsie and Bob enjoyed the next four years in marital bliss. Then suddenly, without warning, Bob suffered a heart attack during a playful moment at home. He was chasing Elsie around the patio when he slipped into eternity. On the surface it seemed tragic, but we realized everyone eventually dies. How sad it would have been had not that old Siamese cat led them to stumble into a loving reunion, and Bob had not discovered that true love surpasses any other kind of joy.

After Bob's death, Elsie moved away. I received a letter from a veterinary hospital requesting their cat's medical history. More out of mischief than from proper medical practice, I detailed the entire account, using medical jargon, of the blessing by Father Joe in my reply. I would imagine those veterinarians figured there are some pretty kooky veterinarians residing in British Columbia.

Elsie and the Siamese encountered another adventure before the move to Alberta.

She told of a day driving in downtown Campbell River when she thought, "gee, people in Campbell River are certainly friendly; everyone is waving to me."

When the waving continued, she thought "some of those bystanders look pretty serious."

She decided to stop and see if the car had a problem. There on top of the car was the cat, spread-eagle with all four sets of claws dug securely into the roof of the hard-top convertible, hanging on for dear life. The cat's name, by the way, is "Lucky."

Sailing Beyond the Sea

CHAPTER 15

Slight Attitude Adjustment

In those days, the jerk in me was beginning to waver. Developments around us hinted there might be more important values in life than the interests we hung on to so tenaciously. In our family, professional and financial lives, occurrences held a common thread...the influence of God in our life and in the lives of others we met. Life continued to be exciting, but with a different twist.

The clients who used the animal hospital at Campbell River were exceptionally gracious people. One young lady, who regularly visited with her two huge dogs, was an outdoor type who loved hunting, fishing, and exploring. One day she and her big dog, King arrived at the hospital. King appeared to be the classic picture of depression with his tail tucked tightly between his legs and head hanging low. A lengthy medical examination revealed no visible reason for his demeanor.

After exhausting every medical possibility, I inquired, "Are there any circumstances in your home that might affect your dog emotionally?"

"Maybe," she replied, "you probably noticed my black eye."

"No, I didn't notice." I had been concentrating on the dog and missed the all too obvious black eye.

"The guy I live with drinks a lot and every time he gets drunk, he beats me. "Would that bother my dog?"

"It certainly could," I replied.

After dealing with the dog's problem, I turned to the lady. "You don't have to put up with this sort of treatment, you know. There is a way out."

"There is," she queried. "Like how?"

Joe, the same clown who conned me into the Cursillo, was my hospital accountant at the time, and faithfully involved in AA. I introduced her to Joe, who in turn arranged a meeting with a couple, Ed and Dedra, who were well qualified to deal with abuse. They convinced her that remaining in her situation would eventually become a fatal mistake, and it was urgent that she leave now!

After the problem was resolved, she dropped by on her way out of town. "I didn't know problems other than animal ailments could be solved in a veterinary hospital." (Neither did I.)

The young lady moved to a safe home, and not long after, met a man who didn't beat her. They were married the next year. In former days, I would have passed that off as none of my business.

Sometimes, when you begin feeling too self-satisfied, a good lesson in humility is healthy. Another client qualified as a burnt-out hooker. She also was addicted to alcohol and drugs...her brains were scrambled from long term drug abuse. She smelled terrible and was almost impossible to understand when drinking or drugged, which was most of the time. Her little dog suffered a variety of ailments and required regular medical help. I would work on her dog and then move her out of the office as quickly as possible, all the while graciously accepting her money for services. We dreaded to see her come and considered her a great inconvenience.

One night, she overdosed on drugs and was rushed to the hospital. I learned that our wise-cracking accountant, Joe, lost an entire night of sleep with this obnoxious person to keep her from falling out of a hospital bed or injuring herself in some other way. Many other friends in AA helped her survive in spite of her many undesirable traits.

We learned only recently that she has kicked the alcohol disease and is living a new life. She would not be alive now were it not for her selfless friends in AA.

They had heard *and* listened to the words of Christ, "the least of my brothers."

Father Peter was the parish priest in those days. He was a wounded man, but by his wounds, he was able to solve problems that more organized people could not understand. Maybe a damaged counselor can relate better to damaged people. I referred to him as "Father Impetuous."

Father Bernie, from the Cursillo movement, passed on a quote that described all of us in profound words. "We are all wounded healers, stuttering prophets and crippled leaders."

The Monday Night Meeting was a little project that Father Peter organized so people could come together, build community, and share their stories. Carole and I had recently attended a retreat. There, we were given a passage from scripture and asked to put ourselves into the place of one of the characters in the story to better understand the teaching. The story given us was the Road to Emmaus. As I read the story to Carole, we became incredibly touched by the event in a way bible stories never before affected me. I asked our youngest son, Mark, to listen in and he too was affected by the story...not interested before, but deeply moved by this event.

The story described how, after the resurrection, Jesus appeared to two disciples on the road to Emmaus, but somehow kept his identity hidden. They were terribly depressed because Jesus, from whom they had expected great earthly triumph, had been shamefully tortured and put to death. In their eyes he was a failure. While they walked, Jesus showed them, through old testament prophecies, that his suffering and death was destined to take place in order to change the course of humanity. Finally, they recognized him when he celebrated the Eucharist, blessed the bread, broke it, and gave it to them. Then he disappeared from their sight, leaving them overwhelmed, but full of joy.

At the next Monday night meeting, Father Peter asked me to explain the mechanism of the retreat. I explained how reading the story of Emmaus brought tears to Carole and I and deeply touched our son. One of the girls present asked what the story was about and why it moved us so. I began to relate the story of Emmaus. Still a little choked, I muddled the story quite badly.

Father Peter, or rather Father Impetuous, barked impatiently, "somebody hand me a Bible. I'll read the story so we can get on with this!"

Taking the Bible in hand, this seeming "in-control-all-the-time" person began to read. He reached the point describing the breaking of the bread, the same place where we were so moved, and he, himself, was overcome by tears and was unable to carry on. A long silence followed.

Not long after the affair, when the same selection showed up as the gospel in the daily Mass, he read it through with no sign of difficulty.

I approached him after Mass and teased, "you did a little better job of reading than the last time you tried, Father Peter."

"Get out of here and don't bug me," he growled.

Carole's mother was affectionately known as "Mudgie." Like my dad, she was a professed non-believer. During her visit to Campbell River, Carole and I were attending Mass every day. Carole prayed daily for her mother's conversion. To Mudgie, attending Mass every day appeared to be pretty ridiculous and extreme radical behavior.

She complained, "don't you think you are carrying this church thing a little too far, going to Mass every day? After all, when you are dead, you are dead, and that's all there is to it."

What could we say to a mother?

The next year, we were in Olympia, Washington, where she lived, to attend the funeral of my sister, Emily. Emily was a sweetheart, but suffered from alcoholism and much heartache in her life. Of all days, Mother's Day, the year before, her youngest son had been killed by drug dealers.

However, as our niece, Sister Patricia, a Poor Clare Nun (and a constant fountain bubbling over with joy) excitedly announced, "we are celebrating Emily's resurrection." There was a tremendous peace surrounding the funeral that made an impression on everyone present.

Carole contemplated, "now I understand how people felt at the resurrection of Jesus."

Mudgie was unable to attend, but joined us for dinner that evening.

During the meal she inquired, "How do you become a Catholic?"

We thought this was just a curiosity question, but she insisted, "No, I want to become Catholic, myself."

"What made you decide that?" I asked.

"Those ladies in your church in Campbell River, they are so full of unselfish love, it has to be real. I want to be part of that."

The next year, Mudgie joined the church and learned to pray. Through the rosary, she learned the joy of having a heavenly mother leading her to Christ. Like my sister, she too, endured many sufferings.

Just before Mudgie died, she spoke of a heavenly visitor whom we believe was the Mother of Jesus. Carole's sister Tudy, Tudy"s husband Bob, and their daughter Arron, were with her.

As she was growing weaker and slipping into eternity, she whispered to the people at her bedside,. "I wish I had the strength to tell you everything the beautiful lady said to me. She told me it was time to leave now and be with my husband and family."

Arron was thrilled. Death is always depicted as a time of grief, but her grandmother's death was a celebration of love.

This same Bob, Carole's brother-in-law, introduced me to a book that became a major element in my attitude adjustment, *"Marguerite, Message of Merciful Love To Little Souls."* It struck me so profoundly that when Carole and I traveled to Europe, we detoured three hundred miles into Belgium so I could meet the future saint, Marguerite. I needed to know for myself if she was authentic. That meeting erased all doubt in my mind. I was impressed to the extent that I presented a copy of the book to the bishop when I returned from Europe, which he obligingly read. I promoted the book so enthusiastically that friends were borrowing the books from me in great numbers. Soon it became obvious that I would have some financial difficulties if the give-away program continued at the present rate. Most were unwilling to part with the book once they discovered what was taking place in their heart.

The thought came, "why not start a book store? Then I could sell the books and solve the financial difficulty resulting from giving them away."

In a short time, friends purchased over 600 of these books and I was asked to become the western Canada representative for the Legion of Little Souls, a group inspired by the book. Then I started stocking so many other titles that I had to move a trailer onto the clinic property to accommodate the increasing numbers of books. This was rather quaint, a veterinary hospital with an in-house, religious bookstore. A friend suggested the name Galley Books, a title that has remained to this day. There are now five Galley Book outlets on Vancouver Island, in most major towns.

Home for lunch one day, I received an urgent call from the office, but the urgency was not about an injured animal. Katherine, a friend from Courtenay who happened to be in the bookstore, was on the line.

"I think you better come down here," she anxiously pleaded. "There is a guy with a problem and I don't know what to say."

It was a young policeman named Barry. His son was seriously ill at Children's Hospital in Vancouver. His wife could not handle the stress and left home. Barry had gone to a provincial self-help group, whose teaching only increased his dilemma and confusion.

Their philosophy said, "if your mate steps out on you, you should do the same in order to get even."

Barry, though not practicing, had been raised Catholic and said, "since that didn't sound like a practical solution, I thought I would search somewhere else for answers."

Our priest sent him to the book store. We selected some books that provided a more positive value than revenge. I then invited him to join our Cursillo group reunion which met every Thursday morning at six. This follow-up of the Cursillo keeps alive the spirit of the Cursillo weekend. There were six exceptionally great guys in our group, any one of which would be a consolation for him.

"I can't make that time," Barry lamented. "I have to take care of my two kids until the baby-sitter arrives."

All the boys agreed, "then let's have group reunion at Barry's home." This worked well and continued for quite a long time.

One aim of a group reunion is to continually realign our goals from purely social to moral values. One of Barry's new goals was aimed at doing something for the young offenders at nearby Camp Snowdon, a reform camp for juvenile offenders.

Slight Attitude Adjustment

"I helped put enough kids in there," he said. "I think I better try to help remove a few."

A year passed and new tragedy struck Barry himself came down with cancer. There followed a long heroic struggle before he died. When Barry had first joined our group, we thought we were doing him a great service. After his death, we pondered over our friendship and realized he had a far greater influence on us than anything we could have done for him. His courage and positive attitude permanently affected our lives. More red-coated policemen gathered at his funeral than we had ever experienced in one event. Evidently, his fellow policemen shared our point of view.

Harry was lying in a hospital bed when I saw him, propped up on one elbow. It had been several months since we had last met. Carole and I were taking Holy Communion to the sick in the hospital that day.

Harry and I met at a twelve-step meeting several years before. He talked about St. Francis at the meeting, so I knew we had some common ground and got together several times after that. The most characteristic trait about Harry was his four-letter word vocabulary. He had difficulty delivering one sentence without at least two very inappropriate four-letter words. At times His attitude was so negative, it was uncomfortable to be around him.

"What are you doing in a hospital bed," I asked.

"I'm just getting over a heart attack," he replied.

"I haven't told anyone except Father Charles about what happened to me here," Harry continued. "People would think I am crazy if I told them. I know you are already crazy so I don't mind telling you."

His back-handed compliment didn't bother me since I was used to his rough ways and there was a lot of truth in his words. We dished it out to each other on a regular basis.

He continued with his story. "I was up north when this terrible pain hit me. The doctor said I was having a severe heart attack. It felt like someone was prying my arm off with a crow-bar. The pain was unbearable. The doctor gave me emergency treatment and rushed me to the Campbell River hospital. There they applied electric shock treatment to my chest because my heart had stopped. They talked as if they thought I was unconscious, but I was aware of everything. The pain was gone and there was no distress when they bounced me around with the electric shock. I was at peace and all fear had disappeared. Suddenly, I was aware of someone else standing near my head. I turned to look. There stood 'a person made of brilliant glowing light'!"

I said, "Jesus Christ! Who the '*Bleep*' are you?" It was him! And he was laughing! He has a sense of humor! He told me that all was OK between him and me and I could go with him now, if I liked. It was up to me. He was so full of love that I could hardly stand it. I didn't dare look him in the face. I knew if I did, I wouldn't be able to resist following him. Then I thought of my children abandoned in Vancouver with no religious training. I told him, 'I think I better stay and do something about teaching my children about you and eternity.'"

I had shown Harry the letter from my dad explaining his experience. That is why he felt comfortable telling me his story. He knew I wouldn't laugh.

The next and last time we saw Harry, he was leaving a twelve-step recovery meeting he regularly attended. An amazing change had come over him. His negative attitude had disappeared and the four-letter vocabulary was totally absent from his conversation. He appeared positive and cheerful.

"I'm leaving town," he offered.

"Where to?"

"I'm moving to Vancouver and try to get my kids into a parochial school."

We prayed the fervor wouldn't wear off.

CHAPTER 16

You Are Losing It, Doc

In the real estate game, it seemed I could do no wrong. Midas-like, everything turned to gold. My real estate holdings were impressive. In Terrace, we owned a one-hundred-acre golf course. In addition, we held three large commercial acreages and a trailer park in Courtenay, two hundred acres of waterfront in Desolation Sound known as Galley Bay, as well as numerous other parcels and buildings on Vancouver Island. So, what if we were two million dollars in debt, the real estate value exceeded six million!

Dr. Paul Burgoyne joined the staff at the veterinary hospital which was growing busier by the day. This freed me to commute to Galley Bay where I developed a large waterfront subdivision. Twice weekly, I traveled by powerboat to carry out the development of roads and buildings. The plan was to, once again, become extremely " wealthy". To be a successful entrepreneur, it becomes necessary to sleep, eat and spend nearly all spare time planning, shifting and developing. A person must dedicate their life to that endeavor.

Carole's brother-in-law, Bob, and I were discussing how rich we would like to become someday.

His wife, Tudy, overheard this conversation and offered her advice. "You guys wouldn't be happy even if you had twice that much money."

"If I had that much money," Bob retorted, "I'd buy me a clown to make me laugh."

All this time, another part of me was beginning to listen to the messages of wisdom that had been stubbornly knocking at the door throughout my life. Was I shifting the deck furniture on the Titanic? Did the close encounters I had experienced and my dad's vision all have a meaning? Had I given my kids the message that accumulating money and things was easy and therein lies the object of life? Mother Teresa's life and the study of St. Francis Assisi left me wondering.

Moving in the financial circles I chose, we crossed the paths of many people financially secure. Somehow, none of them seemed to have found that great contentment they sought and were sure would arrive as soon as they reached a certain plateau of wealth, ownership, and goals. Some of the poorest peasants we met in Mexico and the people in the South Pacific, the "affluent poor", were far more content than any of my wealthy colleagues.

In the gospel, Jesus said, "No one can serve two masters. He will either hate one and love the other, or be devoted to one and despise the other. You cannot serve God and mammon." (Mat 6: 24.) A North American like myself has difficulty swallowing a statement like that since most of us are singularly dedicated to the search for fun, money, quality of life, and things.

The rich young man asked Jesus, "Teacher, what must I do to gain eternal life?" Jesus answered, "If you wish to enter into life, keep the commandments."

"All of these I have observed. What do I still lack?" the young man replied.

Jesus said to him," If you wish to be perfect, go sell all that you have and give to the poor, and you will have treasure in heaven. Then come, follow me."

The rich young man had many "toys" and didn't want to lose them, so he went away sad.

"Whatever you do to the least of my brothers, you do to me." What was I doing for others? Not a lot, but making life pretty comfortable for ol' Jim.

I always assumed these scripture passages were meant for someone else or had some obscure meaning that didn't apply to me. It was easy to rationalize and squirm around those messages, but they wouldn't go away.

. "Okay God," I prayed, "if all this stuff is getting in the way of what You want from me, go ahead and take it away. One thing though, God, if You don't mind, we would like to keep the big sailboat, because it's so nice and if we had nothing else, it's always a place to live, and besides that, our friends really like it."

My brother, Dave, warned me one time, "you should be careful about praying for humility, you might get it."

I continued to be heavily involved in real estate development with many high quality investments. Carole went along with it for the ride, though half-heartedly. At one point, Carole was asked to come to an attorney's office to cosign a $300,000 mortgage.

The lawyer questioned her, "do you understand the seriousness of what you are signing since you cannot read this document? Do you realize that if something happens to Jim, you will be held responsible?"

Carole's saucy answer was "guess I'll have to sell a lot of pencils to pay this one."

I thought it was pretty funny, but the lawyer didn't even smile.

When we first climbed deep into debt, the mortgage rates were fixed at twelve percent, which wasn't a problem since the hospital was doing so well. Then came the financial crash of the early eighties. Interest rates climbed drastically to twenty-six percent. No way could I spay enough cats to deal with those numbers!

God has a tremendous sense of humor. Not long after registering that fantastic conditional covenant with God over the boat, the Canadian economy went down the drain. Real estate sales stopped dead in their tracks.

What did we lose first? Right, the boat! After all, he did tell the young man, "*all* that you have."

The boat was mortgaged for $150,000. It was a sad day when we delivered it to the broker's dock. Carole cried as we walked away. The Maritashan had become an essential part of our life. To Carole, it was a little akin to peddling one of the kids. The next owner was an oil well driller in Vancouver who used it for charter trips to the south. Then, the Stoley family from Campbell River purchased Maritashan and moored it there. The new owners allowed us to pat her on the bow whenever needed and generously offered open visiting rights.

Galley Bay property was next to go and it was the cornerstone around which everything else flowed down the tube. Finally, even the house and office were forfeited to the mortgage companies.

The economy was so poor that no one wanted to buy any real estate, allowing us to occupy the house and office as renters.

When anyone is attached to property and money, and everything is lost, a great depression ensues the first few days. Many, during the 1930 depression, committed suicide for that reason. My biggest concern was for Carole. What did she think now of her real estate tycoon who couldn't possibly lose? I admitted that concern to her.

Carole only laughed. "We have always been taken care of; why should we worry now?"

I became a little envious of St. Francis. He went broke voluntarily for the love of God; he *gave* it all away. I was forced into it for the love of gain (possibly initiated by my little prayer). Oh well, St. Francis was a saint!

Now, when we look back on the whole scene, losing everything was one of the best things that could have happened to our lives. Going down the tube really helps straighten out a person's twisted brain and gave my attitude revision a solid jump start.

A great relief came over me that, at first, was difficult to comprehend. It was as if someone had lifted a piano off my back. Whatever path I took, I must be dedicated to making it work. In order to make the 'money thing' work, that dedication had to be all consuming. To this day, I am still plagued by the thought of how innocent people may have been hurt because of my financial adventures. Does this border on stealing?

We visited a bankruptcy trustee for advice.

CHAPTER 17

Pilgrimage to Europe

We had always wanted to make a Pilgrimage to the holy places in Europe as the faithful did in ancient times. We longed, also, to visit the Marian shrines there. I had never attempted before because taking the time might interfere with my pursuit of wealth. I knew the history of Lourdes and Fatima. There, the Mother of Jesus had been sent by God, like the angels of the Old Testament, to warn the world of coming disaster.

As a youth, I loved the story of Fatima which many scholars believe was the fulfillment of Revelation 12. There, in 1917, Mary appeared to three young illiterate children and warned of the scourge of communism before the world ever heard of the word. She was sent to warn the world through the children that people must change their lives, stop offending her son, and follow her request for prayer and return back to God. If not, another worse war would follow the First World War then raging in Europe. She said further that an unknown light would illumine the night as a sign that her requests were not fulfilled. In 1938 nearly everyone in Europe witnessed that awesome light, just before World War Two began.

The world was warned through the children. "If people attend to my requests, Russia will be converted and the world will have peace. If not, Russia will spread its errors throughout the world, fomenting wars and persecutions of the Church. There will be plagues. The good will be martyred, the Holy Father will have much to suffer. and various nations will be annihilated." Who, in 1917, could dream of anything destructive enough to annihilate an entire nation? She promised that in the end her Immaculate Heart would triumph and there would be peace.

Many other approved apparitions were giving identical messages: Lourdes and La Salette in France; Banneux and Beauraing in Belgium; Akita in Japan; Betania in Venezuela; Kibeho in Africa; and Naju in Korea were some.

Obviously, we ignored her requests, at Fatima. I knew of those requests but only responded with half a heart. Like so many others, I became part of the problem.

I believe God uses young and humble people to receive messages because they are open and not burdened with mental hangups like adults. Also, profound biblical messages are more credible when transmitted by uneducated youth who are not able to fabricate such a complicated message.

Now, in our time, ever since 1981, we were hearing hundreds of reports out of Yugoslavia that the Blessed Mother had returned and was appearing daily to six young children in Medjugorje.

As our desire to make this pilgrimage grew, I consulted with the bankruptcy trustee, "if it becomes necessary to declare bankruptcy, should we make the trip before or after?"

He shook his head. "You better go now; mortgagors don't like people wandering around Europe when they are supposed to be in bankruptcy!"

In addition to Lourdes and Medjugorje, we were anxious to visit Rome. St. Peter, the first leader of the Church, was my favorite saintly hero and I chose his name for confirmation. He was buried beneath St. Peter's Basilica in Rome. I read the intriguing story behind the discovery of the tomb told by the editor of Reader's Digest in his book *The Bones of St. Peter.* As recently as 1950, his burial place was discovered quite by accident.

Marguerite, the writer of the book *Message of Merciful Love* that impressed me so, lived in Belgium not far from Rome. I had this overwhelming desire to meet with her, so we added Belgium to our list of places to go.

Two other family interests called us to Europe. We wanted to visit Chateau d'Urfe, a castle in France, the ancient home of my ancestors. Also we wanted to attend the upcoming wedding of my nephew, Ted, in the Orkney Islands of Scotland, scheduled for June of 1985. The two events set a logical date for the trip. It didn't take us long to decide.

Pilgrimage to Europe

"We have nothing left to lose," we agreed. "Lets go for it."

Carole suggested, "we'll leave our destiny in the hands of the Holy Spirit. Things always seem to work out better when we do it that way."

A priest friend, Father Dan, asks people with problems who are having doubts about turning their lives over to God, "how are things going now that you are running the show on your own?"

Soon we received evidence of the efficiency of our chosen tour guide.

A month before we were to leave, the bishop stopped by our home in Campbell River, only the second time he ever visited. He had made our day with the Pope's visit to Canada, so why not quiz him about what we should do in Rome.

He inquired, "what day do you plan to visit Rome?"

"May 25th," we told him.

He didn't know of anything, but would keep in touch.

Within the hour, he phoned. "You are in luck once again! May 25th is the day of the Consistory, when the Pope consecrates 28 new cardinals. Two of them are Canadians, and I would like you to represent Victoria Diocese at the Consistory."

How come we keep receiving these extraordinary gifts when so long I have been unfaithful? What next?

Soon all arrangements were made. Another veterinarian was located to manage the hospital for the month. Plane tickets and Eurorail passes for Europe were quickly arranged.

Other than my interest in the shrines of Europe, I really never had a desire to see Europe. I personally thought it would be a bore. I am a white knuckle flyer and would rather be sailing or almost anything other than flying. Carole loves flying and ready anytime to go anywhere.

One time, on board a flight to the Yukon over endless frozen peaks, I asked a mechanic sitting next to me, "what happens if these engines fail up here in the air?"

His simple, blunt answer depressed me "we plummet!" He offered. Ugh!

However, when we climbed aboard the 747, we were both about to explode with the excitement of what might be waiting over there.

We landed in Frankfurt and located a train headed for Rome. The bishop's office had even arranged a room for us in a hotel run by Ursulin nuns, just outside the Vatican wall in Rome. Those kindly nuns cared for us as if they were our mothers.

The bishop had provided a letter of introduction to Padre Robideau, the rector of the Canadian College at the Vatican. Men from Canada come here to study for the priesthood. We were given near royal treatment wherever we went in the Vatican, and introduced to the soon-to-be Cardinals Vashon and Gagnon in the college.

One of my greatest desires had been to attend Mass at the tomb of St. Peter. The basilica is the largest church in the world. St. Peter became Christ's first appointed vicar and the first Pope or "Papa" of the Roman Catholic faith.

The site of St. Peters in ancient times was outside the city limits, and therefore, appropriate to serve as a Roman burial ground. This was only discovered in the 1950s by archeological excavations beneath the basilica. This same area earlier was the site of Nero's circus, used for the persecution and martyrdom of the early Christians more often than the Roman Coliseum. Evidence in ancient literature and archeology shows that St. Peter was martyred by crucifixion. He requested crucifixion upside down, because he felt unworthy to be crucified like Christ in the upright position. St. Paul was beheaded near the same time. Paul was a Roman citizen and by law could not be crucified. St. Peter's body was quickly removed and hidden in a nearby Christian burial place to prevent desecration by the Romans. After a short time, his remains were returned to an area near to his martyrdom. In the 4th century, Constantine built the first smaller Basilica over the burial site in honor of St. Peter. Five hundred years ago, the present Basilica replaced the older building.

It was here we learned that the first thirty popes were put to death for their faith. (I wondered if they had trouble finding candidates for the job in those days.)

It must have taken a full day to describe to Carole the grandeur of the architecture and art inside St. Peters. The Pieta was the most striking of all the art, carved from one giant piece of marble by Michaelangelo. A documentary told how he could picture in his mind, the art he was to create from the stone in the marble quarry before it was mined. I stood there gazing at the Pieta like an awe struck school boy. The art was so delicately sculpted, it was as though I could see Mary's veil flowing in the breeze.

Recently a deranged man had attacked the Pieta with a sledge hammer and seriously damaged the figure of Mary. It was meticulously repaired, but permanently weakened. A guide informed us that the Japanese offered several million dollars to have the art piece shipped on loan to Japan for a world fair exposition. They were disappointed to learn this would never be possible since the damaged marble could not take the stress. It would have to remain as is until the end of time.

Our parish priest advised that a quick way to locate St. Peter's tomb was to watch for a priest carrying a chalice and fall in behind. Just as though they were waiting for us, at 7:30 that first morning, we found two priests bearing a chalice with an altar boy in tow. We followed them around a large statue, down a spiral staircase that we never would have found without those guides, directly to St. Peter's tomb. Our great celestial Tour Guide was apparently remaining on duty full time. The priests just happened to be American and spoke English.

"Could we receive the Eucharist?"

"Most certainly" was their enthusiastic reply.

The four of us were the only English speaking of the twelve who were able to squeeze into the tomb. Carole insisted that we sit together on a tiny bench sixteen inches wide. I started to argue, but decided that was no place for a marital flap with St. Peter buried in front, the tomb of Pius The Xll directly behind, and John Paul II, "live" upstairs. I crowded next to Carole in true togetherness fashion.

The Epistle, Gospel, and homily, of course, were all about St. Peter with Jesus after the Resurrection. Jesus said to Peter, "Do you really love me? Then feed my sheep," the words of my favorite song. Well, that was too much for our Carole, and she started to sob aloud. Her sobs were too much for the priests and they became so moved that they had to delay the service for several moments to regain their composure.

When Mass was finished, an elderly Italian lady beckoned me to come forward. She pointed to the spot behind the altar where the few remnants of Peter's bones lay in a small chest. When opened, you can see a few ancient shreds of purple cloth still clinging to the bones.

What an extraordinary and awe inspiring day that turned out to be. We spent the next two days within the Basilica, visiting tombs of great saints like St. Veronica who wiped the face of Jesus on the way to the cross, and the apostle St. Andrew and many great Popes. All the while, we marveled over what a tremendous gift was our Catholic faith. We gave thanks that we should have that gift since it is so easy to lose these days and there are so many other options available. It is said there are now over 26,000 different Christian denominations, all with opposing teachings. As each new church divides, it loses a little more and deviates further from the original truth. My grandfather used to say, "the Catholic faith is a tough one to live by, but a great faith to die by."

At the consistory, the new Cardinals receive their rings and are officially consecrated as Cardinals. For this ceremony, a temporary site was built in front of the Basilica to accommodate the altar. Around the altar they prepared an area for the more than one hundred Cardinals present with their relatives and honored guests. Important heads of government from many countries were in attendance. We arrived early, allowing us to sit in the third row near the altar, the Pope and all the ceremony. (This was not at all like us; back home we jokingly refer to Carole as my "late" wife, Carole.)

Most impressive was a large delegation of black people from Africa, in beautiful brilliant colored attire and bearing extraordinary musical instruments made from bone, intricately decorated with gold and gems.

While waiting for the service to begin, we became acquainted with a priest-chaplain from Philadelphia stationed on a U.S. aircraft carrier in the Mediterranean. He was present as a guest of Bishop John O'Connor from New York, who became a Cardinal that day.

The next half hour turned into one of the greatest experiences of our pilgrimage, completely unexpected. Since Carole can't see what is going on, I try to describe everything in detail. This is always rewarding because she gets so tickled when I describe beautiful and exciting events to her. You would think she was actually viewing the scene.

Pilgrimage to Europe

Often, when we return from a particularly scenic trip, she will tell others, "you should have seen the wonderful things we saw today!" Silly girl.

As I looked toward the huge entry doors of the Basilica, I noticed a diminutive nun dressed in blue and white emerging from the doors. It was obviously the familiar figure of Mother Teresa, no one else is that tiny.

I excitedly reported to Carole and our priest friend, " hey, there comes Mother Teresa! And she is coming this way. Wow!"

She sat in the first row directly in front of our priest who, in turn, was directly in front of Carole. People started to swarm around the poor dear lady, smothering her with hand shakes, touches, and kisses. The ushers promptly built a barricade of chairs to afford her some peace and protection.

Carole, of course, couldn't see the problem and kept imploring, " oh, I want to see her, I want to see her." I was really torn with this quandary. I didn't want to impose on Mother Teresa, the way others were pressing her, but Carole was so excited and sincere in her pleading.

In my dilemma, I tapped our priest on the shoulder, explained the problem, and asked, "what can I do?"

Without hesitation, he reached forward and tapped Mother Teresa on the shoulder. I don't know what he said, but Mother immediately stood from her chair and spoke to the priest.

Our friend said, "bring her out. Mother wants to meet her."

Now Carole fairly floated out to the aisle, many loving hands guiding her way.

Mother and Carole grasped each other. Carole was too emotional to speak very much other than to sob, "peace of Christ, Mother."

Carole meeting with Mother Teresa

Then, you should have seen her tears come down like falling rain. I looked and saw the priest was in tears. I looked around and everyone in sight was in tears. Then, I couldn't see any longer, for my eyes too, were full.

Carole is a convert to the Catholic faith, and as I commented in a letter back home to Monsignor Mike, "we really should screen our converts better, some of them are way too emotional."

Mother Teresa once said she so dislikes having her picture taken that she believes a day is removed from her purgatory every time she is photographed. I did my part and knocked off several days of her purgatory. Just writing about this causes me to choke up with tears once again. Time for a Kleenex break.

When we returned to our room, Carole remained on cloud nine, reminiscing over the fascinating events of the day. She told me Mother Teresa's hands were as strong and rough as a dirt farmer. Carole took out her little micro-cassette tape recorder. This we call her photo album. The voices of all the grandkids are recorded on it. She regretted not having the presence of mind to turn on the recorder when she talked to Mother Teresa. It would have been so nice to preserve the moment. We replayed the recordings she did make, mainly the music from the service played on the huge mobile organ from the church. "But what was this?" There, in between musical recordings, was the voice of Mother Teresa. Somehow when Carole was working her way out to greet the nun, the recorder accidentally turned on and recorded the entire event, complete with Carole's sobs.

The next day was the Mass for the feast of Pentecost, commemorating the day when the Holy Spirit descended on the Apostles, a fitting time to install the new apostles. This tradition has been going on for 2000 years, replacing the apostles or "cardinals and bishops" who have died and increasing their numbers as needed. It was a spectacular and beautiful Mass, with the music of St. Peter's choir and giant organ.

We met another interesting priest from Montreal who had taught several years in Central and South America. He filled us in on what is really happening there...quite a different story than what we hear from the news media and some of the liberal Catholic press. He asked if we knew what the red of the Cardinals' clothes symbolized. He informed us it was a sign that the Cardinals should be willing to be the first to give their blood for Christ.

The following day, we toured the Vatican and more of the Basilica. To demonstrate how on the ball I am *not*, I described to Carole, at great length and detail, the unbelievable art on the walls of the chapel where we met with the Cardinals. Two days later, we learned this to be the Sistine Chapel, and I had described to her the priceless works of Michelangelo and other great artists.

Many opportunities arose for us to visit the two Canadian Cardinals. I think Carole was not highly impressed with my manner. We were trying to decide how we should greet these great men. Do you genuflect and kiss their ring which we heard contains a sliver of the true cross? Do you just shake hands or what? When we abruptly ran into the impressive figure of Cardinal Vashon, impulsively I blurted out, "hey, Cardinal Vashon, red is your color!" Carole keeps reciting this incident to others so she must have felt my protocol was off. Carole was embarrassed, but the Cardinal laughed heartily.

After four days, it came time to move on to another event. We returned to the College to show our appreciation to Padre Robideau for the arrangements he had made.

One of our fondest desires was to visit Medjugorje, where the Mother of Jesus was reported to be appearing to the peasant children, not just a few times such as at Fatima and Lourdes, but 1500 times up to that date. When I was young, I wished Mary would come back since I wasn't around for Lourdes or Fatima. Wouldn't it have been something to be present at the time of Fatima? In Fatima, she appeared six times to those children. At the end of the apparitions, the Miracle of the Sun was displayed before a crowd of 70,000 to bear witness to the truth of the events. I had read the old articles reporting the news. She did not perform miracles on her own, only by the will of God. None of the Fatima messages conflicted with those of Medjugorje. In fact, the messages were in agreement with all the many other church approved apparitions.

Witnesses claimed that God was confirming the authenticity of Medjugorje by displaying all sorts of celestial phenomena and miracles. Jesus worked miracles while on earth so that people would believe. Now God was working wonders around the Blessed Mother to show those who are open that she was authentic and we should listen to her words, all of which are in agreement with the scripture.

The Bishop of Split Yugoslavia commented, "by their fruits, you will know them. The apparitions have done more to spread the gospel in four years than our works have done in forty years." Pope John Paul said in 1984, "Medjugorje is the fulfillment and continuation of Fatima." He said also, "if I were not the pope, I would be there already."

Detractors of apparitions argue that they aren't necessary since the gospel is all that we need. The response to this is that people are not listening to the gospel. Hopefully, Mary can wake us up before it is too late. Others argue that maybe it is the devil, but the devil is not noted for promoting the love of God or peace and conversion.

We debated the controversy. If there is a chance Medjugorje is authentic, why not be there? At that time, controversy was rampant in an effort to dissuade pilgrims from coming. The same difficulties prevailed at first in Fatima and Lourdes which are now approved by the church. The Church has to be very cautious, as there are also fakes, which could be damaging to individuals of weak faith. We did not know how our bishop felt, and did not want to offend him after all he had arranged for us. I suggested to Carole maybe we should skip Medjugorje.

"Now, the Holy Spirit has been the best tour guide we have ever run across, " Carole argued. "Look what he has done so far. Why not use him for the rest of the trip?" So far, we had set no agenda for time.

As we were saying good-bye and thank you to Padre Robideau, he questioned us, "where are you headed next?"

We replied, "we had planned on Medjugorje, but due to the controversy...we wonder if maybe we shouldn't."

"Don't let a little thing like controversy hold you back," he advised.

He then introduced us to two priests who had recently returned from there. They were ecstatic!

"Don't go home without Medjugorje," one encouraged. "We are waiting to return, ourselves at the first opportunity."

"Be sure to go to confession while you are in Medjugorje," added the other. "That's where the greatest of graces are received."

After three positives and no negatives, it seemed obvious; going to Medjugorje was the right thing to do.

No one should use the excuse that since he is a jerk, the creator has no further use for him. I discovered that, in spite of being unfaithful in the past, God still had some use for me, depending on how open I was to change. During our last conversation with Cardinal Vashon, Carole described all the gifts that had been heaped upon us. We were on a spiritual roll, receiving the Eucharist from the pope, being here to witness this great celebration in the church, Carole's encounter with Mother Teresa, and now on our way to Medjugorje.

She asked the cardinal, "what are we supposed to do in view of all these gifts we keep receiving?"

In an emphatic tone, he presented a challenge. "You go home and put them to use."

If that is God's will, were we willing to try?

Sailing Beyond the Sea

CHAPTER 18

Medjugorje

Two days after our flight from Canada landed in Frankfurt, a bomb went off in the Frankfurt airport, killing several airline employees. One day after we visited Buckingham Palace in England, a bomb was discovered there. All the while we were in Europe, Lebanese terrorists were holding a plane load of U.S. air passengers hostage.

A month later, near the end of June, we drove to the airport on our return home from Europe. The news headlines that morning reported an Air India plane, originating in Canada, was blown out of the sky by a terrorist's bomb, killing over 300 passengers. The stewardesses on that flight home were most entertaining. They did their level best to divert people's attention from the morning news. They danced down the aisles wearing ridiculous hats which they changed at regular intervals. They made jokes out of everything. I think they would have fared well on any talent show that day. The passengers were offered all the liquor they could consume. Triple shots were the order of the day.

But would a few trivial incidents like these concern a couple of brave world travelers like us? Yes, as a matter of fact, a lot! Carole didn't seem to be as concerned as I, the white knuckle flier. Maybe she is a good actress or maybe there is an advantage in not being able to enjoy the headlines.

Meanwhile, back in Europe, we had arrived in Yugoslavia early in June of 1985, the country was still under Communist rule. The police, military and customs people seemed dedicated to intimidate everyone, almost as if they had a mandate to keep everyone in a constant state of fear. Somehow, we were not concerned. Most pilgrims visit Yugoslavia with the benefit of tour guides. We planned to try it on our own. We knew that millions of pilgrims had gone to Medjugorje and reported that somehow all their needs had been taken care of without fear or effort. Some twenty million pilgrims had visited since the first apparitions, and to the best of my knowledge, no one had yet been harmed.

Now, after that first visit since 1991, the Serbs, who are the remainder of the Communist empire, are devastating the towns, churches and people of Yugoslavia. Journalists report that the cruelty and destruction exceeds that of the Nazi holocaust. Strangely enough, Medjugorje remains unscathed, while the towns all around have been flattened. The score to date, was one cow, one dog, and one chicken killed in Medjugorje. Of all the thousands of people killed in the war, none to this date from Medjugorje had yet been killed. Stories abound from enemy pilots, recounting how many times they have tried to bomb Medjugorje and some freak phenomenon prevents the attack. Bombs have been dropped on the village and they either go off in the air with no ill effects, or they land and fail to explode. One failed bomb was left stuck in the church yard as a sign and reminder.

Several people have complained to me that they have difficulty believing the apparitions in Medjugorje. How could all this evil take place if Mary is appearing in Yugoslavia? "The answer seems obvious to me." Medjugorje is the only town in Yugoslavia where people are answering the requests of the Blessed Mother, known as the Gospa in the Croatian language. The messages explain that this lesson is for the entire world. We can listen to the pleading of the Mother of Jesus and have peace like Medjugorje, or ignore her as we did at Fatima and the whole world will soon suffer the plight of the rest of Yugoslavia.

Mary in Medjugorje calls herself *The Queen of Peace*. She appeared precisely to the hour and the day, one year after the Chernobyl accident. In Kibeho, Rwanda, she appeared in 1981. There the visions warned the country, through the children, of a great disaster coming to their country. In the vision, they saw hundreds of bodies floating in rivers colored red with their blood. In 1994, thirteen years later, we viewed the fulfillment of that vision on national TV, exactly as it was predicted.

In the little village of Medjugorje, much prayer and fasting is offered in answer to the request of the Gospa. The Gospa told the children we have forgotten that by prayer and fasting, even natural disasters and war can be prevented.

The first positive information on Medjugorje in Canada spread by means of an audio tape with Father Bob Bedard telling of his pilgrimage to Medjugorje. We followed his path from Rome through Yugoslavia. Our travel agent in Canada advised that we take a ferry from Barri, Italy, to Dubrovnik, Yugoslavia. Upon arrival in Barri, we discovered the ferry would not start its run until August. A poster in Barri advised that a ferry would be leaving Pescara for Split, Yugoslavia, in a few hours. We reached Pescara in the nick of time for that ferry and crossed the Adriatic Sea to Split.

A series of mini-miracles arranged for us to reach every destination we sought. The one and only glitch was a detour from Split to Dubrovnik, only to discover the bus for Medjugorje actually leaves directly from Split. That cost us an hour. The singular advantage I could discover in favor of communism was cheap bus fare. Returning to Split, we soon found a bus leaving for Mostar.

The countryside around us was mostly barren of trees from logging without replanting five hundred years before. The remaining rain leached rocky soil made it difficult for trees to gain a foothold. Bushes and small plants struggled for survival and gave the hope that someday nature would make a stand once again. In spite of the missing trees, the rugged mountain terrain was awe inspiring as we wove our way up the long winding road.

We could speak only two Yugoslavian words, "Dubro Utro". This means "Good Day". Since our total vocabulary consisted of only two words, it seriously limited our conversation skills. We had just seated ourselves on the bus to Mostar when a seemingly friendly Croatian couple came to speak with us. They spoke many words, none of which we could decipher. The translation book was no help to either them or us. At one point, it sounded as if they might be telling us they had recently been married. We tried that translation, but that only created a barrage of laughter from all those seated near by who, by this time, were becoming extremely amused with the whole affair. We wondered why the couple was so persistent and determined to stand there next to our seat. Were we that charming?

Finally, an hour later and 50 miles into the trip, the driver stopped the bus. He marched military fashion, back to our seat, and in no uncertain expletives explained to us that in Croatia all bus tickets have a seat number printed on them identical to the number on your seat *and that is the seat you are to sit in!*

Our lengthy conversation with the two strangers was all about, "you are sitting in our seats. Would you please get up, go sit in your own seats, and let us sit where we belong." Two rows behind were two empty seats...our very own.

Mt. Krizevac, Medjugorje.

When we arrived in Mostar, history leapt backward a thousand years. There Islam and Christianity meet. Ancient buildings and structures surrounded us and a culture we had not yet experienced. In Mostar, we rented a car. The next half-hour brought us another wild adventure weaving through the switchback mountain roads. We dodged daring Yugoslav drivers who seemed to enjoy challenging fate driving at top speed. If anyone ever went over the edge of those high mountain roads, it would be a long time before they would hear the crunch of landing. Next time we would take a professional tour bus.

After a half-hour of this thrilling stock car race, we arrived in Chitluk, only three miles from Medjugorje. Two miles before we reached Medjugorje, the great stone cross erected by the villagers in 1933 loomed into view. It stood high on a mountain top overlooking the little village we sought. At first sight of this great monument, the hair literally stood up on my neck. What if all this about the Mother of Jesus is true? What if she is really here? What if God *is* using her, as he used her and the angels for centuries past to deliver warnings to the world? This is supernatural stuff. If the messages are true, then the event is monumental! A point that could rival the great flood or any momentous turning point in history.

Straight to the church, we drove down a tree-lined dusty road. People welcomed us on our arrival as if we had known them forever. We marveled at the vast crowds of people in such primitive surroundings. All roads and paths were dirt, no pavement or concrete was present.

The enormous crowd around the church in Medjugorje

There were only two public toilets for about 50,000 pilgrims. These were fashioned out of four sheets of galvanized roofing leaned together. Only one water faucet served the same numbers. Most astounding was the peace and lack of hostility by all who shared the limited facilities. Never in my life have I witnessed such a peace and joy as I felt in that little village. Even the thousands who couldn't speak English were full of love and friendship toward us. Never have I seen the faith so alive and vital as there. Oh, if only the rest of the world could be like this!

We were able to talk to the children who actually see the Blessed Mother. The children acted very sincere, very humble yet positive. After the service, they disappeared into the crowd, unwilling to be noticed. All our apprehension immediately faded away.

There were no hotels or hostels in Medjugorje in 1985. When we inquired about a place to stay, Father Peter, one of the assistant pastors, promptly drove us to the home of a lady named Yella and her four children. As in many homes, the father worked in Germany to support the family. We lived with them during our five day pilgrimage in Medjugorje. There was no common language, but we managed to create a tremendous communication of love, friendship, and sign language. They treated us like members of the family, even taking us with them to visit relatives in a neighboring town. They insisted we eat all our meals together which was no problem as their diet, though simple, was most appetizing. The bread was especially memorable. Most villagers lived in simple stucco homes without central heat and most without inside running water. There were not many lawns, but flowers grew everywhere. Long rows of vineyards, fruit trees, and gardens surrounded the village. The peaceful farm scene contrasted with the countryside we had witnessed earlier on the way. Chickens and ducks ran free and many homes were mini-farms with pigpens and cows either fenced or tethered. The familiar sound of roosters crowing, donkeys braying, and sheep bleating was almost musical in that atmosphere.

Following the suggestion of the priests in Rome regarding confessions, we sought out the first English-speaking priest we could find. This was a stroke of our now familiar boundless tour guide. Father Bill Frazer, visiting from Scotland, was one of the most inspiring priests we have ever encountered. He consecrated his life completely to Christ, and is deeply devoted to the church and the Blessed Mother. We appreciated the deep discussions on faith and his revelations to us on the troubled state of the church, life after life, and the significance of the Gospa's messages. For several years after our meeting, we corresponded by letter. We have since lost track of him, but hopefully our paths will cross again another day.

Father Bill introduced us to a variety of interesting people that we would never have met otherwise. First, we met Sister Briege McKenna, an exceptionally warm and happy lady. Several months later, we learned she is a world-renowned personality with extraordinary gifts of healing and insight. Sister Briege holds retreats for priests, bishops and cardinals.

On another occasion, he introduced Father Michael O'Carroll, who is, at this time, the spiritual director for Vassula, a controversial but well known seer from Egypt. I was touched by the heartfelt prophetic blessing he administered to Carole.

Forming the Sign of the Cross over each of her eyes, he prayed, "may your blindness teach others to see."

Three years before our pilgrimage, I had met Betty Hoy in Powell River. Betty introduced me to a book, *To the Priests, Our Lady's Beloved Sons,* written by Father Don Stefano Gobbi, a priest from Milan, Italy. The book has ecclesiastic approval from the Vatican, as well as imprimaturs from many bishops around the world. A very humble and holy priest, Father Gobbi receives locutions like Marguerite, but his messages come from Mary rather than from Jesus. His book contains these messages and is the source of the movement known as the Marian Movement of Priests. The MMP has spread throughout the world. Members include over 100,000, or one-quarter of the priests in the world, as well as many bishops and cardinals. Pope John Paul II holds frequent private audiences with Father Gobbi. When I first received the book and read a few passages, it seemed preposterous to me. It was too supernatural for my abbreviated faith. I stuffed it away high on a shelf. Father Bill produced a copy and asked if I was familiar with the work. I related to him my impressions, and that I had stashed it away on a shelf.

He explained the purpose and truth of the messages. Emphatically, he stated, "when you go home, you had better take it off the shelf and read it."

Of all the gifts of wisdom Father Bill passed on to me, that became the most valuable. The book became an incomparable source of consolation and the beginning of fascinating events which the future held for us.

As many as twenty priests heard confessions throughout the entire day, and sometimes into the night. Long lineups were everywhere. By the end of the day, the priests were exhausted, but overwhelmed by the change in peoples' hearts in numbers none of them had witnessed before. Several official confessionals lined the church inside and many unofficial outside...against a car hood, leaning against a stone fence, on a chair in the field, or under a tree. Before we left for Europe, our parish priest requested that I to go to confession once a month, from then on. Under a tree in Medjugorje, I started following his advice. During that first visit to Medjugorje, the children reported that Mary asked everyone go to confession once a month. I think our priest was impressed that Our Lady agreed with him.

We met many holy priests, nuns and lay people during those five days. Most people in the valley attended daily Mass. Most prayed the complete fifteen mysteries of the rosary daily, generally on their knees. Nearly everyone, young and old, fasted on bread and water only, one to two days per week to pray for peace. The priests living there stated that serious sin had disappeared from the valley. Most who visit Medjugorje find this love, peace, and holiness contagious and return home to pass it on wherever they go. Every day, ten (and sometimes up to a hundred) priests concelebrate the Mass. The Mass is celebrated several times each day in different languages.

Carole wanted to see the room where the daily apparitions took place. When I showed her the area where the Gospa appears, I should have known. What does Carole do every time we get near something holy? The sobs and tears come flooding down! Pilgrims told us of many signs announcing when the Gospa was about to appear to the children. The numerous chirping birds in the area become suddenly quiet. Others could tell because they turned the rectory porch light on to announce the time. I was fortunate. I had my own little high tech signal system. Whenever the Gospa was about to appear, Carole began to cry.

Maintaining my dearth of faith, we prayed that last night for a sign or miracle to show us this was authentic. Oh, we of little faith! At that very time, we squeezed into the isle to sit on the floor of a church large enough to accommodate twenty towns that size. We were on the floor because there was no room in the pews to kneel; in fact, no room in the aisles or on the porch outside. (Why was this old church built so large?) Thousands were standing or kneeling in the parking area. Hundreds of souls, even Moslems, were being converted to Christ through the prayers. (And we were looking for a sign?)

When we left Mass that evening, we went to reclaim some medals and rosaries which we had entrusted to an Irish girl so they could be blessed by the Gospa. This girl volunteered her support to any English-speaking pilgrims. We were conversing with her and Father Bill, when Father Svedt, the parish priest, approached. He invited us to be the first to view a new video made in Germany, with Father Rene Laurentin showing the church's investigation of the apparitions. *The Queen of Peace Visits Medjugorje* is produced by Hans Schotte. Father Laurentin is probably the world's foremost authority on Mariology. The video solved all my doubts and was the answer to our prayer of that evening. I questioned Father Svedt on how we might obtain a copy of the video. He informed us that the only possible source would be the "Voice of Freedom" broadcasting station in Munich, Germany, who was producing the film. How interesting. We were headed for Munich the very next day to meet relatives of our daughter-in-law, Ingrid. "Thank you, *Tour Guide*." I now have that video available for anyone to view.

We were continually warned not to let the signs and wonders which accompany the apparitions cause us to loose sight of their purpose. The most important reason for Medjugorje are the messages. We are asked to listen, but most important, to live according to them. The signs and wonders are to show they are real, not simply to impress us. Jesus produced tremendous miracles on earth to show that his words were true. God is using Mary now, and miracles surround these messages to show that they are truly from God. On our second trip to Medjugorje, we were privileged to witness several of these fascinating signs and wonders which I will relate further on.

We left Medjugorje with reluctance and a resolve that we would return again to that holiest and most peaceful place on earth. After only five days, we became as attached to that village, as to any of our homes in the past.

I thought this must be similar to what heaven is like. If we could only convince others to listen and accept these messages, then the rest of the world could share the peace so abundant in Medjugorje. If so, then one person could make a difference in preventing the world from entering into the disaster, where it is now headed.

As yet, the church has not given a final opinion on the authenticity of Medjugorje apparitions. This usually takes several years. So far, the messages are in complete harmony with the many already approved by the church. Neither is there any discrepancy between the messages and Holy Scripture or church teaching.

I believe the best way to summarize the message of Medjugorje is to quote a letter from Father Tomislav Vlasic, explaining the phenomenon of Medjugorje to the Pope. The letter follows.

Holy Father:

After the apparition of the Blessed Virgin on November 30, 1983, Maria Pavlovic came to see me and said, "the Madonna says that the Supreme Pontiff and the Bishop must be advised immediately of the urgency and great importance of the message of Medjugorje.
This letter seeks to fulfill that duty.
1. Five young people (Vicka Ivankovic, Maria Pavlovic, Ivanka Ivankovic, Ivan Dragicevic, and Jakov Colo) see an apparition of the Blessed Virgin every day. The experience in which they see her is a fact that can be checked by direct observation. It has been filmed. During the apparitions, the youngsters do not react to light; they do not hear sounds; they do not react if someone touches them they feel that they are beyond time and space. All of the youngsters basically agree that: "We see the Blessed Virgin just as we see anyone else. We pray with her; we speak to her, and we can touch her.

The Blessed Virgin says that world peace is at a critical stage. She repeatedly calls for reconciliation and conversion. She has promised to leave a visible sign for all humanity at the site of the apparitions of Medjugorje. The period preceding this visible sign is a time of grace for conversion and deepening the faith. The Blessed Virgin has promised to disclose ten secrets to us. So far, Vicka Ivankovic has received eight. Marija Pavlovic received the ninth one on December 8, 1983. Jakov Colo, Ivan Dragicevic and Ivanka Ivankovic have each received nine. Only Mirjana Dragicevic has received all ten. These apparitions are the last apparitions of the Blessed Virgin on earth. That is why they are lasting so long and occurring so frequently."
2. The Blessed Virgin no longer appears to Mirjana Dragicevic. The last time she saw one of the daily appari-

tions was Christmas, 1982. Since then, the apparitions have ceased for her, except on her birthday (March 18, 1983). Mirjana knew that this would occur.

According to Mirjana, the Madonna confided the tenth and last secret to her during the apparition on December 25, 1982. She also disclosed the dates on which the different secrets will come to pass. The Blessed Virgin has revealed to Mirjana many things about the future; more than to any of the other youngsters, so far. For that reason, I am reporting below what Mirjana told me during our conversation on November 5, 1983. I am summarizing the substance of her account, without word-for-word quotations.

Mirjana said that before the visible sign is given to humanity, there will be three warnings to the world. The warnings will be in the form of events on earth. Mirjana will be a witness to them. Three days before one of the admonitions, Mirjana will notify a priest of her choice. The witness of Mirjana will be a confirmation of the apparitions and a stimulus for the conversion of the world.

After the admonitions, the visible sign will appear on the site of the apparitions in Medjugorje for all the world to see. The sign will be given as a testimony to apparitions and in order to call the people back to the faith.

The ninth and tenth secrets are grave. They concern chastisement for the sins of the world. Punishment is inevitable, for we cannot expect the whole world to be converted. The punishment can be diminished by prayer and penance, but it cannot be eliminated. Mirjana says that one of the evils that threatened the world, the one contained in the seventh secret, has been averted, thanks to prayer and fasting. That is why the Blessed Virgin continues to encourage prayer and fasting: 'You have forgotten that through prayer and fasting, you can avert war and suspend the laws of nature."

After the first admonition, the others will follow in a rather short time. Thus, people will have some time for conversion. That interval will be a period of grace and conversion. After the visible sign appears, those who are still alive will have little time for conversion. For that reason, the

Blessed Virgin invites us to urgent conversion and reconciliation. The invitation to prayer and penance is meant to avert evil and war, but most of all, to save souls.

According to Mirjana, the events predicted by the Blessed Virgin are near. By virtue of this experience, Mirjana proclaims to the world, "Hurry; be converted; open your hearts to God."

In addition to this basic message, Mirjana related an apparition she had in 1982, which we believe sheds some light on some aspects of Church history. She spoke of an apparition in which Satan appeared to her disguised as the Blessed Virgin. Satan asked Mirjana to renounce the Madonna and follow him. That way, she could be happy in love and in life. He said that following the Virgin, on the contrary, would only lead to suffering. Mirjana rejected him, and immediately the Virgin arrived and Satan disappeared. Then, the Blessed Virgin gave her the following message in substance.

Excuse me for this, but you must realize that Satan exists. One day he appeared before the throne of God and asked permission to submit the Church to a period of trial. God gave him permission to try the Church for one century. This century is under the power of the devil; but when the secrets confided to you come to pass, his power will be destroyed. Even now he is beginning to lose his power and has become aggressive. He is destroying marriages, creating divisions among priests. and is responsible for obsessions and murder. You must protect yourselves against these things through fasting and prayer, especially community prayer. Carry blessed objects with you. Put them in your house, and restore the use of holy water."

According to certain Catholic experts who have studied these apparitions, this message of Mirjana may shed light on the vision Pope Leo XIII had. According to them, it was after having had an apocalyptic vision of the future of the Church, that Leo XIII introduced the prayer to Saint Michael which priests used to recite after Mass up to the time of the Second Vatican Council. These experts say that the century of trials foreseen by Leo XIII is about to end.

Holy Father, I do not want to be responsible for the ruin of anyone. I am doing my best. The world is being called to conversion and reconciliation. In writing to you, Holy Father, I am only doing my duty. After drafting this letter, I gave it to the youngsters so that they might ask the Blessed Virgin whether its contents are accurate. Ivan Dragicevic relayed the following answer. "Yes, the contents of the letter are the truth. You must notify first, the Supreme Pontiff and then the Bishop."

This letter is accompanied by fasting and prayers that the Holy Spirit will guide your mind and your heart during this important moment in history.

Yours, in the Sacred Hearts of Jesus and Mary,
Father Tomislav Vlasic

Sailing Beyond the Sea

CHAPTER 19

Munich to Lourdes

The rickety, yet low-cost, Yugoslav bus carried us to Split from Medugorje. As I looked out over the steep and rocky, sometimes barren countryside of Croatia, my thoughts wandered over all that we had heard and seen in Medjugorje. The messages and signs were all so profound and scriptural that there was no longer any doubt of their authenticity. How fortunate we were to witness this monumental turn in history. I reflected on the words of David Duplesis, a leader in the Pentecostal church, "truly, God is here in Medjugorje."

On the ferry once again, we returned to Pescara where we boarded the train to Venice on our way to Munich. My wife was gifted with a built-in romantic nature as part of the package. She insisted we go for a ride through the city of Venice on a Venetian gondola and have an Italian gondola baritone sing "O Solo Mio." We acquired the gondola easily enough, but as luck would have it, our skipper couldn't sing a note. Anyway, we enjoyed the gondola ride, sipping Italian red and chewing on pistachios.

On the third day, we ventured toward Munich to meet our daughter-in-law, Ingrid's family. They lavished German hospitality upon us. Fortunately, Ingrid's sister spoke some English. Without delay, she led us to the Voice of Freedom broadcasting station, where we were able to obtain the video we sought, *The Queen of Peace Visits Medjugorje*. Videos are produced under a different format in Europe than in North America, so European videos cannot be viewed until converted. For a mere $375 we were able to accomplish the conversion in Vancouver. The following year, this same video became available at centers for peace in the U.S. for $24. I couldn't wait; we had a job to do.

In Munich, our new family treated us to a downtown parade. There, leading the parade, was Cardinal Ratzinger whom we had so recently encountered in Rome. He is head of the Congregation For the Doctrine of the Faith, probably the second most important position in the church. On the other hand, it is probably the least enviable job in these days when so many within the church are trying their best to destroy it under the guise of modernization; wolves in sheep's clothing.

From Munich, we traveled by train south to Lourdes, France, in the Pyrenees mountains. In 1858, fourteen year old Bernadette Soubirous received eighteen apparitions from Our Lady in the cave of Massabielle along the River Gave. During the last apparition, the lady identified herself as the Immaculate Conception. This is an intellectual term, understood only by theologians in those days. Bernadette was an uneducated child at the time and would have been completely unaware of the term. She was instructed by the Lady to wash in the spring under the rock of Massabielle, but no spring was there. Muddy water was the only result of her effort to obey the lady. A likeness of her in the museum shows her facing ridicule with a mud smeared face. Later that day, after enduring a shower of heckling from the townspeople, a generous spring blossomed and spewed out from that spot into the River Gave. The bountiful spring continues even now, producing 32,000 gallons a day. This incredible spring, and the visions and reports of many miraculous cures, attracted hoards of pilgrims. In 1862, the Church officially approved Lourdes as a place of pilgrimage. It gradually became second only to the Holy Lands as a pilgrimage site in the Christian world. A great Basilica was dedicated in 1901, and in 1958, a vast underground church was finished. An estimated six million pilgrims visit Lourdes every year. A medical bureau and a hospital have been established to study and authenticate the reported miracles.

Rows of baths are there for pilgrims to immerse themselves as they pray for intentions. Carole and I took the plunge. Yes, they are cold! I always wondered how they managed the enormous laundry system that it must require to deal with the millions of towels needed for the pilgrims. I discovered that it was actually quite simple. There are no towels; you crawl back into your clothes dripping wet.

In 1993, over 300 apparition sites were reported around the world. Some, such as Bayside, New York, are obviously fraudulent. The Church does intense study before accepting apparitions, and in many cases for very good reasons. This process takes many years. A recent question and answer column explains this.

Question: You say the devil imitated Our Lady at Lourdes. Please explain, as I have never heard this before. I believe Our Lady did appear at Lourdes.

Answer: Certainly, Our Lady did appear at Lourdes, but the reader above was not alone in wanting us to "explain" the devil's "appearance" at Lourdes. It has dawned on us that many Christians are unaware of this fact, one of the basic reasons why the Church is so cautious in accepting reports of apparitions and the like.

The devil is real. Christ was tempted by him. St. Paul warns us that we wrestle not against "flesh and blood, but against principalities and the powers of darkness." Scripture speaks of the devil nearly as often as the creator. Our generation alone has fallen victim to his greatest lie, to persuade us he doesn't exist.

In an excellent book, *Evidence of Satan in the Modern World* by Leon Christiani (Macmillan, N.Y., 1962), accounts of demonic intervention, some of it grotesque, are presented, all from the most reliable sources. As the author notes, Satan would scarcely have been so active in "troubling" the saintly Cure of Ars, yet remain indifferent to the appearance of the Woman at Lourdes, whose warnings for our age would surely save many from falling into his snares.

Witnesses to Satanic activities at Lourdes range from the mayor of the town to clergy, to the superintendent of police, and to many notables.

The first occurrence was reported by Bernadette Soubirous, herself, on February 11, 1858, when she became aware of a "young girl in white" (Our Lady) in the hollow of a rock at the entrance to the grotto of Massabielle. Bernadette reported that the vision was "disturbed" by strange noises, apparently coming from the River Gave - voices, that seemed to echo and reply to each other. One, more distinct than the rest, kept shouting the furious, menacing cry, "Flee! Flee!"

(Why "Flee! Flee!" from such a beautiful lady? Obviously, because the Lady was there with a world-wide message of saving souls.)

Then came so many other visionaries that Bernadette could no longer compete with so many. The accounts are given by Father L.J.M. Cros, a Jesuit priest who had access to the official records and testimony of the witnesses.

These visionaries ranged from a "virtuous twenty-two year old girl, very religious, but with a powerful imagination, to a woman of forty-five, married, of bad reputation, and addicted to drink. All believed they had seen Our Lady, but, significantly, none reported seeing her on the spot where Bernadette had seen her. "Some invisible protection seemed to encircle the spot and also the person of Bernadette herself," says the author.

Literally, there were scores of "visionaries" including school girls, some going into ecstasies, some howling like dogs, some giving weird commands ("Kneel down and kiss the ground forty times, because Our Lady says so!") and all, manifestly, the work of the devil.

Father Cros questioned some of the visionaries twenty years later, and most had, at best, "only a vague recollection" of the events in which they starred - and which created such incredible confusion among both the civic and religious authorities.

This priest was convinced they *had* "seen something"; they *had* heard voices; but "they came from the Devil." Why? - To discredit the reality of Our Lady's genuine appearance to Bernadette. The devil is often referred to as "God's ape." He is an imitator....

Sometimes it takes inspired souls to discern the difference. This is why it is foolhardy to ignore the judgment of the Church that Christ founded in the matter of "signs and wonders," wrought by Satan; "to deceive, if it were possible, even the elect." This same phenomenon was reported all around Medjugorje in the first years, but was soon discounted.

Carole and I experienced a confrontation similar to this in Medjugorje during our second visit. It was enough to make the hair on your head stand on end.

CHAPTER 20

Short but not so Sweet Sojourn in Paris

After Lourdes, we traveled northeast to the city of Roanne, France, for the next stop on the itinerary that we had set for ourselves...my mother's ancestral castle, the Chateau d'Urfe. The ruins that remain, mentioned in her d'Urfe family history, are located not far from Roanne. The last d'Urfe to live there was hacked to death by his servants in the year 1100. (Maybe the jerk in me could be hereditary. Hope springs eternal, though. The family is also said to be connected with Joan of Arc.)

Paris was our next significant stop and my memories of that city are not so fond. We arrived in the early evening by train. Immediately, we set out in search of a hotel. Since there was no place to leave luggage, we packed the cumbersome load with us wherever we drifted, from one hotel to the next. Every hotel was full; "there was no room at the inn." We returned to the street in front of the depot. Darkness was rapidly descending on the great city.

The station manager observed our bewildered appearance. "You folks better come inside the gate and bed down until morning. The streets of Paris are no place to be at night."

His voice carried an ominous tone. We accepted the proposal with no hesitation. That night, Carole slept (a little) on a hard wooden station bench. Two gentlemen reeking of stale alcohol stretched out on benches adjoining hers. I slept the most uncomfortable sleep of my personal history; atop the three suitcases laid out on the not so sanitary concrete floor. I kept one eye watching over Carole most of the night.

The following morning, bleary eyed from the effects of sleep deprivation, we set out to indulge in some culture. The famous Louvre Museum, where stands Venus, and where hangs the famous Mona Lisa, and many other illustrious art pieces.

Outside the subway, we studied the street map of Paris. We must have appeared as the ultimate depiction of two greenhorn tourists. A group of four youngsters approached. They held out a newspaper with several green lines scrawled over the front page; I presumed to serve as a map. Their behavior was odd as they jabbered incessantly, pointing to various sites on this home-style map. This drawing, they held over our map and over our little day bag which I carried in my hand. For the life of me, I couldn't understand what they were up to. Then suddenly, a car on the busy street came to a screeching halt. A lady leaned out of the car window shouting, waving her arms excitedly, and swearing at the kids in words I didn't understand. She motioned frantically at the array of maps and our bag. Obviously, something was amiss. I lifted the map only to discover these slick little varmints had skillfully unzipped the bag and were rooting through it, all the while keeping my attention with the phony map and their excited chatter. I shouted at them and conjured up the meanest look I could muster. The kids flitted in all directions, and in seconds they were out of sight.

My next thought was, "How many big bandits are there lurking around who won't run away from a few angry words?"

These little adventures shattered my interest in hanging around Paris. I performed my obligatory visit to the Louvre Museum and became properly impressed. My brother-in-law, Joe Revlock, covered the subject well when he proclaimed, "When you have seen one museum, you have seen a lot." This really disappointed Carole, who was ready to experience it all and paint the town red.

CHAPTER 21

Marguerite

Maybe, since our tour was under celestial guidance, we weren't to waste our time in the secular world of Paris. Another reason for my lack of interest in Paris was the compelling urge to meet Marguerite. She is the humble housewife living in Belgium whose book, *Message of Merciful Love To Little Souls,* consoled me so much when I was most in need of a guide. Marguerite, like Father Stephano Gobbi, is one of the first of the modern locutionists. A locution is a private revelation, through means of an inner voice, giving messages to a person generally of great personal holiness. The claim is that Marguerite receives messages from Jesus as did Saint Theresa of Avilla and St. Augustine, as well as many other saints throughout history. The church studies these locutions meticulously, as they do the apparitions. The devil has been known to dupe people in the same manner with fictitious messages. It is important to listen to the authority and wisdom of the church to discern this sort of phenomenon. Her book, detailing these locutions, has imprimaturs from sixteen approving bishops, more than any book I have yet run across. To receive an imprimatur, a book is "judged to contain nothing contrary to scripture or authentic church teaching." Unfortunately, most authentic visions and locutions, like prophets, are not appreciated until centuries after they pass. Pope John Paul II is reported to have recommended this book to priests when he held the office of bishop. Passages in the book are identified with a J. when Jesus speaks and an M. when Marguerite speaks.

Joan of Arc received locutions and was interrogated by the king. He was quoted as demanding, "Who are you, Joan of Arc, to say that God would speak to you, a peasant. I am a king. Why, instead, does he not speak to me?"

Joan humbly replied, "He probably does, Your Royal Highness, but you fail to listen!"

Maybe many of us might receive some supernatural insights if we became more open.

It was the distribution of this book among friends back home in B.C. that led to the establishment of the five Galley Book stores on Vancouver Island.

Time after time, I received reports how profoundly this book had changed someone's life, especially a person who didn't realize every sin under the sun, no matter how serious, will be forgiven by God if the person will only ask and accept forgiveness. Evidently Marguerite needed a great deal of forgiveness herself.

Two close friends living near Campbell River, Jack and his wife Virginia, helped distribute the book. They were impressed with the messages for the consolation it gives to nearly all who study the work. Everyone finds passages that seem to address themselves directly, solving all sorts of formerly unanswerable problems. At the same time, it produces a profound thirst for Christ and Holy Scripture.

Critics of this sort of devotion seem to stubbornly overlook the mire that the world wallows in, while those changed by listening to the message experience a new and boundless joy. I often answered critics with the questions. "Have you another book that actually and singularly brings hundreds of people back to the sacraments and their faith? Show me another book with sixteen imprimaturs from good and holy bishops?"

The December 30, 1972, message reads, "The Legion of Little Souls is no human undertaking, but the work of salvation issuing from My wounded Heart which has compassion on the world's misery."

Jack's sister, who had been away from the sacraments for some twenty years, had been injured in a serious car accident during a tour of Italy. While she was recovering in hospital, Jack presented her with a copy of the book. Her first reaction was one of severe distaste, and she shoved the book away. After several days in the hospital, she once again ventured into the pages to discover that all the messages were dated the month and year they were received. A message that was given on the anniversary of her own birthday struck her like a bolt of lightning. She then read the entire book and discovered all the messages had the same effect. She then returned to God and the sacraments.

No one claims that these messages are only for a person on their birthday, and definitely not like astrology. This is only an element that Jack and I enjoyed. All the messages are for all of us every day. They are all biblical and approved by sixteen holy bishops. A biblical message on a birthday seems to make a more penetrating impression than it would on another day.

Coincidences have always intrigued me anyway. Our friend Linda was assigned an hour to pray in the middle of the night during a Cursillo. She fell asleep and dropped her bible. When she picked up the open book, the passage that loomed before her read, "so you could not stay awake with me one hour?"

Jack's family has a fascination for names. They came to northern Vancouver Island to visit another island nearby. It held the same name as their ancient Gaelic family name. They liked the area so well, they moved and are still living near Campbell River. After his sister's conversion, Jack was disappointed because his birthday anniversary, November 3rd, was nowhere in the book. I received a new edition the following year with a one hundred page supplement. Jack took several of these home. There, in the new supplement, was a message on November 3rd. The family had recently moved to a new house on the hill overlooking the ocean. Earlier that morning, his wife had said to Jack, "isn't it interesting Jack, that we now live in a house which means the same as our name?" (In an ancient Gaelic dialect, their name means "house on a hill".)

The message on November 3rd, 1973 reads:

(Jesus) "On this hilltop, I am at home and I am here in a very special way. Here My Spirit reigns completely, and great graces are waiting for men of good will." That message fit their family to a "T".

When they discovered this, Virginia urged Jack, "phone Jim and tell him to read the message."

"No," Jack protested, "he'll think we are fanatics!"

When they finally did phone, not to be outdone, we decided to look up our own birth anniversaries. Carole's birthday is October 11th. When I read the message on October 11th, 1967, I broke into tears, and a long time elapsed before I could choke out the words so Carole could understand.

> *October 11, 1967. J. "Look at Me, in you and around you.*
> *See the Face of your God, sad with the world's*
> *sadness, radiant with the beauty He has created.*
> *My little child, it is sufficient to look in order to see.*
> *You see because you love Me."*

Many people, to whom I have related this story, have looked up messages that fit their own life, read it and exclaimed, "oh my God," bought the book and went away to discover a whole new outlook on life.

When I was in the process of accumulating wealth, my accountant recommended that I invest in old silver dimes and quarters, as well as a good stock of one ounce gold coins. They would soon be worth a lot more, especially if there was an economic crisis. This sounded like a prudent choice to make. I followed the advice and stored away about thirty thousand dollars in coins. As I was starting to loose everything, I cashed these in to pay off some of the mortgages. My bookkeeper, Brian, was reading messages daily out of Marguerite's book.

When I returned from the bank that day, he read, with a mischievous tone in his voice, a passage he was saving for me. "All of you saving that silver and gold, shame on you, place your treasure in heaven where it will neither rust nor decay."

Marguerite herself often doubted the source of the messages.

One of the messages tells Marguerite, "you will find enough little miracles in these writings to prove their authenticity."

Feeling a little nervous as we entered Belgium, we went about the search for Marguerite. One problem nagged at me that I found difficult to erase. Here was a great mystic who I do not doubt would someday be declared a saint. Who were we to think we should be afforded a personal audience with her? What words could we possibly find to say if we were able to meet with her?

Marguerite

We traveled by train to Liege, Belgium, and then boarded a bus to the end of the line, Chaud Fontaine. After we checked into a hotel, the clerk directed us to a cab driver who delivered us to Chevremont, the village where Marguerite lives high on a mountain. We knew Marguerite did not speak English, but once again, being of little faith, I had to discover for myself if she was 'for real.'

There were no house numbers in Chevremont and none of the streets were named. How do you find someone in a town in a foreign country, not speaking the language, not knowing her last name and even realizing the name Marguerite is not her real name? She has been requested in the messages to remain anonymous and humble in this life, and her real name, even now, is unknown to any of us. The cab delivered us to a huge basilica and monastery on the outskirts of the village of Chevremont. No one in the basilica spoke English and even when I unveiled the little red book, *Message of Merciful Love to Little Souls,* no one seemed to understand. Had we traveled 300 miles for naught? Finally, a sympathetic lady introduced us to a monk who spoke fluent English.

He gently alleviated our anxiety. "No problem, go to the large stone building next door. It is the center for the Legion of Little Souls. You will learn all about 'The Message' there."

We approached the old stone building, and once again, great fear and embarrassment descended over me like a dark cloud. My mind raced...who are we to think that we can walk in and talk to a holy lady who receives locutions from the Son of God? If she were a fraud, it would be easy to talk. I labored over the authenticity. The message had the approval of Cardinal Sin, the chairman of the movement in the Philippines. Who do we think we are, anyway? I truly suffered those few minutes of despair as we ventured toward the center.

Relief came when the only person present, a most fascinating lady named Yetta, greeted us at the door. She, the Spiritual Director Father Ancart, and one other lady are the closest associates of Marguerite. Yetta quickly disarmed our anxiety and was so delightful and informative that we stayed talking to her for four hours. She spoke better English than we. She relayed considerable information concerning Marguerite, the message, the state of the world, Our Lord and his Mother.

We didn't notice the time fly by until, all of a sudden, Mass time had arrived. The rosary is prayed and mass celebrated daily at 5 o'clock in the chapel located in the center. We were advised that a fairly large group generally attends with Marguerite. Yetta informed us that there was a schedule interruption and Marguerite had gone away. Too bad the three hundred mile trip might be for nothing; except that the meeting with Yetta made it worth while. Marguerite is normally there every day, Yetta explained; but because of the crowds and the demands on Marguerite's time, our meeting would have been limited to shaking hands and greeting Marguerite. That would have been enough for me.

To our surprise and delight, as we entered the chapel, we learned Marguerite had arrived after all. Because of the unusual schedule, no one else was present except Marguerite. We had her to ourselves! Marguerite was a diminutive lady in her early sixties at that time. Her hair was evenly divided between silver and black. She was highly animated and had a great bubbling sense of humor which often bubbled over. Her most striking feature was her holiness. According to her autobiography, she was a most unworthy person in her youth.

When she asked Our Lord why he allowed her to be unworthy for so many years,

he replied, "So you would understand the difference."

In later years, she was severely persecuted for the faith she had found.

There we were at Mass, kneeling next to one who many are convinced will someday be canonized a saint. When she passed by after communion, she smiled gently and filled us with peace. Even that would be enough. Then, as we rose to leave, Marguerite held out her hand and said "momente." She gave each of us a big hug and invited us to join her and the vivacious spiritual director, Father Ancart. Yetta became our interpreter. We were fortunate to be with them for nearly an hour. Marguerite sometimes laughed whole heartedly, while at times her demeanor became gravely serious. She was keenly aware of the pressing spiritual problems in the church and in the world.

We told her about our visit to the d'Urfe Castle. Marguerite teasing, asked what we thought my royal title should be. When I suggested King d'Urfe, she frowned and shook her head.

"Well how does Count d'Urfe sound?" I parleyed.

She laughed good naturedly and voiced her approval, "that sounds much better."

She was delighted that we had been to Medjugorje, Rome and Lourdes. She told us she corresponds with Father Gobbi whom she had met twice - once at the request of Pope John Paul II. She explained that the crisis in the church and the world is far more serious than most people understand. She speculated that Mary spends more time on earth now than ever before, trying to bring people back to God. Carole was a little dubious about the *Message of Merciful Love* before meeting Marguerite, but was so impressed with her sincerity, simple piety, and great humor, that she now listens to the messages on tape.

We were greatly blessed for that month in Europe with more gifts than we will ever deserve. One of my most precious moments was the Mass and the time with Marguerite. Our Tour Guide deserves the credit for not allowing our fear to keep us from following our hearts.

The messages encourage all to start cenacles, using the book as a guide. We have since started and encouraged several cenacles. There are many operating faithfully throughout the world now, similar to the cenacles of The Marian Movement of Priests.

After leaving Marguerite, we traveled to the Orkney Islands, north of Scotland, where we attended the wedding of my nephew Ted and his bride Helen. Seventy people, mostly from North America, attended. St. Magnus Church was confiscated by the Church of Scotland at the time of the reformation. The, wedding was reported in the *Glasgow News* as the first Catholic wedding in St Magnus church in 500 years.

Following the wedding, we returned home, determined to put our gifts to work as recommended by the cardinal.

Sailing Beyond the Sea

CHAPTER 22

Native Pilgrimage and Cursillo

Retired Bishop O'Grady, from Prince George, B.C., once predicted that the Native Indian might be the humble instrument used by God to bring white man back to himself. I, and many like myself who are obsessed with "quality of life", have forsaken the creator, searching for happiness in stuff and things. Never in history have we owned more stuff and never have we been more depressed, worried and forlorn.

I often chide Native friends that they better get busy; if Bishop O'Grady is correct, they have a monumental task ahead of them.

Another gift from Dad was his appreciation for the Native Indians in Montana. He taught us respect and admiration for the natives and many became his closest friends.

Father Frank Salmon was responsible for our interest in the Native Pilgrimage and Native Cursillo. Father Salmon is a unique priest from the order of Oblates of Mary Immaculate. His life is dedicated to the Native's faith like no one else I know. He lives in Ahousat, on Flores Island, and ministers to all people on the west coast of Vancouver Island. His adventures could, and should, fill a holy and humorous book. When the bishop was about to move him off the island, natives gathered a petition to keep him from leaving. The slogan they used for the petition read, "Help Save Our Salmon."

On one of Father's frequent visits to Campbell River, he informed our friend Ed Fauchon that several hundred Natives had moved to Campbell River. They were now removed from their normal environment and, as Father Salmon mused, strangers in their own land, distressed and uncomfortable.

"It is up to you people to share your love and let them know they are appreciated." he said. "Don't try to turn Natives into white men. It would be better for you to become like them. Their faith is uncomplicated."

Jesus said, "unless your faith becomes like that of little children, you cannot enter the kingdom of heaven." So much for the cliché, "mature faith," zealously proclaimed today but in sharp contrast to the gospel.

Alcohol and drugs have created havoc and tragedy for the natives. They speak of alcohol and drugs as their last major war. I know of no other group that works as hard to overcome that problem. They say the devil desires them to drink.

One theory that has gained considerable acceptance was explained to us by Father Tom, a Jesuit therapist from Washington.

The theory goes as follows: the Jewish nation has had alcohol available for over 3000 years, and enjoys the lowest rate of alcoholism of any race. The majority of the Caucasian race has been drinking for two thousand years with twenty percent of their population afflicted with alcoholism. The west coast Indians were introduced to alcohol one hundred and fifty years ago. They have the potential of eighty percent alcoholism. Inuits have only been drinking for fifty years and their rate of alcoholism approaches one hundred percent. This is a sort of "survival of the longest." The ancestors of the Jewish race who were susceptible to alcohol died off a long time ago and have fewer descendants who are susceptible. Some Natives, as well as individuals from other races, can become alcoholic after one drink and their addiction can be stronger than heroin is for another. Many other factors enter in to complicate the problem. So, to assume that a native who can't stop drinking is necessarily a bad guy is unfair and shows a lack of knowledge on our part, akin to criticizing someone for having diabetes. The pursuit of freedom from drugs is a long, painful and sometimes terrifying trip that rarely can be accomplished alone. People who don't have the disease of drugs or drink have a much easier cross to bear. The therapist who proposed this theory admitted that the Irish are a population who don't fit the hypothesis. He admits it's only a theory, but worthy of consideration by the very observation of the facts.

Native Pilgrimage and Cursillo

Neither Ed nor I had a clue how to follow Father Salmon's advice, but we were learning how to pray, especially the rosary. Wayne Weible describes the rosary as a mini-bible. Father Jozo called it the "biography of Jesus."

Some of our friends, who are not familiar with the rosary, are surprised to discover that the first half of the Hail Mary prayer is a direct quotation from scripture. The second half is a request asking Mary to pray for us. We take the Apostles Creed literally when we say, "we believe in the communion of saints." This means when people pass away, only the body is dead and we can still communicate by prayer to saintly people in heaven. We don't mind asking holy people and ministers on earth to pray for us, so why not ask the greatest of all saints, Mary the mother of Jesus, to pray for us. In praying the rosary, the Our Fathers, Hail Marys and other prayers become the back-ground music like the song Ave Maria, which is the Hail Mary in Latin and in song. Meanwhile, the high points of the life of Christ become alive as we meditate on the joyful, sorrowful and glorious mysteries of his life.

So we prayed. Our answer came in the person of Jim, a young Native leader. When he moved to Campbell River, we 'grabbed' him. Jim was a recovering alcohol and drug abuser who knew the problem well. He and his wife had developed a successful rehabilitation center in Powell River which continues to this day. Deeply concerned about his people and their problems, he joined us in the rosary, begging the Creator for help.

We decided to try a fifty-four day rosary novena; we pray the rosary every day for twenty-seven days petition, and then for another twenty-seven days in thanks. Jim said he tried, but could never complete it on his own. Perhaps, if we prayed together, we might succeed. We met every day without fail, at either his home or mine for the rosary. Jim assured me that it mattered not what time of day or night for him to pray.

"Come whenever you can make it," he urged.

One night I didn't return from Gold River until 1:00 AM. The lights still burned in his home so I took a chance and knocked on the door. I was surprised to find Jim, his wife, and five young children still awake and about. A little guy, Ian, one and a half feet tall, answered the door.

Bonnie, his mother, called out, "who's at the door, Ian?"

"It's that crazy white man here to pray the rosary again," Ian yelled back.

We completed the novena several times. One thing led to another and Jim suggested we organize a Native banquet and retreat. Ann Haig Brown offered her home on the Campbell River for the occasion. About eighty people turned up and a happy tradition was born. Eighty new friends were found. Father Salmon attended and eight beautiful new babies received their baptism.

There are forty-eight different Native bands located on Vancouver Island and forty-nine thousand native people. All bands were welcome to these banquets, and the banquets grew and continued on for several more years. Good things were beginning to happen.

At these banquets we met two of the most important families in our lives and the lives of our spiritual community, Bill and Susan Blaney from the Holmalco band at Church House and another Jim and wife Pat Nicolaye from Kyuquot on the west coast of the island. Both men had been chiefs of their bands. Here was another answer to prayer.

The Native banquets, were going well. However, like most good things, they were only a stepping stone to another plateau. We read in a Vancouver paper that the Korean community held a Korean Cursillo. It had been one of the most successful events they ever experienced.

"Why not a Native Cursillo?" After a few inquires, we learned that Natives in Montana and Alberta had already been holding Cursillos for two years. They were spreading like wild fire across the prairies. I conveyed our interest to Bob Breaker, a leader in Gleichen, Alberta, on the Blackfoot Reserve. Without hesitation, he invited four of us to join their native Cursillo at Gleichen.

The white man's Cursillo was one of the most moving weekends I have ever experienced, great fun and immensely rewarding. Now the Native Cursillo was another story. The people in Alberta pull out all stops when they have a function, complete with professional musicians and amplifiers. I had a dislike for country western gospel music up until that time, so my psyche had to be rebuilt. The Natives gently removed that stigma from my brain.

The Native Cursillo movement started in Browning, Montana. It spread to the surrounding reserves, spilled over into Washington, and then to Alberta, Canada, where it was held regularly throughout the province.

Father Jackson, the provincial of the Oblate order, told us that before the Cursillo, only a handful attended Mass on the Blackfoot reserve. After the Cursillo started, the church was full. At that Cursillo, closing Mass where he spoke, there were 600 present.

His nephew, a local police officer, asked, "what is going on here? The crime rate is dropping ten percent a year and the tragic death rate is declining fifty percent per year. The police are going to be out of a job if this keeps up."

Father figured the nephew, an unbeliever, would never understand that this was related to the Cursillo so he didn't bother to explain.

Browning, Montana, had boasted twelve taverns in the recent past. Since the Cursillo and Pilgrimage, they were reduced to two, both struggling for survival. Tavern owners had mixed emotions about Cursillo.

Besides being immensely entertaining, these functions were more successful in healing than anything we had witnessed. I purchased a fifteen passenger Ford van. We shared the costs and the original four proceeded to bring many of our friends from Vancouver Island to the Alberta Cursillos. The hope was to someday hold a weekend on the Island. All the while, the Natives were teaching us the real meaning of love and change of heart.

Through the Cursillo, we discovered the Pilgrimage. The Cursillos were doing great things in Montana, but not quite addressing the alcohol and drug problem as well as the people desired. A group of Montana Natives including, Dave and Myra Knopfl and a man known as Blue, together with two Jesuits, decided to try to combine the Cursillo with a twelve-step program like AA. They called it "Pilgrimage." It turned out to be another grand success which spread out into adjoining territories as did the Cursillo. The effort aimed, in part, at encouraging people to seek help in treatment centers and AA. Conventional pilgrimages are a spiritual journey to a holy place. The Native Pilgrimage was a journey through life.

When I sold the Veterinary practice in Campbell River in 1989, we decided to take our VW camper across North America and visit the kids we had scattered across the continent, as well as relatives and friends along the way.

When we arrived in Browning, we phoned Dave Knopfl.

"What a neat coincidence," Dave chuckled. "We just happen to be on our way out the door to work on a Pilgrimage at Heartbutte, Montana. Why don't you come along and join us?" That tour guide we adopted in Europe was apparently staying on for the second act.

We had never attended a Native Pilgrimage, although we had heard a great deal about them.

We replied in the typical modern way, "sorry, we would love to, but we've got places to go and things to do."

Dave persisted, "well, then just come out and have a cup of coffee. Heartbute is on the way to where you are going anyway."

"OK," we agreed, "but just for a quick one."

We wove and twisted through the hills and plains of Montana for what seemed like several hours. Finally, we reached the little dried up poverty-stricken village of Heartbutte. (Sure it's on our way, if we were headed for Timbuktu!)

Once Dave gained our attention, he turned on his gift of persuasion, "you might just as well stay for supper; you have to eat somewhere."

We agreed. There we met another group of unbelievably wonderful people.

Talk about Con-artists! Dave and Myra are champions. After dinner, the Pilgrimage began.

Dave moved in again. "It is really too late to start on the road tonight, you have to sleep somewhere, so why not here; then you can join us for breakfast and get a good start in the morning."

Next morning, sure enough, "you might as well stay and listen to the first talk so you can tell the folks back on the island what it's all about."

I thought I had some good stories to tell, but I couldn't hold a candle to the life stories shared that weekend. It seems the tragedies and hurts we receive in our lives add up and result in abnormal behavior. Then, it's our obligation, once we learn this, to bring about a change. There is no value in the damage, or in grieving over the damage we have received, but there is great value in how we overcome the damage. Most of the people who make it, discover it happened only when they began to follow the path described by Christ. The Natives have discovered that only by opening up and telling their story can they start to recover. The people listening to the stories of disaster and triumph, in turn, learn there are stories more hopeless than their own and discover hope for anybody who will put out the effort to try. This is the start of recovery. However, we are warned not to lay back and wallow in our sad story, or blame someone else for our behavior. Some therapists had recently caused a great deal of harm by convincing people to blame everything they do on someone in their past. We have to get out of it. Break the link ourselves and then turn our lives over to God. It is a giant step to struggle out of the quagmire of selfism and self pity; impossible for some.

The pilgrimage is designed to show us how to quit being a jerk.

There was no way, once we entered into that weekend, at Heartbute that we could leave. The beauty and loving care of those people was beyond compare. First tears and then the joy of friendship and laughter seemed to wash away the grief. At first, the group I was with remained very aloof toward this outsider. During the pilgrimage they had each of four groups develop a skit. Ours was a comedy depicting a drug and alcohol addicted family. Preparing and performing the skit was a riot. The distance between us soon disappeared and all were saddened when the time came to part.

Several years after that Pilgrimage, we attended a Native music festival in Washington state. An elderly man approached me and inquired, "aren't you Jim Proctor?" I confessed that I was.

He chuckled, "back in Browning, we are still laughing about you two, the couple who came only for a quick cup of coffee."

We laughed with him and thought how interesting the way things work out. By this time, we had brought the Pilgrimage home to Vancouver Island and several hundred island people had taken part in a Pilgrimage weekend. It is continuing here twice a year, in Campbell River and Kakawis on Meres Island. We now have teams of experienced "Pilgrims" who will go to any community to promote another Pilgrimage; often they are joined by leaders from

Washington and Montana. The Cursillo and Pilgrimage both seem to slow down in cycles for a few years, then become revived again by new enthusiastic leaders; or in some cases, a new movement will come along to take their place. The Pilgrimage and Cursillo were a great start.

In some areas, a different type of pilgrimage has formed. It is centered on The Mother of Christ bringing the people back to Christ. This follows the tradition of Jesus on the cross when he presented his mother to John and to us. *He said, "Woman this is your son," to the disciple he said, "this is your Mother." From that moment on, the disciple made a place for her in his home."* John 19:26 We, like John are asked to make a place for her in our homes. This is appreciated by Natives. Their admirable dedication to family and mothers fits well into the concept of the Father, his Son, and then our adopted heavenly Mother, the spouse of the Spirit of God, who loves her children beyond any earthly love. Through her, Christ was brought to us the first time and through her Christ will come again.

Of all the gifts we ever received, the Pilgrimage and Cursillo were among the most rewarding. We witnessed, over and over, the Natives' spiritual depth and subtle humor. Most of all, we discovered the joy they experienced once they turned their life over to their creator, compared to the pointless search of those in the world too proud yet to search in the right direction.

Besides the spiritual gains we received, the Natives provided us with some very entertaining moments.

Bill Williams was a delightful character from central B.C., who turned up on a Cursillo weekend. He shared many adventures and told of his assignment to deliver Holy Eucharist to the sick and old people on his reserve.

He would knock at their door and announce, "hey, it's Bill and Jesus come to see you."

"One problem with this job," he continued, "you can start to think you are too darn wonderful. When that happens to me, when the ego gets too big, I just go down to the bank of the old Fraser River. I stand there, extend my arms out over the river and say *"Part"*. It is no surprise when the old Fraser River doesn't part, but just keeps rolling along like it always has and then I'm okay again for a good long time."

Native Pilgrimage and Cursillo

Sam and Violet Johnson, of Gold River have been long-time supporters of the Pilgrimage. Some of their stories illustrate the Native sense of humor which makes them so enjoyable.

Gold River had it's first ever anniversary parade, celebrating Gold River's twenty-fifth anniversary. The community took well-deserved pride in this first grand exposition. The timing of the event followed close on the heals of the Mohawk Indian blockade in Oka, which nearly developed into a war between the Canadian Army and the Mohawks. The first-ever parade was doing nicely. Then suddenly, right in front of City Hall, the local Gold River Native band threw up a blockade bringing the parade to a shameful halt. Everyone was dismayed. Would this develop into the same disaster as Oka, or even worse? Were all the great preparations for naught? The Mayor and police were summoned and hurried to the scene. It looked like the end of the parade, and possibly a serious confrontation. Then, who should appear as spokesmen for the blockade, but Sam and Vi, holding a large banner which read "Happy 25th birthday, Gold River." Sam and Vi, wearing very sly grins and an obvious twinkle in their eye, joined in the parade. The prank was featured on national TV news.

I found evidence of Sam's grandchildren playing on the deck of our new smaller sailboat moored in Gold River.

I sternly reprimanded the children, "now, I don't want you kids to ever go on my sailboat unless I am there and tell you it's OK. Got that?"

The eldest shook his head and with deepest sincerity replied, "oh, we never, ever go on your boat...sometimes."

Whenever the church seems to be dying in a community, there is always one or two who preserve the faith until the grace arrives to revive it. That is the story of the Gold River reserve. Sam and Vi, hopefully, are the ones chosen to preserve the faith. We all pray for the grace that will bring the spiritual life back to their homes.

Jim Nicolaye always joined us on the early Alberta Cursillos and Pilgrimages. Jim, and his wife Pat, were two of the most admirable friends we ever met. Jim's faith and sense of humor were his outstanding features. When traveling by van, he would keep a joke alive and prolong it for a hundred miles...everyone in stitches, while he toyed with different versions of the same joke for an hour or more.

His favorite story was the saga of Chief Walking Eagle. It seems a certain Minister of Indian Affairs visited the Blackfoot reserve in Alberta and spent considerable time talking to the people. The people were so 'impressed', they gave him the honorary title of "Chief Walking Eagle." The minister returned to Ottawa, quite impressed with himself for making such a hit that the Natives would honor him with the gift of a personal title. He announced this over TV, to the newspaper media, and reported the honor to everyone who would listen. He was so well liked, they gifted him with the title, "Chief Walking Eagle."

Meanwhile, back on the reserve, the people were splitting their sides with laughter. To them, "Chief Walking Eagle" meant "he's so full of 'bleep' he cannot fly."

On one of our Cursillo trips, Jim introduced himself to the crowd. "My name is Jim Nicolaye. I am here as bodyguard for Jim Proctor, to prevent him from being scalped."

One of the old timers present matched his humor by replying, "we don't scalp white guys anymore. We found that if we just wait a while their hair will fall out on its own."

This remark brought the roof down and served to dissolve any Native-white-man tension.

Jim also used to delight in telling a true story on his wife, Pat, much to her chagrin. Pat was extremely shy. They had stopped at a restaurant en route to Port Alberni. Pat ordered chicken soup. Jim liked the description of their split pea soup on the menu so he ordered that.

After some reflection, Pat decided the pea soup sounded like a better choice so she shouted across the crowded restaurant to the waitress, "hold the chicken and make it pea."

The embarrassment was almost more than she could bear when everyone in the restaurant burst into laughter. Poor Pat relived the moment often as Jim regularly retold the story.

Jim's kidneys had been damaged by drinking in his early days, leaving his health in a condition continually on the edge. For three years, he was hooked up to dialysis waiting for a kidney transplant.

After Jim finally received the transplant, his medical condition fluctuated for many months. We had not seen him for three months and decided to visit him at the Vancouver General Hospital, especially since the reports on his health were not encouraging. He was shaking uncomfortably when we arrived, and Pat was very concerned. He displayed a genuine delight on seeing us. Wouldn't you know it. He started joking about the hospital and his condition. Pat asked for a priest to anoint him, but for some reason the priest was unable to attend. We remembered some holy oil in the car that Father Mel had blessed for a Pilgrimage in Penticton. Carole and I returned to Jim's bed. Carole anointed his forehead and I his hands, hoping that would help until a priest could be found. He stopped shaking then and a peace seemed to come. We returned to the island. At seven that evening, we received a call that Jim had passed away shortly following our departure. The passing of Jim was one of the greatest losses we have ever felt. "Why him?" His influence was so powerful on everyone he met. Everyone who knew Jim loved and revered him as an ideal to follow. His legacy remains as a model for all his relatives and especially the kids who knew him.

Maybe Jim would be like Saint Theresa who promised to shower the earth with heavenly bouquets after she arrived in paradise.

Jim, Alfred Vincent and I, in the past, had taken Holy Communion to Kyuquot, Jim's home village. It was difficult for Father Salmon to be there as often as he would like. Kyuquot is near the northwest extremity of the island, and only accessible by boat or plane. I also traveled there for veterinary clinics from time to time. My relations with the people were normally quite good, but recently some of the people seemed to hold some resentment. I wasn't sure why. There was some evidence of some overzealous religious leaders working Catholics over to gain converts to their own church. Sometimes, religion is used like politics. A zealous person will run down another religion, the way politicians do, to gain converts to their belief. There are hundreds of books in circulation, written for this purpose against the Catholic Church. There is a great deal of room on the Father's lap. Why do we keep trying to push each other off?

Jim's funeral, in Campbell River, attracted a huge crowd. After the funeral, he was moved to Fair Harbor by car and loaded onto a skiff for burial on an island near Kyuquot. Carole and I were the last to arrive at the harbor. I noticed that Alfred had failed to turn off his headlights. I hurried out through the crowd on the wharf to reach him at the far end. When I informed Alfred about the lights, he passed me his keys and asked if I would turn off his lights. On the way back through the crowd, I came across a little two year old boy poking at something over the edge of the pier. All of a sudden, he lost his balance and plunged headfirst deep into the dark and icy winter water. All we could see were the bottoms of his little white runners descending to the bottom, rapidly going out of sight in the cloudy water. Everyone was stunned...unable to move. Sailors become accustomed to people going overboard. I desperately grabbed at his foot under water but too late; it was well out of reach! The only hope was to follow, suit and all. Boy was that water refreshing! Grasping his foot just before he went out of sight, I was able to bring him to the surface and raise him up to no shortage of outstretched hands on the wharf. He came out sputtering and spewing, as did I. Our friends, Bonnie, her husband Lyle (who is also our God Child) and Alfred saw me come out of the sea, shivering and dripping wet, but didn't know the reason.

They took the opportunity to make fun at my expense. "There goes Jim, goofing off again. What's he up to this time? Let's call him Jim the Baptist."

That's all the sympathy I ever received from that quarter.

I wondered, did Jim Nicolaye and a couple of his angel friends arrange that perfect timing for me to be in that exact spot at that time. Was it his final act as peacemaker...a role Jim played so well in life? The boy would certainly have drowned had I passed by either seconds earlier or seconds later. After the dip, the negative attitude by those few disappeared. I received several hugs from some who were cold toward me before, and the elders made a large honorary fuss over me at the funeral banquet.

The older brother of the drowning boy took my hand and announced emphatically, "boy, you sure did save my brother, didn't you?"

Those loving gestures made the frigid plunge well worth the effort.

CHAPTER 23

Medjugorje Two More Times

During our first journey to Medjugorje, we fully expected to commence bankruptcy proceedings upon our return. We prayed for guidance and also forgiveness, because greed was the cause of our gigantic debt. As things worked out, we avoided bankruptcy. All real estate holdings were surrendered to the creditors, and they agreed to accept the income of three years to work off a good share of the remaining debt. In spite of the depression, the hospital continued to grow to the extent that soon we were able to repurchase the house and office. The great wealth was gone, never to return. We decided, furthermore, that flipping real estate was not any kind of spiritual calling. I couldn't recall any saints who had been inspired in that direction. The economic climate improved rapidly and a fantastic opportunity arose, once again, to create a bonanza in the real estate game. Somehow, after the experience of Medjugorje, wealth and the crusade for the good life had lost its appeal. The temptation still glitters when I see another sweet, sure-fire deal pass by. Some of our friends had difficulty understanding that losing everything could be anything but bad. "Are you crazy or what?" I found it best not to bring the subject up in many of my former circles.

When I enrolled in history of the Far East at university, we studied the thinking of people belonging to the great dynasties such as the followers of Genghis and Kubla Kahn. They sincerely believed stealing, lying, and cheating were great virtues and arts for which to strive. The only sin was being clumsy enough to get caught. I compared this to our modern philosophy. Like most, I had been indoctrinated with North American philosophy that ego stroking, wealth and success were the cardinal virtues.

Now, when I am confronted with a decision, I ask myself, "how would Mother Teresa or St. Francis handle that situation?"

I will never approach their level, but their attitude provides a far better goal for which I should aim.

Business continued to improve. Dr. Burgoyne returned and joined the business as a partner in the veterinary hospital. Now the time was ripe to revisit Medjugorje for another shot in the arm. The memory of the astounding peace and joy of that little hamlet was difficult to resist. It lay smack in the middle of a pagan Communist country, a contradiction to the thinking of that government and the entire world, especially at home.

Old 1917 newspaper reports and books on Fatima told of great throngs of people who witnessed the miracle of the sun, while a woman clothed with the sun appeared to three shepherd children. Seventy thousand terrified people watched as the sun left its orbit and careened toward the earth with violently swirling cartwheels. Luke 21:25 states *In those days there will be signs in the sun, the moon, and the stars.* This was a great sign to authenticate the message of the apparitions. The people fell to the muddy, rain soaked ground, certain this was the end of the world. However, the sun returned to its normal orbit and all were bewildered to find their clothes completely dry. Revelations 12:1 describes those days to come, *A great sign appeared in the heavens, a woman clothed with the sun, with the moon under her feet and on her head a crown of twelve stars.* The children reported that the clothing of the woman who appeared shown brighter than the sun, but did not hurt their eyes.

Now, strange reports were coming out of Medjugorje, like Fatima, the same woman, clothed with the sun, was appearing, accompanied with great signs and wonders in the sun and the moon. There was a difference this time. All the experiences in Medjugorje were pleasant and peaceful. The woman, this time, appeared with *a crown of stars on her head.*

The woman told the children on August 25, 1991, *"with your help, everything I wanted to realize through the secrets which began in Fatima, will be fulfilled. I call you, dear children, to grasp the importance of my coming and the seriousness of the situation."*

All those who saw her were astounded at her heavenly beauty.

One of the youngest of the children asked her, as only an innocent child would do, "How come you are so beautiful?"

She answered, *"if you loved God as much as I do, you would be just as beautiful."*

Before leaving for Europe this time, we watched a Sally Jesse Raphael show on TV. Her three guests had recently returned from Medjugorje. They were Wayne Weibel, a Lutheran and author of the book, *Medjugorje, The Message*; Mary Lou McCall, a non-practicing Catholic; and Jim Bailey, a reporter who belonged to the Baptist church. The three of them arrived in Medjugorje as skeptics. They simply wanted to make a TV story and increase their ratings. They returned amazed and converted. The experience had dramatically changed the lives of all three. Unable to photograph the sun, they showed photographic reproductions of some of the celestial events, as well as the faces and shocked expressions of the onlookers during the miracle of the sun. They, too, were most impressed with the great sense of peace in Medjugorje.

Once again, we boarded a plane bound for the European continent, free this time from the black cloud of financial disaster hanging over our heads. Unlike the overcrowded airplane on the last trip, we encountered a most fortunate ticket mix-up. We were mistakenly booked into the first class upper room on a Boeing 747 with all kinds of special service, champagne and fancy delicacies offered at no extra cost. This is mortification?

That was June, 1987. Millions of people were descending on Medjugorje, especially since June 24 was the anniversary of the first apparition. There were probably fifty thousand people, daily, in the village where only a few hundred people normally reside. Pilgrims were left to wonder how local residents could stay peaceful and friendly with the vast crowds pouring over their land by the millions.

On the second European journey, Medjugorje was our sole destination. Along the way, we visited a former Campbell River friend, Joyce Pogacic in Zagreb, Yugoslavia. We departed from that city by plane for Sarajevo, by bus to Mostar, and finally by taxi to Chitluk, three miles from our destination. We arrived in Chitluk at two in the morning. With fifty thousand pilgrims visiting, where do you find a place to stay in a tiny town in the middle of the night? As usual, and as many have found, these things were provided. Just by chance, the first hotel we approached had the only room available in the area.

I woke early in the morning, my mind pondering over the wonders and strange celestial events reported by returning pilgrims. I wouldn't mind seeing a real miracle myself. I thought of the Gospel verse, "In those days, there will be signs in the sun and in the moon." Medjugorje was worldwide news by that time. I remembered the reports of the sun changing so that it could be viewed directly without harming the viewer's eyes. Normally irreparable eye damage occurs from even a thirty second exposure to direct sunlight.

That morning, deep in thought, I watched the reflection of the sun in the bi-fold window of the hotel room. Even the reflection was too brilliant to view.

I thought, "maybe only really holy people see miracles."

Then, in the other half of the bifold window was the figure of something like the moon, sort of a white disk. After a moment, the disc-like object moved to cover the reflection of the sun in the other pane. Now, I was looking directly at the sun's reflection with no discomfort at all.

The only thought that came to me at the time was, "what a strange optical illusion my eyes are experiencing," not thinking that anything was seriously out of the ordinary. (One has to remember my faith is handicapped and I have to be knocked off my feet before anything registers.)

That morning another cab delivered us to Medjugorje and probably the most phenomenal experience of our lives. A warm feeling came over me when the towers of St. James church and the familiar peaceful countryside of Medjugorje came into view once again. We were coming home!

Things in the village had changed considerably from the primitive state we had witnessed two years before. Many families had built onto their homes to accommodate the ever increasing flow of pilgrims. Considerable new construction at every stage was visible. Dozens of Gypsy kiosks lined the streets leading to the church property unlike the few solitary fruit wagons and two small stores present on the previous visit. Restaurants and stores were under construction everywhere. Some consider this commercialization a contradiction to the authenticity. We were reminded that God isn't into removing free will or striking down every worldly endeavor. There was, however, the case of the only pornography store in the village that was struck and destroyed by lightning at the start of the apparitions. No one found the courage to rebuild it.

Now, we were confronted with the problem of a place to live for the next ten days, unlike the thousands who arrived under the guidance of organized pilgrimages where billeting was prearranged. In a town built for a few hundred, where do you host fifty thousand people? We asked our cab driver if he knew of a place to stay. He suggested a friend, another taxi driver by the name of Marco, who might have room. They lived only two miles from the center. The driver introduced us to Marco, his charming wife, Svetlena, and young daughter, Yellena. They seemed overjoyed to have us, but caused us pangs of guilt when they moved from their relatively comfortable bedroom into a cramped spare storeroom so we could use their bed. They fed us the usual simple, but delicious, Croatian meals, and Marco always had a cold drink waiting each evening when we returned.

Once again, neither family could speak the other's language. We had great fun using the translation book and sign language to carry on conversations. This helped to improve our Croatian vocabulary. The process produced some good laughs, especially when we tried to explain the occupations and schooling of our six children.

Student and doctor were both simple to find in the translation booklet to describe our son, Jim junior. Student nurse easily described our daughter Marggie. Carita had recently graduated from travel agent school. That was no problem. Our middle boy, Bob's profession, plant pathology, presented a more difficult problem to translate. We tried "vegetable doctor," but that only produced amused frowns from our hosts. This dilemma was finally solved when we came up with "plant scientist." Mark, our youngest, was the most difficult to describe. He was drifting from job to no job, unsure of a goal in life. We wrestled with this translation for a long while. Finally, Marco grasped the idea! Laughing, he threw both arms into the air and loudly proclaimed, "I understand, I understand; *Taxi Driver!*" We all had a good laugh over his good-natured, self-deprecating conclusion.

Marco drove us to many of our destinations. We had to force him to accept any pay, even though his borderline-poverty was obvious.

Many pilgrims were reporting the sight of an unusual white object appearing near the sun. They described its appearance as somewhat like the moon. This object would then be seen to cover the sun. When this took place, they were able to view the sun directly with no ill effects. We were warned several times, "don't try this at home; you could lose your eyesight." Of course, this was no big deal for Carole as she had nothing to lose.

We headed for Mass that afternoon and I noticed several people staring at the sun to the west of the church. I looked, and there again was that same disc-like display I had observed in the hotel window. Once again, it moved over the sun. I felt no more discomfort than looking at the moon. The locals explained this to be a sign of the Eucharist; that the Eucharist was here to protect us. Whatever the meaning, we were fascinated. We entered the church and knelt down. When I closed my eyes, I could still see the sun as it appeared outside. Only now it broke in two from top to bottom, the same as the priest breaks the large host after the consecration. Several times it separated and then resumed it's original whole appearance again.

Beggars were attracted to the village as they are to many shrines, probably capitalizing on the charitable mood of pilgrims. We were asked not to offer them money; this would encourage their numbers to increase. Officials explained that the government took good care of the handicapped and they were better off than the average citizen. The truth of that was not possible to learn. There was one beggar I could not resist. She was a lovely young mother with a small child in her arms, all dressed in white. She met us on the trail as we descended Mt. Krizevac. What a perfect Madonna and child the two of them made. Carole agreed we better give them a gift just in case, by a slim chance, they might be who they resembled!

Everyone who goes to Medjugorje tries to gain entrance to the apparition room during an apparition.. Although not necessarily true, it was human nature to assume chances for a healing would be improved if we could be near the apparition. Many cures have been reported in Medjugorje, far removed from the apparition site. Walls and space mean nothing to a heavenly messenger. Why not ask Mary to intercede with God to restore Carole's vision? It would certainly be appreciated by our family and friends; although everyone who knows Carole considers her blindness a gift.

The location of Mary's apparition moved several times since the beginning. The first apparitions took place on the hillside above the village. Religious gatherings outside of a church were outlawed by the government. The military authorities soon put an end to that location. The apparition site then moved to the sacristy of the church, until the local bishop intervened. In obedience to the bishop, the children moved to the rectory, where the apparitions were taking place during our second visit. It didn't seem right the way the Mother of Jesus was being kicked around, although her son received the same treatment two thousand years before.

A lady suggested we arrive at the gate leading to the rectory stairs two or three hours before the expected apparition. This would allow a chance to talk to the young man who regulated the gate. Possibly, he might allow a blind person access. (We milk that white cane for all it's worth.) Because of the large crowds, access these days had been reserved for the press and some of the priests. The apparition room was small and could only accommodate a dozen people. At least a thousand had the same request as ours. Needless to say, we remained outside. We were completely unprepared for the unsettling scenario we were about to experience.

As the hour of five approached, the crowd around the rectory began to swell. People from different ethnic backgrounds were invited to stand on the steps and lead the crowd in songs or the rosary in their particular tongue. As always, peace and kindness prevailed in spite of the massive gatherings. The common buzz-word in Medjugorje is "Peace," a most appropriate motto for the place, especially since the Madonna of Medjugorje calls herself "The Queen of Peace". I was fascinated listening to people's experiences while we waited. One lady told of her priest delivering a small rock from the apparition site to the home of one of his parishioners dying of cancer, too sick to withstand the arduous journey to Yugoslavia. The day after she received the rock, her symptoms began to disappear and she was now completely recovered.

Wherever the Blessed Mother appears, we are told her adversary, the devil will move in and try to destroy her work, the same as his attempt in Lourdes. Gen 3:15 *I will make you enemies of each other: you and the woman, your offspring and her offspring.* Rev.12:13, *As soon as the devil found himself thrown down to the earth, he sprang in pursuit of the woman, the mother of the male child, but she was given a huge pair of eagle's wings to fly away from the serpent into the desert.* In the messages to Father Gobbi, the Mother of Jesus describes that desert as the hearts of her earthly children who are preserving devotion to her for the sake of her Son. The children dislike talking about the devil and chose not to divulge the details, but have spoken of times he showed up to disturb their prayer meetings.

When I was a youngster in the 6th grade, I attended Sacred Heart Grade School in Spokane. My favorite nun, Sr. Mary Francis Eleanor, reassured us, "if ever confronted by evil, you should make the sign of the cross on yourself. Evil cannot withstand the cross of Christ."

She explained the power of that ancient sign and prayer, a truth almost forgotten by many today.

During my life, I have experienced only two Technicolor dreams, revealing messages. Analysts say that men rarely have Technicolor dreams. One concerned the power of the Eucharist, the other the power of evil. I am unable to forget either dream. In the evil dream, a beautiful blond girl was tempting me to go along with her. I accepted the invitation. The instant I touched her, her face changed to the most hideous gray features I have ever seen or imagined! Nothing was said in the dream, but the message came loud and clear, "Gotcha." This dream left me with a sickening feeling that returns whenever I am reminded.

Meanwhile, back in Medjugorje, we were all feeling pretty excited that the woman in Genesis 3:15 and the Book of Revelations 12 was soon to appear in the room above. She would, no doubt, provide another profound biblical message for us and the world.

All of a sudden, a terrible lady showed up directly behind me, cursing and screaming in a language I didn't understand. She yelled, pushed, jumped up and down, completely disrupting the former peace everyone had been enjoying. This is most unusual for Medjugorje. She pushed in front of me and it looked as if her bizarre antics were going to crush Carole against the stone stairway! I thrust my elbow and upper body in her path to protect Carole. Her fingernails were exceptionally long! With these, she clawed at the sweater-covered arm of the young man managing the gate! Then she retreated to a spot directly behind me! Those around her shouted, "Peace!" "Peace!" All to no avail. Then she started screaming louder and leaping high into the air.

A frightened woman behind me pleaded, "somebody do something about this woman! She's an animal!"

I don't remember at what point, but it suddenly dawned on me. "This was the same wretched face as the girl in that awful dream I had experienced, years before!"

Carole remembered what the nun had explained to me regarding the power of the sign of the cross when confronted with evil.

Emphatically, she advised, "make the sign of the cross on her forehead!"

One look at that hideous mug and I knew I wasn't going to touch her with a ten foot pole!

Carole, impatient with me and very brave, but blind, waded right up to the woman and made a bold sign of the cross on herself, in front of the woman's face. Instantly, the ferocious woman stopped. Dead silence; not another peep was heard.

Wondering what was going to happen next, I turned to look. The woman had disappeared from sight; not an easy task in such a tightly packed crowd. No one said anything more. We all just stood there stunned and amazed.

Inclusive language advocates will, no doubt, be pleased to learn that maybe the devil can be a she.

Most people have loving and happy experiences in Medjugorje. Why this for me? Am I being told again? Is this what happens to men who succumb to temptations of lust? I certainly would hate to spend eternity with that wench. Is this whole thing a sign of the dangers of temptations that confront me? If a simple prayer like the sign of the cross has such power over evil, how much more power is in the Mass, or an entire rosary?

I have been close to temptations that could have turned out that way. We have all experienced that Satan can use the weakness of even good people or innocent damaged people with problems to lead us down his path and destroy the peace. Now, whenever I have fears of evil or temptations, I make the sign of the cross on myself, several times if necessary, and always I'm left in peace. When in public, I make the sign mentally on myself. I have discovered this to be equally effective for conquering nagging doubts of my faith. Obviously, doubts originate from the same source.

The next day turned out considerably more inspiring. Attending Mass is an unforgettable experience in Medjugorje. The enthusiasm of everyone is exhilarating. We only wished that the real presence of Jesus in the Eucharist could be appreciated back home to the degree it is in Medjugorje. The priests especially become endowed with vibrant enthusiasm.

When apparition time arrived the next day, our eagerness to wait near the entrance of the rectory had waned. We chose an area in the shade of the trees, fifty feet from the rectory. The heat of the sun was intense. A small cloud passed over the sun and suddenly the glaring brilliance disappeared. We all found ourselves staring into the sun once again. I thought to myself, "is this maybe what happens, a cloud film stays over the sun? No, the cloud was now gone."

A lady standing nearby handed me her little Instamatic camera and exclaimed, "look at the sun through this!"

I looked, and there was the sun but with that white disc clearly lying beside it when viewed through the camera. We looked at each other and just shook our heads. We agreed, "this certainly doesn't happen at home!"

As Mass time approached, we headed for the church, some three hundred feet beyond. Many people, who weren't in the shade to avoid the heat, were staring at the sun.

I said to Carole, "lets go inside. The children remind us the miracle there is even greater."

The visionaries confessed that the Eucharist was more important to them than the apparitions. Just as we approached the front steps, we noticed a group of people in front of the doors watching the sun to the west, through an opening in the trees. A young blond lady in the group screamed, jumped backwards several steps, then stood there pressing her hands to her cheeks in awe! Then she started giggling with joyful glee!

We rushed forward to see what had provoked such an emotion. To my utter astonishment, giant, brilliant, golden plumes were billowing out of the sun in every direction, covering the entire western sky! Their brilliance turned the trees and everything in sight to gold! I have never experienced such an extraordinary sight. I fairly dragged Carole back to the edge of the trees where it was less crowded, so we could gain an unobstructed view. By this time, the scene had changed. All around the sun was a great and beautiful fuchsia colored ring that was undulating in and out like a giant amoebae. Wow! What an extraordinary sight to behold!

Carole's last tiny perception of light was rapidly disappearing in those days. I pointed her head in that direction and she could just barely make out the beautiful fuchsia color of the halo-like ring. This was probably the last thing she was ever able to see. A man watching behind me was completely overcome. He just kept gasping over and over, "Jesus, Jesus, Jesus, Jesus!"

I have sometimes been accused of being a sensationalist, like sailing across the seas when normal people are satisfied with a good game of golf. This accusation is also made of my spiritual search. However, my idea of the sensational is "zip" compared to the marvelous extravaganzas that God can produce...either in the miraculous marvels he performs, or in his fantastic creation around me. (We had better get used to the supernatural.)

It's not right, I know, but whenever I have trouble with my poverty stricken faith in the power of God, I think back to that scene. I long to be like those with great faith who don't need this sort of proof. *"Blessed are they who have not seen and yet they believe."* I guess God knows guys like me need all the help they can get.

When I shared with a priest about the sun phenomena, I received the usual blank stare you get when you relate a supernatural experience to the average priest. I appreciate the caution displayed by priests, however, we would be in rough shape if they believed everything they hear. They must receive some pretty bizarre tales. Many persons reading this probably feel I am in serious need of therapy.

I liked Wayne Weible's suggestion at a luncheon we held for him and the priests in Vancouver.

"Don't try to impress your priests with rosaries that have turned to gold or other wonders, just wear them out hearing your confessions. That will impress them far more."

I remembered the advice from the priests in Rome who recommended that great graces were received from going to confession in Medjugorje. I searched out the shortest confession line. (I was reminded of our Native friend, Bill Blaney, who used to say, "they should have express confessional lines for people with three sins or less.") I located a likely-looking priest sitting on a chair beside the church. He looked a little odd with a handkerchief stretched over his bald head to protect it from the hot sun.

I was having a conscience problem over a real estate deal. The salesman had offered to give a low appraisal on a property I was losing, so that I could make a better deal. I didn't say no to the man or ask him to give a fair appraisal. The thought dawned on me afterward, "if I cooperate in this, it would result in something like stealing on my part." I related my concern to the priest.

"The Holy Spirit must have sent you to me," he smiled. "I used to be a real estate broker before becoming a priest."

We had a good laugh and I asked, "how did you get to be a priest?"

He jokingly quipped, "oh, sales were lousy so I went to the seminary."

Then, with gentle sincerity, he explained how to solve the problem without hurting anyone.

The first visit to Medjugorje was too short, lasting only five days. That was not quite long enough to remove the world from my brain. The second and third visits lasted ten days and provided a much better duration for a pilgrimage.

As one priest pointed out, "you need enough time to chase the noisy monkeys out of your tree."

We have made three trips to Medjugorje. That second voyage was, by far, the most astounding, both for spiritual growth and interesting adventure.

We returned to Zagreb via Sarajevo on our way home to visit with Joyce. The Olympic games were hosted in Sarajevo a few years before. It was interesting to see many storefronts full of modern conveniences, but no one buying. Joyce explained that this was the communist government's propaganda effort. This showed tourists that Yugoslavia shared all the modern conveniences that the developed countries possess. Few people in Yugoslavia could afford to buy anything but food. It seemed sad that TV sets and electronic gadgets were the symbols of greatness for any country.

Since our time in Sarajevo, and since the recent war in Yugoslavia, the once beautiful historic city has become a shambles. This destruction is a more accurate symbol of atheism. While waiting for our plane to Zagreb, we prayed the rosary on the bank of a beautiful river flowing through the city

In Zagreb, we rejoined Joyce who introduced us to her life's work of teaching values to young people and caring for the handicapped. At that time, she was teaching a group of young girls the art of Jewish folk dance. Her life seemed always on the edge. Joyce is a U.S. citizen who lived and married in Canada. Unusual circumstances surrounded the death of her husband who came from Yugoslavia. She moved to Zagreb so her sixteen year old son could appreciate his heritage. She was being watched a good share of the time. Joyce became so involved with helping people and the Third Order of St. Francis, that Zagreb became their home. Her efforts are solely supported by donations from friends in the U.S. and Canada.

While waiting for Joyce outside the cathedral, we sat on a stone wall decorating the city street to pray another rosary.

She approached our little retreat with a look of concern. "you should not be praying in public. You could be arrested and jailed."

I wondered to myself, the way persecution of the church and her teachings are progressing so rapidly at home, could this soon be the same in the streets of North America?

Medjugorje inspires everyone who visits and encourages them to live a more devout life. There is a great sense of urgency about all the messages. We have very little time left to change our lives. The Madonna explained that very soon, faith will no longer be a gift or virtue because everyone in the world will be assured that God, heaven and hell exist. For this and other urgent reasons, it is very important to accept faith now, before it is too late. The world soon will be subject to unparalleled consequences if we do not change. This sense of urgency, which is not shared by many back home, creates a disturbance when people return. Why should anyone turn away from the good life? After all, we have been taught that a good income, retirement benefits, quality of life, and "toys" are most important of all.

Aren't they?

The quote from Malcolm Muggeridge kept ringing in my ears, "all that is not about eternity, is eternally worthless."

We returned to Medjugorje for a third time in April, 1990, shortly before the war erupted there. We helped organize a large pilgrimage of a hundred people through Marian, with Split Travel in Edmonton, who is, herself, a native Croatian. This organized trip had many advantages, such as visits with the visionaries and a trip to see Fr. Jozo. Many rosaries turned gold along the way. Many of our friends from Vancouver Island joined us this time. The trip was made especially enjoyable by having my sister, Margaret Duran from California, along. I wish someday we could share that little glimpse of heaven with all our six children.

An interesting side trip took us to Mostar and a visit to a Muslim Temple. During the tour through the temple, a fellow pilgrim beat me to a question I was going to ask. He asked the Muslim priest if it was true that the Muslim religion held great respect for the Mother of Jesus.

The priest replied. "This is true. There is only one female mentioned in the whole Book of the Koran and that one woman is the Mother of Jesus."

We speculated that maybe she would be the cause of their eventual conversion once they discover who her son really is. Many Muslims have already been converted to Christianity through Medjugorje.

On the return flight, a member of our group from Montreal approached me and asked, "I understand that you have been to Medjugorje several times. Could you give me some advice?"

"Sure," I said, "but I'm no expert."

"Have you ever heard of a non-religious object turning gold?" he continued.

"No," was my honest reply.

He pulled up his shirt sleeve. "I don't want to make a big deal of this, but look at my watch. It is a Timex, a gift from my son sixteen years ago. It used to be silver colored and well worn. The lens used to be scratched and worn from age. Look at it now."

The watch looked like one fresh off a jeweler's shelf. It was gleaming gold. The lens was clear as new.

"What does this mean?" he asked.

"I honestly have no idea what it means," I replied, "but I sure would like to keep in touch. It has to mean something pretty profound!"

Back in Canada, we landed in Toronto. The signs of peace and joy ended abruptly as we entered the hotel. Out on the street, a policeman and another man were in mortal combat with a barrage of loud cursing, swearing, and slugging. That night, the hotel fire alarm went off at three AM and several hundred people filed into the street in there nightgowns. We learned later that a distraught teenager, who was angry at his girl friend, had set off the alarm. It was clear. We had come down off the mountain. As the Queen of Peace implied, we have a huge job ahead of us.

We organized a fourth large pilgrimage which we were unable to join. I became quite concerned because the war broke out during that trip, but all returned safely.

It is heartbreaking to see on TV news, the beautiful places in Yugoslavia where we have been, now transformed into tragic piles of rubble and death. My friend, John, the travel agent Marian, and I had a memorable visit

Mostar Bridge, now destroyed in the war.

together in a little patio restaurant over-looking their beautiful azure colored river in Mostar. A recent issue of Time magazine showed this restaurant as a bombed out, desolate battle field. The ancient, spectacular bridge was shown, covered with old rubber tires in an effort to preserve it. Since then, it has been completely demolished. Most towns in Bosnia and especially the churches, have been destroyed, while Medjugorje, where people are living the messages left by the Queen of Peace, remains untouched.

Several years after the last pilgrimage, I had an interesting encounter with some doctors. I visited one of the better eye specialists to have my glasses checked. The doctor, I knew, was a Catholic skeptical of Medjugorje. When he examined my eyes, he stated that I had the start of macular degeneration. This is the most common cause of vision loss in people over fifty. Macular degeneration can also result from direct sunlight or welding light damaging the retina. He asked if I had been looking at the sun. Since there was only room for one blind person in this family, I became concerned. For fear his view of Medjugorje might cloud his diagnosis, I consulted another specialist and explained the phenomena of Medjugorje to him. This doctor confirmed the first diagnosis, but thought the damage was very slight and not likely caused by sunlight. He wished his sight was as good as mine. To be certain though he referred me to a retina specialist. This doctor concurred that there was no serious problem as yet. When I explained to her that I had peered into the sun for over a half hour while in Medjugorje, she became unglued!

She was a rapid-talking individual and the speed was intensified in her response. She evidently had gotten word of the sun thing in Medjugorje from one of the previous doctors. "No! you did not look into the sun! No you didn't! No! No! You probably looked at the moon. Yes, that's it, you looked at the moon. You could do that all right, but you didn't look into the sun like that, not without being blinded! No! You couldn't have done that! No you didn't!"

"Okay, okay," I thought. The poor dear, for fear she might have a breakdown, I changed the subject. Obviously, the things of Medjugorje are not good subjects to bring up around the average doctor.

I still am concerned that someone reading this or one of the hundreds of other similar reports might be tempted to look at the sun. Please don't. It will cause permanent blindness under most ordinary circumstances.

CHAPTER 24

Cenacles and Marian Conferences

I once knew an old time mule skinner who maintained that some mules needed a blow over the head with a two-by-four in order to gain their attention. I resemble those mules. Why, really, am I here? I was good at receiving gifts, but it never dawned that anything might be expected of me.

The words of the Cardinal in Rome to Carole struck a nerve. "What should we do in view of all those gifts we were given?"

"You should go home and put them to use."

Some turn to scripture, when they need an answer. *James 2:14, What good is it my brothers, if someone says he has faith but does not have works? Can that faith save him? If a brother or sister has nothing to wear and has no food for the day, and one of you says to them, "go in peace, keep warm, and eat well," but you do not give them the necessities of the body, what good is it? So also faith of itself, if it does not have works, is dead. For just as a body without a spirit is dead, so also faith without works is dead.*

The signs given me either mean something or are just coincidence. I'm convinced they are too frequent and pointed to be coincidence. They must have a serious meaning. Now, whenever I pray the part of the Our Father, "Thy Kingdom come, Thy will be done on earth as it is in heaven," I ask, "show me what I can do to help that prayer be answered."

Medjugorje removed all doubts of the reality of God's message and his love for me. It affects nearly everyone the same who travels there with an open mind. The messages from the Mother of Jesus are true and it is necessary and urgent that I take them to heart. Sometimes, she is in tears when she appears, pleading with us to wake up and listen. The messages are imperative, and they are for everyone, not just Catholics. She warns that the time is very short. When the apparitions come to an end, there will be very little time to convert. There will be a warning, then a great miracle, so that all may believe, then a chastisement or great tribulation. She tells us the great tribulation predicted in the Book of Revelations and the great apostasy predicted by St. Paul have already begun.

I have searched the authors who study the messages. Many private revelations speak of the Second Pentecost. They describe the warning as, the Holy Spirit coming to everyone in the world, the way He first came to the apostles. Everyone will see clearly the state of their soul as heaven sees a soul. This will be so powerful that some may not live through the experience. Those, who have changed their life, will be happy. Shortly after this will come the great miracle. Finally, the chastisement, the severity of which depends on how well and how many are converted. The chastisement can be mitigated by our response, but not stopped, since it is already so late. The Gospa pleads, "don't wait for the signs to convert. Convert now, before it is too late!"

Mirjana from Medjugorje asks us to listen to the pressing invitation of our good Mother Mary. "after this time of grace will come the time of purification which will culminate with the third warning. Then...the visible sign for all. After this sign, the world will certainly know that God exists. But it will be too late to convert. The encounter with the heavenly reality will be sad for those who have not profited by the warnings and have not converted. But there will be great joy for those who have opened themselves up to God during this time of calm."

Mary pleads that unless we turn back, the world is headed for the greatest calamity since the flood in Noah's time or the destruction of Sodom and Gomorra. She is telling us that mankind has turned away from God worse than ever before in history, that in our pursuit of pleasure and gain, we have destroyed peace throughout the world. The messages tell us that prayer, especially the rosary, penance, fasting and conversion can stop wars and even prevent natural disasters. She asks that three hours a day in prayer and bible reading should eventually be the minimum since the time is so late, but at least start small. Jesus told us in the gospels to pray always. Even a dedicated atheist watching the news can see that the world is at the brink. Non-Catholics are invited to pray in all the ways they know.

The Gospa tells us, *"I am here to tell you God exists, that Satan also exists and is causing great havoc over the earth. He knows that his power is about to end and is, therefore, very aggressive trying to destroy families, the priesthood, and the church."*

This was predicted in Rev. 12:12, *For the devil has come down to you in great fury; for he knows he has but a short time. When the dragon saw that it had been thrown down to the earth, it pursued* **the woman who had given birth to the male child**. *"She could fly to her place in the desert, where, far from the serpent, she was taken care of for three and one-half years.* (Possibly the time of the antichrist. The desert is the hearts of those who listen to her.) *Then the dragon became angry with the woman and went off to wage war against the* **rest of her offspring**, *those who keep God's commandments and bear witness to Jesus."*

The following message is reprinted with permission from the book, *To The Priests Our Lady's Beloved Son's.*

> "The evil one, Satan, the ancient serpent, the great dragon, has always acted and works in all kinds of ways to take away the precious blessing of peace from you, from the Church and from humanity. It enters, then, into my function as a Mother to bring you all to a great communion of life with God, so that you may have the sweet experience of love and of peace.
>
> "Never, as in your days, has peace been so threatened, because the struggle of my adversary against God is becoming stronger and stronger, more insidious, continual and universal. You have thus entered into the time of the great trial.
>
> "The great trial has come for all of you, my poor children, so threatened by Satan and stricken by the evil spirits. The danger you are in is that of losing grace and the communion of life with God, which my Son, Jesus, obtained for you at the moment of redemption, when He delivered you from slavery to the evil one and set you free from sin.

"Now, sin is no longer considered an evil; indeed it is often exalted as a thing of value, and as something good. Under the perfidious influence of the mass media, the awareness of sin as an evil has been gradually lost. Thus, it is committed and justified more and more, and is no longer confessed.

"If you live in sin, you return again to slavery under Satan, subjected to his wicked power, and thus the gift of redemption which Jesus accomplished for you is made useless. Thus, peace disappears from your hearts, from your souls, and from your life.

"O my children, so threatened and so ill, accept my motherly urging to return to the Lord along the way of conversion and of repentance. Recognize sin as the greatest of evils, as the source of all individual and social evils. Never live in sin. If you should happen to commit it out of human weakness, or through the subtle temptations of the Evil One, have recourse quickly to confession. Let frequent confession be the remedy which you make use of against the spread of sin and evil."

In Fatima, and many other approved apparitions, Mary has promised her Immaculate Heart will triumph very soon. Then she promises a tremendous period of peace where times will be better than ever before, but first we must pass through the period of purification. She promises those who live her messages fervently will receive special protection during the tribulation.

In September, 1987, Our Lady told Father Gobbi, *"In this period of ten years there will come to its culmination that purification which, for a number of years now, you have been living through and, therefore, the sufferings will become greater for all. There will come to completion the time of the great tribulation, which has been foretold to you in Holy Scripture, before the second coming of Jesus. All of the secrets which I have revealed to some of my children will come to pass and all the events which have been foretold to you by me will take place.*

On December 5, 1994, The Blessed Mother announced, through Father Gobbi, *"I confirm to you that, by the great jubilee of the year two thousand, there will take place the triumph of my Immaculate Heart, of which I foretold you at Fatima, and this will come to pass with the return of Jesus in glory, to establish his Reign in the world. Thus, you will, at last, be able to see with your own eyes, the new heavens and the new earth.*

During a retreat, when I was sharing my dad's experience, a dear friend admonished me, "Jim, I think you take this supernatural stuff too seriously." My spontaneous response, without thinking, made sense to both of us, "we better get accustomed to the supernatural, Rita, because all of us are going to die one of these days and from then on, everything will be supernatural." She accepted that argument, and knows better than I now. Cancer took her life not long after we talked.

Galley Books is restricted solely to books accepted by the church or those which by special permission do not need an imprimatur. About ten percent are Marian books. The volume was growing daily. It was simple; just keep the shelves full and people helped themselves. The nurses at the animal hospital took care of the sales even though they didn't really understand what was going on. Most of the time I never knew who was purchasing the books.

One of the young animal health technicians found a book in the store called, *Teens and Sex*. Her brief investigation produced a troubled comment. "You should screen these books better; some are pretty naive." I've noticed, since her comment, reports that one in every 250 people in North America have become infected with HIV, and predict one in ten will be infected by the year 2000. Nineteen percent of North Americans have some form of VD, three times the world average. Half of pregnancies...end in abortion. I felt helpless to explain to the girl what thinking was *really* naive.

Whenever our friends discovered a new fantastic book loaded with answers, we became so enthused that we had to tell the world. Our enthusiasm was contagious and the books moved in great numbers. We never really made any money, because it seemed necessary to give away books to those who were curious, but afraid to invest. Somehow, we always had just enough to pay the bills and expand.

When Dr. Burgoyne joined the veterinary practice, space became a problem so the book store had to close, but not for long. We gifted most of the store to St. Patrick's parish, where it continues operating today. I retained some of my favorite books and distributed them from home. The interest in Marian devotion grew so rapidly that now we have expanded to five home Galley Book stores on Vancouver Island; Victoria, Nanaimo, Port Alberni, Comox and Gold River. It is a challenge to keep up with the orders and run a veterinary hospital at the same time.

Mystical phenomenon has been recorded in the history of most churches, and especially the Catholic Church, for it's entire two thousand years of existence. The Bible is full of apparitions of angels or people who once lived on earth and are now used as messengers; Moses, Elijah and Gabriel, to name a few. Now, more than ever before in history, Mary, the Mother of Jesus, is reported to be appearing as a messenger. In some areas such as Scotsdale, Arizona, Jesus himself is said to be giving messages. Marguerite informed us in Belgium that Mary spends more time on earth now than ever before. It has become obvious that almost everyone has a tremendous thirst for knowledge of the supernatural. This is also evidenced by the clamoring toward the dangerous cults like new-age, even within the churches, and psychic readers.

Catholic books on mystical life are outselling the philosophical works twenty to one. Some people have a problem with the supernatural, but as Rita and I concluded, "we better get used to it."

In the Second Vatican Council document, *Lumen Gentium*, it is stated, "the Holy Spirit distributes special gifts among the faithful of every rank. Such gifts of grace, whether they are of special enlightenment or whether they are spread more simply and generally, must be accepted with gratefulness and consolation, as they are specially suited to, and useful for, the needs of the Church. Judgments, as to their genuineness and their correct use, lies with those who lead the Church and those whose special task is not, indeed, to extinguish the spirit, but to examine everything and keep that which is good." (confer 1 Thess. 5: 19.21)

Official Church teaching on this states that publications about new apparitions, revelations, prophecies, miracles, etc., have been allowed to be distributed and read by the faithful without the express permission of the Church, providing that they contain nothing which contravenes faith and morals. This means no imprimatur is necessary under the above conditions.

Pope Urban V111 wrote "in cases which concern private revelations, it is better to believe than not to believe, for if you believe, and it is proven true, you will be happy that you have believed, because our Holy Mother asked it. If you believe, and it should be proven false, you will receive all blessings as if it had been true, because you believed it to be true."

To the chagrin of some, Galley Books stayed scrupulously faithful to the official guidelines of the church. Books like *Christ Among Us* and the books on Creation Spirituality by Matthew Fox were removed when they were found by the teaching authority of the Church to be contrary to Church teaching and scripture. These works only caused confusion in a world already overrun by confusion. If its all right to discredit one teaching of the church or scripture, why listen to any of them? Who decides for "cafeteria Catholics" which teachings to accept and which to reject? Literature is continually being scrutinized by the Church. Fictitious phenomena such as Bayside or The Little Pebble are soon uncovered by church investigators and discarded.

As I became more involved I discovered elements inside the church trying to destroy it from within. One philosophy was attempting to rid the church of, holy tradition, loyalty to the pope, orthodoxy, and devotion to the saints in order to propagate a philosophy of new age and modernism. Many on the island have been taken in by these erroneous new age teachings.

On the other hand there are now movements and periodicals being distributed, dedicated to a philosophy which causes the loss of faith at the radical conservative end of the scale. They are nearly as dangerous as modernism and liberalism, but more subtle. These militant periodicals and their movements start by defending the Church in the most heroic ways and appear commendable for this. However, they continue by insinuating that certain popes especially Pope Paul VI and now John Paul II are weak in certain areas and that Vatican 2 is somehow flawed and we should not accept parts of the teachings. Some tend to follow the schismatic Bishop Lefebvre. These over zealous groups in an effort to combat the evils of modernism, end up unwittingly holding hands behind their backs with the modernists who twist the teaching of the Church and Vatican 2 to support their own agenda and defy the teachings of the popes. Grave doubts about the faith and confusion are created while in their own mind they believe they are defending the faith against modernists. Both extremes are in grave danger of eventually loosing their faith.

Cardinal Ratzinger said in his book *The Ratzinger Report* that "Every error has a seed of truth, and the more seeds of truth it has the more dangerous it becomes."

It was interesting to watch how authentic, Church approved, Marian and Eucharistic devotion developed on Vancouver Island. Carole and I were probably the first on the island to visit Medjugorje. None of the messages there have been found to contrdict scripture or church teaching. In fact they reinforce both We have been invited to several parishes to give talks, share our life adventures and faith. It became obvious, by the interest shown that there is a great thirst for this information and many who were confused by modernists now desire to return to the teachings of the Gospel. We discovered that many had stopped listening to the Gospel message, but will listen to the same message when presented by the gentle loving Mother exhorting us to return to her Son.

Many were confused about the roll of Mary and we found it necessary to explain this to those who were unaware. Jesus is the Son of God. Mary is the Mother of Jesus. Since Jesus is true God and true man, then Mary is the Mother of God. Even though my earthly mother did not create my spirit or soul, she is still known as my mother. We are the mystical body of Christ. Mary by becoming the Mother of Christ became the mother of that mystical body, the Mother of all humanity. We are the family of God. A family without a mother is a disfunctional family. God took Mary for his spouse. No one devoted to her could ever come close to honoring her to the degree that the God Himself honored her? No one is to worship Mary, only honor her. Genesis 3:15 together with Rev. 12 and many readings in the Bible between these explain the roll of Mary by scripture.

Martin Luther, who is considered the father of Protestantism, wrote in his commentary on the Mother of God, "O Blessed Virgin

Cenacles and Marian Conferences

and Mother of God, how hast thou been able to be considered as nothing, and disdained as of little consequence, and yet God has, none the less, regarded thee with all his grace."

The Angel, Gabriel, said to Mary, "Hail full of grace."

Jesus said to Mary, at the foot of the cross, "this is your son," and to the apostle, John, he said, "this is your Mother." (John represented all mankind.)

In the messages from Jesus and His Mother in the books, *Marguerite* and *To The Priests Our Lady's Beloved Sons,* both urged those listening to start *Prayer Cenacles* to keep the faith alive. Thousands of Cenacles were springing up throughout the world. We discovered, that to keep the fires burning in any movement, a follow-up was necessary. This was true with the Cursillo and Pilgrimage, as well. We needed something to keep the Pilgrimage alive.

The message from The Marian Movement of Priests 419 reads, *"now that you are entering into the last decade of this century, during which the decisive events that will bring you to the triumph of my Immaculate Heart will be completed, I am asking you that cenacles among priests, cenacles among the faithful, and especially family cenacles be multiplied even more. I am asking, in particular, that there be formed everywhere children's cenacles, as a crusade of innocent prayer, in order to form a great barrier against the spread of evil and sin, and allow God and your heavenly Mother to bring about the victory of goodness and of love."*

The Natives in Washington initiated a cenacle prayer meeting for Pilgrimage follow-up. We copied their example and started a prayer cenacle along with the Natives in Campbell River at Bill and Susan's home. This was the first Marian Prayer Cenacle on Vancouver Island. (Maybe the Prince George Bishop was right when he predicted the Natives might be the instrument that God will use to bring the rest of us back to God.) Now, Vancouver Island hosts over twenty such cenacles, with many faithful followers.

In 1989, shortly after the cenacle started, we sold the veterinary hospital and moved fifty miles west to the little town of Gold River where we now live and practice between Gold River and the village of Tahsis, another forty miles west. This move allowed us to stay close to our kids and grandchildren in Campbell River and Comox.

We always asked and hoped that we were guided to where we should be. We presumed God didn't need us anymore and led us into the wilderness and spiritual retirement. Wrong! We continued to support the cenacle at Bill and Susan's home in Campbell River, which was producing wonders, bringing people together. A second cenacle developed in Gold River.

The greatest boost to cenacles on the island came when Fr. Francis Jerimiah, the translator for Fr. Gobbi, visited the city of Vancouver to organize a one-day cenacle. Many from the island attended, and as a result, some fifteen new cenacles evolved, all of which are still thriving. New cenacles are continually forming.

The word cenacle, comes from the gathering of the apostles with the Mother of Jesus at the cenacle in the upper room. They waited and prayed for the coming of the Holy Spirit.

Since the advent of Medjugorje, another exciting celebration developed world wide, almost overnight; the celebration, known as "The Marian Eucharistic Conference". From three to a dozen, or more, world renowned speakers are invited to a three-day celebration. These speakers are generally noted for their holiness, speaking ability, zeal, and loyalty to church teaching. The weekend develops around those modern day evangelists who, by the power of their presence, remind us of the early apostles. The conferences are billed as *Marian Conferences,* but invariably concentrate more on Christ and the Eucharist. All authentic Marian devotees recognize that Mary's calling is to bring Christ to people the way she brought Christ to the world two thousand years ago. In spite of critics, it is a simple matter of fact that she has been more effective in that roll than any other evangelist in history. Her appearance in Guadalupe, Mexico, alone produced twelve million converts to Christianity, away from a most atrocious paganism, the largest conversion in the history of the world. Medjugorje is causing countless numbers to change from their unhappy and pointless ways.

These conferences are powerful witnesses to faith. The Mass is concelebrated daily with the many priests present, and the talks are punctuated with moving spiritual devotions such as living rosaries, Benediction, Chaplet of Divine Mercy, healing services, or any other devotion chosen by the organizers under the guidance of a spiritual director and with approval of the local bishop.

Cenacles and Marian Conferences

In the summer of 1991, Carole and I attended our first Marian Conference in Eugene, Oregon. Here, we witnessed for the first time, three of the greatest of the modern day apostles, Wayne Weible, Fr. Ken Roberts, and Jan Connell. All three are authors of best-selling books. This was a most inspiring and exciting three days. A thousand people attended, all equally impressed as ourselves. We concluded that this was what Vancouver Island needed to help renew our faith. The big question was, "how do you make it happen?"

Soon, people from island cenacles were attending Marian conferences in Washington, Oregon and Arizona, featuring more dynamic witnesses. Each conference we attended increased our enthusiasm. We returned with inspiring conference videos to show our friends and keep the enthusiasm alive.

August of that same year, Port Alberni invited all cenacles on the island to come together for a cenacle reunion. At that cenacle, I presented the question, "what would you people think of having a Marian Conference of our own?"

The response was a resounding unanimous, "yea, lets go for it!"

Two months later, several of us attended Lacy, Washington's, first and very successful conference. There I met one of the most popular conference speakers, Father Stephen Barham. He is a convert from the Assembly of God and is noted, not only for his powerful oratory, but also for his holiness, dedication to the Church, and contagious sense of humor. Father Barham agreed that if we could put it together, he would be there.

I hope that in these dangerous and decisive times, all those Protestant and fundamentalist religions who splintered away so many hundreds of years ago, and are now breaking apart themselves, will bury the hatchet, come back home, and join forces against the real adversary. The Protestants that I know are great zealous people and full of life; unbelievable strides could be made if we ever got back together. Jesus said, "a house divided against itself cannot stand." The adversary knows that better than anyone, and loves the division. Another time Jesus prayed that all may be one, as he and the Father are one. Twenty-six thousand opposing denominations indicate that we have a long way to go toward unity.

Also In Lacy, I met Steve Ellis, a professional organizer from Richland, Washington. He traveled 300 miles regularly to help us organize and keep on track. I doubt if the task could have been accomplished without him.

He advised that we should let the Holy Spirit run the show. When that happens, anyone can pull off a conference. A committee of thirty-four of the most humble and generous people I have ever worked with, joined in. Away we went, running as fast as we could to keep up with the Holy Spirit. It was obviously out of our hands from the very beginning, and the results exceeded our wildest dreams. The Blessed Sacrament was exposed during all of our meetings in St. Michael's Ukrainian Church, and heaven was stormed with more prayer than we had ever offered before. This was the secret of success. Never in the history of Vancouver Island has there been such a large, powerful, inspirational and orthodox event. Up to a thousand people attended the three days, and hundreds of them witnessed to the change; it made in their lives. The conversions, as a result, are continuing today. Many people smelled a strong odor of roses at the conference, a common sign of Mary's presence, and asked if we had put perfume in the air conditioner. No we hadn't.

The Island Conference, entitled, "Vancouver Island Marian and Eucharistic Conference", was well on its way when we discovered it to be the first of it's kind in Canada. We were then able to encourage Vancouver city to start a conference as well as the Natives in Edmonton, Alberta. Honolulu Hawaii used our format and records to help organize their own. Many others are planned and now taking place across the nation because of the seed planted here.

In the final analysis we are invited to consecrate our life and our everything to Jesus through The Immaculate heart of Mary. The great battle has started. No one will remain alone. Either Satan will have hold or The Immaculate Heart of Mary. There are now two choices; either the soul will be protected by grace or snatched by evil. The consecration prayer is found in the back of the MMP book To The Priests My Beloved Sons, or The Consecration according to St. Louis de Montfort may be used. Be prepared for a grace filled and awesome experience. *For those who find me find life, and win favor from the Lord. Prov 8:34.*

CHAPTER 25

Whatever is not Dead is Alive

Before and after the Marian Conference, we needed inspiration to keep the fire burning. We arranged for Michael Brown to come to the island and tell his story. Michael is an investigative journalist who uncovered the "Love Canal Scandal," where a town was built over a toxic waste dump. Michael is author of the *Final Hour*, co-author with Josyp Terelya of *Witness,* the story of a man who spent seventeen years in a soviet prison camp, and his most recent books, and *Bridge to Heaven,* the story of the church-approved visions in Betania, Venezuela and *Trumpet of Gabriel.*

Next, I had the honor of introducing and guiding Tom Rutkoski on a speaking tour of the island. Tom is the author of *Apostles of The Last Days.* In 1989, he founded Gospa Missions, a non-profit foundation, to fulfill a promise to Christ to take pilgrims to Medjugorje in gratitude for his conversion. Tom's change of attitude is an intriguing story. When I introduced him, I told the people he should be paying me royalties from his book because he was telling my story.

Shortly after Tom's visit, we invited Steve Wood to make a tour of the island and I was honored to guide and introduce him. He is founder of Family Life Center in Florida. Steve was a well known Presbyterian minister and theologian. He, with Scott Hahn and an ever increasing number of Protestant ministers, has returned to the original faith. They formerly taught that the Pope was the antichrist and the Catholic Church was the "whore of Babylon." Now, after being surprised by the truth, they work full time defending the Catholic faith and the church from the thousands of myths that have been propagated against it. At the same time, they harbor no ill will against their former faith. Wayne Weibel was next and probably the most sought after speaker available. He was a Lutheran who shared the change in his life received from Medjugorje.

We talked to many who said they were taught to hate the Catholic Church when they were young. Many now are looking into the facts and are *Surprised By The Truth*. This is the title of a very well written new book by Patrick Madrid, which relates the stories of eleven people, mostly ministers, who were surprised by the truth and returned home to the original faith. Bishop Sheen once said there are only a handful of people who oppose the Catholic church for what it teaches. but there are thousands who oppose it for what they imagine it teaches.

Recently, I made the rounds of Vancouver and Vancouver Island with Ted Flynn, author of *Thunder of Justice*. This is a powerful book which catalogues and compares modern predictions, most already approved by the church, and ancient biblical prophecies. One reader commented, "all you have to do is watch the news on TV, then look up in *Thunder of Justice* to see on what page it has already been reported." Ted has been most helpful in the writing of this book.

Spending days traveling and eating meals with these powerful people is a tremendous gift, and this opportunity has had an positive effect on my faith. I asked again, "why am I so fortunate?"

In 1995, Father Gobbi, himself, came to the island to spread his love and devotion.

One cause shared by modern orthodox spokesmen is a deep respect for all stages of created life. All of them are actively defending the very young and the very old and otherwise helpless. At the same time, having compassion for innocent mothers and fathers who have been conned into destroying their children, not realizing until too late, what really has happened. And it is paramount to realize that anyone causing or having an abortion is totally forgivable as long as they repent. We probably should quit using the cliché "Over my dead body", because each time the prolife cause loses another court case, the reality of that cliché becomes more and more a possibility. The propaganda machine has so thoroughly and cleverly glazed the vision of the world, that even some

Whatever is not Dead is Alive

who are very intelligent accept the killing of the unborn and the elderly with impunity. To save a life has now become a crime; to kill an innocent, a virtue. The answer that best covers the argument of life for me is. "Anything that is not dead, is alive."

My cousin, Elizabeth, has spent twenty-five years defending the unborn, even to the point of running for public office in Washington.

She is seventy years old now, and complained to a friend, "when am I going to be old enough to quit fighting for the unborn?"

Her friend pointed to a picture of Mother Teresa and said, "ask her she's eighty-two."

Our friend, Bruce Lenz in Campbell River, presented me with a challenge. He suggested we put our neck where our mouth is and spend a day picketing the abortion mill in Vancouver. I agreed and our bravery was beyond compare, right up until we arrived at the abortuary.

There is a strong stigma attached to carrying a picket sign. "Only freaky radicals do that." We were even more downcast when it appeared we were the only people on the side of life present that morning. Sheepishly, we entered the fabric shop next door and asked for picket signs. My lack of humility showed again and I found this quite unnerving. We stood looking at the signs in the shop for a long time.

Bruce suggested, "lets go have a coffee, Jim, and we can talk about this."

That seemed like an excellent plan so we sailed out of the fabric shop to the nearest restaurant down the street.

The shop owner smiled as we passed him. "Chicken, huh?" We agreed and hurried on.

After bolstering our courage with coffee, we decided we had to return, shouldered our signs and went out feeling extremely conspicuous. There, we encountered two rough and determined women "manning" the place. Then much to our relief, others began to join us, mostly women, young and old; some pushing baby strollers; none of them radical freaks.

When I listened to the stories of those selfless people, I felt pretty cheap for being so cowardly. Many of them had spent time in jail and had been physically abused for defending the defenseless. They were persecuted beyond belief, but relentlessly carried on. Some passers by waved encouragement while others gave us an unkindly hand signal, accompanied by a snarl or non-complimentary epitaph.

We returned home that evening, inspired by the faith and courage of those saintly people. While many are now trying to squeeze the last ounce of pleasure out of life, those people were laying their lives on the line for their innocent brothers.

It is most amazing how the human mind can be manipulated with continued propaganda. Hitler once proclaimed that if you tell a lie often enough, people will eventually believe it. Many innocent people have been caught up in the propaganda to promote the culture of death. Mother Teresa countered the propaganda of overpopulation with an interesting comparison. If all the people in the world were put into Texas, everyone would have fifteen hundred square feet of space. (This could present a problem if they all decided to go to the shopping center at once.) The rest of the entire world would be vacant. It only appears overpopulated because people tend to pile up on top of each other in relatively small areas of big cities. At one time I was flying over a good share of North America. After listening to the propaganda, I was surprised to see that most of our continent is uninhabited.

A doctor friend described a meeting of doctors that he attended twenty-five years ago in Vancouver. They were discussing the idea of providing contraception devices for prostitutes. One doctor explained how the mentality of contraception naturally leads to promiscuity, and promiscuity will naturally lead to abortion. All present were appalled that he or anyone would even suggest that doctors might be condoning abortions in years to come. My friend said he would like to confront that same group now, twenty-five years later.

One day, we joined several thousand people in front of the parliament buildings in Victoria to promote life. An exceptionally beautiful lady stepped up to the microphone.

She spoke in a strong and positive tone to the crowd which had gathered. "My parents discussed having me killed by abortion when I was only three months old, and I am so thankful they were convinced not to kill me."

Another person then stepped up behind her and removed the white knit sweater from her shoulders. "She had no arms!"

When everyone had caught their breath, she continued, "Take a good look. Yes I have no arms. I was a thalidomide baby." She then went on to describe her philosophy and her family. "I now have two beautiful loving children of my own and a very loving husband. I am very happy to be alive."

I have heard since that her two children eat with either their hands, or like their mother, with their feet, not able to distinguish which is normal.

I was discussing our trip to the Vancouver abortion clinic with another friend, Joe Regan, several years after. He mentioned that he had also picketed the same clinic. When I asked him how often, I was humbled once again. (I should be very humble, I get so many opportunities.) He told me he devoted six hours a week to protesting at the abortion mill for a year. The following is Joe's amusing story.

"In April of 1992, I moved to Vancouver, B.C., in search of employment. With the extra time I had on my hands and not knowing anyone in the city, I felt I needed a worthwhile project. I have always been strongly pro-life, so decided to call the office of The Vancouver Right to Life. They told me a group picketed regularly each Monday outside the abortuary at 44th and Victoria. I was certainly welcome to help. Picketing was something I had never experienced, but the next Monday, I joined their group.

There were eight other people, all women, all elderly. I was the only male. I thought they would probably feel more secure having me around. They gave me a placard, and I ventured out on the street. I admit I was nervous. The street and the sidewalk in front of the abortuary were much busier than I expected. We were in full view of everyone around. At one point, a truck came by and the driver yelled out obscenities. I was shocked that these women had to listen to that kind of language. However, the obscenities didn't seem to faze them at all.

In fact, one of the women after one of these verbal attacks, joked with a smile, "a friend of yours?"

When I attempted to strike up a conversation with the women, they politely exchanged a few words and then moved away. At first I felt shunned, but then realized they were praying their rosary. I learned quickly that we were not here to socialize. As the weeks went by, I began to understand why the rosary was so important, and just how powerful it was. Around abortuaries, you are on the front lines of a spiritual and sometimes physical, war. Evil is ever present and very real. On one occasion, several hood types picked up one of the old ladies and threw her, bodily, into the street.

One Monday, all the women were a little late, so I started to picket by myself. I was suddenly overcome with fear. It seemed as if everyone on the street was out to get me that day. Out of habit, I started to say my rosary and within a few minutes, I could feel anxiety replaced by courage and peace. Many times I experienced the same when I needed it most.

It didn't take long to discover that those women's arsenal possessed some powerful weapons for defense. They surrounded the entire building with blessed Miraculous Medals. They had thrown medals onto the roof and inserted medals into the cracks of the building wall . I grew to recognize the inner strength they possessed and their commitment to winning the war. In the worst of weather, be it heat, snow or freezing rain, they were always there. I discovered that some of their husbands and families did not approve of their picketing. Defending the cause they knew with all their heart was so important, but which resulted in a great deal of heartache at home. Being arrested and charged by the police was always a real possibility. I was surprised to learn that the year before, some had spent long periods in jail for rescue attempts.

To me, these women were specialists in spiritual warfare, who trusted completely in the protection and guidance of Our Blessed Mother. They were a shinning example of how Our Lord works through the meek and the humble, and how it is through them that this battle will eventually be won for God.

One day, we experienced a terrifying moment. A man on a bicycle raced up directly behind Maureen, an elderly lady well into her seventies. A few inches from her back, he screamed. She was terribly shaken. For the next twenty minutes he terrorized all of us. We tried to talk and explain to him why we were there; that at this very moment unborn babies were being put to death in that building. He looked at the building and then looked at me, confused. He didn't understand what I was saying. All his obscenities had nothing to do with abortion, but were directed against Our Lady , the Pope, and the fact we were Catholic. This fellow was obviously deranged. He was a powerful individual as he ridiculed and leered at me. He spit on us, and rode up and down the sidewalk, trying to run the women down with his bike. At one point, three of the women were at one end of the building and three at the other. I ran from one group to the other, trying to put myself between them and him. Margaret was a frail lady, not at all well. Sometimes, she could not picket for the whole two hours and would have to sit in her car for the remainder of the time. When he approached the three women at one end of the building, Margaret produced a spray bottle from her purse and sprayed in the direction of the biker. Although he was about ten feet away, it had an obvious effect. He yelled out something that sounded almost scriptural. Although I didn't know what the bottle contained at the time, I got the impression he did. He immediately quit and fled from the scene. All of us were relieved. I said to Margaret, "what kind of spray is that you have? Mace?" She smiled and said, "no, it's Holy Water. This is a dangerous place you know, and you must come prepared if you are going to confront evil like this."

Sailing Beyond the Sea

CHAPTER 26

Sailing On

A number of events and discoveries have left a deep impression on me, and help adjust my attitude as I sail through life.

The Natives played a roll in this. Their humble and uncomplicated way, became an important influence in my life. Hobema, Alberta is a large Indian Reserve south of Edmonton and is an exciting land of contradiction. Some past governments relegated relatively poor ground to Native reserves. Unlike most reserves, oil was discovered near Hobema, and the land was no longer poor.

I met Alex at a Native Cursillo in Hobema. He was, at the time, one of only two Native Parole Officers in western Canada, in spite of the fact that the majority of prison inmates are Native. The story he told accurately describes the paradox of Native problems and bigotry against religion.

Alex attended a government meeting in Vancouver for all people and programs involved in Native drug and alcohol rehabilitation. Each program leader was asked to explain his program, relate the cost of the program, and then describe the results.

"This went on for hours." He explained, "if you kept track with a pencil, you would discover countless millions of dollars were spent on these programs. When it came to results, up to that time, there were none."

A little man stood up in the meeting and spoke, "you know the reason we are not showing any results with all this effort and money is that we are leaving the Creator out of the programs."

The lady moderator sternly rebuked him. "We do not get involved in religion here." The little man presented a bible and attempted a quote to demonstrate his point. She promptly summoned the security guards and had him removed from the meeting.

The Hobema Reserve is the wealthiest reserve in Alberta, and paradoxically, the reserve with more problems than many others. In spite of this it was one of many reserves that were making great strides toward recovery from the desperation of alcohol and drugs.

Wearing a bewildered look, Alex complained, "would you look at this? Hundreds of people are turning their lives around, and families are being healed and reunited by means of the Cursillo; obviously the work of the Creator. It isn't costing the taxpayer a nickel and yet the government is telling us that we are not to involve the Creator in their programs, which are all failing."

On another occasion, I drove a van full of ladies from Vancouver Island to Hobema for a Native Ladies' Cursillo. While waiting for the ladies, I stayed at the home of another Alex, Alex Twin, for the three days. This Alex is one of the foremost Native artists in Canada. After we became acquainted, he and his wife opened up and both related experiences similar to my dad's. Mrs. Twin's story was especially intriguing. Several years ago, she had been taken to the hospital in critical condition with pneumonia. She, somehow, watched the frenzied attempt to resuscitate her as they announced she had gone into cardiac arrest and then pronounced her dead. She then described an adventure similar to my dad's. Even though her face was covered over with a sheet, she was quite amused as she watched the removal of the resuscitation and I.V. equipment and as they cleaned up around her bed. She said she watched from above. She noticed the family ring slip from the finger of a nurse and become lost in the folds of a bed sheet. Her body was left for several hours in the room. When the aids came to remove her body, the entire hospital staff went into shock when they found her sitting up in bed. Later, when she was describing the events to her doctor, she asked to see the nurse who had lost her ring. The nurse was again amazed how Mrs. Twin could possibly know the ring was lost. The returned Mrs. Twin then advised the nurse to go to the laundry room in the basement and look in the third laundry basket from the light switch. Sure enough, there was the ring. We shared many of our other unusual past adventures.

Alex believed that the discovery of oil was the downfall of his tribe. The wealth changed the ways of the people and many became addicted to alcohol and drugs worse than other reserves. Consequently, family life was destroyed. In contrast, he believed the Cursillo was the greatest thing to come to the reserve. Many families were being repaired through their return to their Creator and the sacraments.

Alex had been arrested seventeen times and spent eighteen years of his life in prison. He admitted jail is where he belonged. According to his story, he was an incorrigible drunk and charged with a multitude of crimes. During this time he had no interest in spiritual matters whatsoever. One day, the chaplain recognized his artistic ability and approached him with a request to produce a picture of the crucifixion of Christ for the prison.

"I was doing just fine," he explained, "until I painted the hand of Christ. Next I painted the hole for the nail and the nail. As I began to paint the blood dripping from his hand, the whole truth and reason of the Gospel came to me loud and clear. I discovered the love of The Creator and why Jesus had to suffer excruciating pain and die to make up for my wrongs. With deep remorse and regret, I had a change of heart, finished serving my time and vowed to change my life."

After Alex was released from prison, he helped the prison chaplain develop the Edmonton Native drop-in center. In a short time, it grew beyond expectations and helped many to have hope and a new life. Age and eye failure were creeping up on Alex when I knew him, but he was happier than any time in his life. His art is in such demand that he will never be able to complete all the orders. Anyone going to Hobema can visit the teepee church. Everything is modeled after the teepee, including the tabernacle. The stained glass windows depict the major bible stories with Natives as the bible characters, all done by Alex.

I pondered over the meaning of what Jesus went through for me. I think if it were possible for an artist to accurately reproduce how he looked on the cross after his torture, no one could bear to look at the scene, or if they could, they probably would throw up.

While the Natives were continuing to help change my attitude, the meaning of a great mystery began to unfold. It was like knowing the sun is in the sky, but not understanding from where the light came.

Before he died, Jesus promised to be with us until the end of time. Oblivious to many, hidden in the bible, is this astounding mystery of how he would accomplish the feat. The secret requires a great amount of faith to understand. It is known, but not fully understood by many "cradle Catholics", and unappreciated by most. One author, John Haffert, wrote an entire book on the subject with the title, *The World's Greatest Secret*. My appreciation for the secret only developed after observing the remarkable excitement of non-believers when the mystery was unveiled for them. To many, the obvious is impossible to see, even when carefully explained. A short story partially explains the secret.

A "good" Catholic skipped Mass one Sunday, and spent the day working in his garden. The next door neighbor, an observant and sincere Protestant, leaned over the fence and struck up a conversation.

"Do you Catholics really believe that the little piece of bread you receive at communion in your church has actually been changed into the *real* body and blood of Jesus, the Son of God?"

The Catholic replied, "sure we do. Why do you ask?"

The neighbor answered. "Well, for the life of me I can't understand why you are here, working in your garden. If I could possibly bring myself to believe what you say you believe, I wouldn't be here. I would crawl on my hands and my knees, if necessary, to be in your church, that close to the real presence of God." Hopefully, the Catholic was justly humiliated.

"I tell you most solemnly, if you do not eat the flesh of the Son of Man and drink his blood," Jesus said, *"you will not have life in you. Anyone who does eat my flesh and drink my blood has eternal life, and I shall raise him up on the last day. For my flesh is real food and my blood is real drink. He who eats my flesh and drinks my blood lives in me and I live in him."* John 6: Many of his disciples couldn't stomach his words and departed never to return, just as many do today. They couldn't believe God can do anything, even if it sounds like cannibalism to our unlearned ears. He didn't say, "come on back guys, I was only kidding, I meant to say it's only a symbol." He let them go and as the scripture says, they never came back, just as many do not believe today. When he broke the bread at the last supper, he proclaimed, *"this is my body,"* and likewise, when he took the cup, he said, *"this is my blood."*

Saint Paul re-emphasized this in very strong words. *"For as often as you eat this bread and drink this cup, you proclaim the death of the Lord until he comes. Therefore, whoever eats the bread or drinks the cup of the Lord unworthily will have to answer for the body and blood of the Lord. A person should examine himself, and so eat the bread and drink the cup. For anyone who eats and drinks without discerning the body, eats and drinks judgment on himself. That is why many among you are ill and infirm, and a considerable number are dying. We are being disciplined so that we may not be condemned along with the world."*

Carole told me that when she joined the church, that she would have no problem belonging to another faith if it weren't for discovering the center of our belief, the genuine real presence of Jesus in the Eucharist in the Catholic faith. It takes very serious and long study to determine why only Orthodox and Catholic priests have been given the authority to accomplish this miracle.

Observing the history of the world, it appears that science and religion have been waging an unending war, trying to prove each other wrong. Recently I have seen signs that they may be coming closer together as history and scripture unfold.

The TV program, "Sixty Minutes", aired a documentary, produced at Berkeley University, showing various studies on aging. Researchers demonstrated with two groups of mice. One group was fed all they wanted to eat. The other group was fasted and were denied food on alternate days. At the age of three the well fed mice were shown to be fat, lethargic, and many had contracted cancer. Most could no longer reproduce, and many were dying. For the most part, they sat and stared into space or slept. The fasting mice were running around, climbing the cage walls, acting like "three year olds." Generally they seemed to be in excellent health. (Besides promoting grace, the Blessed Mother may be improving our health by encouraging us to fast.)

Next, they explained how it had always been assumed that human tissue cells artificially grown in a test tube would continue to grow and multiply indefinitely. The research demonstrated they do not. The cells multiply fifty-seven times; then they die, and this limit of fifty-seven divisions is built into our genes. Running this information through a computer, it was discovered that the human body is limited to exactly 120 years of life, providing all circumstances are perfect and metabolism is normal. The body then will shut down completely at 120 years. This is coded into the body of all humans since creation. This same calculation in the bible, written several thousand years before, went unnoticed by the researchers at Berkeley.

I might never have noted this "coincidence" had I not watched "Sixty Minutes" and attended a Baptist bible study the same week. In Genesis 5;32, there are reports of men living a very long time. *"The whole lifetime of Methuselah was nine hundred and sixty-nine years; then he died. The whole lifetime of Lamech was seven hundred and seventy-seven years; then he died. When Noah was five hundred years old, he became the father of Shem, Ham and Japheth."*

In the next chapter, Gen. 6: 3, is written, *"then the Lord said, My spirit shall not remain in man forever, since he is but flesh. From now, his days will comprise one hundred and twenty years,"* the exact same number of years discovered by scientists at Berkeley.

A story is told of my favorite scientist. He was responsible for most of the early veterinary medical breakthroughs. This scientist was traveling by train, seated next to a young college science major. During their conversation, the young man commented on how well his scientific education had pleased him. Science showed there was no longer a need to believe in God or religion.

The scientist countered, "that is strange, because the more I learn about science, the more I understand and believe God is a reality."

When the scientist got up to leave, he presented his business card to the student. The student was surprised to learn the scientist's identity, Louis Pasteur, Pasteur Institute of Chemistry.

Sailing On

The Book of Revelations 8:10-11, describes how *"when the third angel blew his trumpet, a great star burning like a torch fell from the sky. It fell on a third of the rivers and on the springs of water. The star was called "Wormwood". It polluted a third of the waters. Many people died from this water, because it was made bitter.*

On July 25, 1986, The New York Times printed an article reporting how a prominent Russian writer recently produced a tattered old bible, and with a practiced hand, turned to Apocalypse. "Listen," he said, "this is incredible." He pointed in the Book of Revelation (Apocalypse), to the great star falling from the heavens, the name of which was *Wormwood* (a bitter wild herb used as a tonic in rural Russia). The translation for wormwood in Russia, Yugoslavia, and other European countries is *Chernobyl!*

When Hiroshima was bombed in 1945, there were eight men who survived the blast. They were located at the epicenter of the holocaust. Scientists are still trying to discover how they could have survived. One of the survivors, a Jesuit priest named Fr. Shiffner, stated on TV, "in that house, we were living the message of Fatima, prayer, fasting, and penance."

In AA, people learn that in order to stay sober, they must help others become and maintain sobriety. I have discovered this concept to be true also with our faith. We have to spread the faith in order to keep it. "No one gets to paradise alone; it is necessary to bring others along."

St. Francis of Assisi, in his great simple wisdom, said, "evangelize, evangelize, evangelize and, then if necessary, say something." The Mother of Jesus tells us the same in Medjugorje. The most important thing is to change our lives continually. Pray, fast, do penance, convert, and by the example of change in my life and the power of grace from prayer and sacrifice, the rest of the world will change. This is like a chain reaction. When this change is universal, there will be peace. If we don't change, then the creator will be forced to do it for us, and that could be a most unpleasant experience. The time is extremely short.

Another saga in the life of Native friends had a remarkable influence on our lives when Susan and Bill moved to Campbell River. We thought they were the obvious answer to our prayers, and those of Father Salmon, for the natives.

As always, though, the adversary had to rear its ugly head into the scene. Bill and Susan had been snared by alcohol and the resulting depression. When we first met, most evident was what beautiful, and gentle people they were. Unfortunately, this couple, who would be ideal and loving parents, could never have children. And further they wanted to quit drinking, but discovered, like most, the odds of recovery from that monstrous disease are slim. They had grown up believing excess drinking was the norm. Everyone around them, white or Native, drank from childhood, on. No way was the demon going to turn loose of its prey. When Bill lost the position of Band Chief, the depression from alcohol only magnified. We tried to console him. It was obvious to all that both he and Susan's greatest talents lay in spiritual leadership, far more valuable than political leadership.

Bill and Susan

Our friendship and our admiration for them was just beginning to blossom when the bottom dropped out of their world. The hopes we had envisioned were dashed. During one of their frequent drinking parties, Susan entered their bedroom to behold the most heart-rending scene any wife could possibly experience. Lying prostrate on the floor, in a pool of blood, was the most important person in her life, her precious Bill, the center of her world. There was a hole in his chest, and a rifle lying nearby. You could only imagine the terror and anguish that ripped at her heart that awful night.

Bill was rushed to the hospital for emergency surgery. The bullet narrowly missed his heart, but left him in critical condition. Somehow, he recovered only to disappear from society in deep remorse.

When they, once again, ventured into the community, our friend, Jim, invited them to pray the rosary with us in the chapel. They felt extremely uncomfortable in regular twelve step groups, so decided to turn to prayer and God for help.

For three years, they joined us with the rosary every weekday morning. Every day, without fail, we found them waiting for a ride to the chapel. No matter if they were still suffering from the night before, relentlessly, they hung on to the rosary. Then, one memorable day three years after the start, they invited their many friends and relatives to the first anniversary; one entire year without a drink! That was seven alcohol-free years ago. I have never witnessed a more authentic answer to prayer. The demon was foiled, once again, by the simplest, yet one of the most powerful weapons on earth, the humble rosary. Those prayers on a chain result in a chain reaction surpassing nuclear fission. As Archbishop Sheen once said, "The Rosary is more powerful than an atomic bomb." I have since met others who have won the battle using the same weapon. It appears to be the most efficient method to solve the problem, yet the most difficult to keep up. If the rosary and AA were combined, no telling what monumental gains could be made.

Bill acquired a good job shortly after, and a year later, his picture was printed in the Campbell River paper with the caption, "Man of the Year". To this day, they have continued to be a model for all people.

We all have our cross to bear; theirs was tougher than most. Because they proved themselves courageous and faithful, they were gifted with the adoption of three beautiful children. Bill is in demand continually for his music, played western style. His music was especially appreciated by all at the at the Island Marian Eucharistic Conference. Susan and Bill are the central figures in all our native gatherings and his music often brightens the Saturday evening Mass in the parish church.

When I attended university, I had the tendency to skip classes and laboratories, especially social studies and humanities. When exam time arrived, panic ensued. Every few years, I have a dream that returns to haunt me. In the dream, it is time for state board exams. I am never ready for these exams and have completely skipped all my laboratories and I'm not even ready for graduation. I wake up in a terrible sweat, relieved that it is only a dream, but left in a troubled mood. This same uncomfortable dream had been returning, even though over thirty years have elapsed since graduation.

I experienced the same dream one night before I accompanied Father Charles to Sayward, B. C., to help him celebrate the Mass. I related the dream to him while we were on the road. He borrowed the theme for his sermon that day by comparing it to the end of our life. Will we be ready when we are called, or will we be like my dream, having failed our calling in all that God asked, and put off all that was necessary for safe entry into everlasting life?

Mother Teresa and Pope John Paul II have both proven old age and health problems are not a legitimate excuse to keep from following God's will. I've learned that even a jerk can be used if he opens his life and his heart.

When we were young, we used to joke saying, "since we can't take it with us, we decided not to go." Life doesn't work that way and in the near future, I expect to meet Christ face to face; the same Christ I meet in the Eucharist.

His question to me, may well be, "so, you call yourself a Christian?"

I hope that I will be better prepared to answer that question than I was when the lady dumped the whisky over my head in Telkwa. I wasted a lot of time chasing quality of life. I regret that I didn't wake up when I was much younger, but on the other hand, thankful that I have started to catch on before it's too late.

A lot of well meaning people think that a life dedicated to the Creator must be a dull or syrupy existence. We haven't found it that way. Life gets more exciting every day.

I have a long way to go, but I'm trying to follow St Paul's example when he said, "I'm not there yet, but I will run the race to the finish."

I just wonder what's over the next horizon as we sail beyond the sea.

Where from Your love can I flee?
If I take wing to the sunrise or sail beyond the sea,
still you are present even there. (Psalm 139)

Sailing Beyond the Sea

EPILOGUE

The crew of the Maritashan:

Jim Jr. with the help of his good wife Ingrid, discovered his place in life and is now a compassionate successful doctor practicing in Campbell River. They live in Campbell River B.C. with son Ryan.

Marggie is now a nurse in in Little Rock, Arkansas. She lives with her husband Doug and two children, Lindsay and Brian.

Carita is a travel agent in Courtenay B.C. Living with husband Keith and three children. Brett, Landon, and Kaylan.

Shannon works in art and carpentry. She and husband Bob have two children, Connor and Marley and one on the way. They live in Campbell River.

All six, even the girls, turned out to be quality carpenters after helping to build 10 veterinary hospitals.

Bobbie has a PhD in plant pathology. He is working for the U.S. department of agriculture in Peoria, Illinois, as a scientist studying DNA in plant fungus. (This family can handle any medical problems in living organisms, whether it be people, plant or animal.)

Mark is a carpenter with aspirations of becoming an architect. He lives on Long Island New York. One of his mottoes is Give Blood, Play Rugby.

Cenacles and Total Consecration:

For information regarding Cenacles or Consecration to the Immaculate Heart, or the Marian Movement of Priests, contact

The Marian Movement of Priests
P.O. Box 8
St. Francis, Maine 04774-0008
USA

The Marian Movement of Priests
1515 Bathhurst St.
Toronto, Ontario M5P 3H4
Tel 416-653-6814

Speaking of True Devotion and Total Consecration, according to Saint Louis De Montfort, Pope John Paul II said, "...This 'perfect devotion' is indispensable to anyone who means to give himself without reserve to Christ and to the work of redemption. It is from Montfort that I have taken my motto: *Totus Tuus* (I am all thine)..."

For information on the above, contact

Montfort Publications
26 So. Saxon Ave.
Bay Shore, NY 11706

Epilogue

From the book, *To The Priests, Our Lady's Beloved Sons*

My maternal task is that of interceding each day for you, before my Son Jesus. As an attentive and concerned Mother, I am asking for all the graces that you have need of in order to walk along the road of goodness, of love and holiness.

Beloved children, the Lord who has come in his first birth is about to return to you in glory. His second and glorious birth is close at hand. And so, in the night of your time, it is my maternal duty to prepare you to receive Him, as I received Him in his first coming.

You must now all enter right away into the safe refuge of my Immaculate Heart. Just as Noah, in the name of the Lord, called into the ark those who were to be saved from the flood, so now must you, my littlest child, in the name of your heavenly Mother, call into the refuge of my Immaculate Heart those who must be protected, defended and saved from the great trial which has now come for the Church and for all humanity.

From my shrine in Fatima, I renew today the pressing invitation for you to take refuge in me, through your consecration to my Immaculate Heart, and to multiply everywhere the cenacles of prayer, which I have asked of you, cenacles of priests, of little children, of youth, and cenacles within families. Do not be afraid. Do not allow yourselves to be seized with discouragement. I am with you always.

The most efficacious prayer, is that of the holy rosary.

In the end, after the time of the great trial, there awaits you the time of great peace, great joy, great holiness, the time of the greatest triumph of God in your midst.

In the cenacles, you will be aware of my extraordinary presence. In the cenacles, you will experience the security and peace which your heavenly Mother gives you. You will be preserved from evil and defended from the great dangers which threaten you.

Sailing Beyond the Sea